To Asia With Love

A Connoisseurs' Guide to Cambodia, Laos, Thailand & Vietnam

To Asia With Love
Edited & with contributions by Kim Fay
Photography by Julie Fay

Cover and book design by Janet McKelpin/Dayspring Technologies, Inc.
Editing assistance provided by Robert Tompkins
Contributor photos by Rachel Whitty

Please be advised that restaurants, shops, businesses and other establishments in this book have been written about over a period of time. The editor and publisher have made every effort to ensure the accuracy of the information included in this book at the time of publication, but prices and conditions may have changed, and the editor, publisher and authors cannot assume and hereby disclaim liability for loss, damage or inconvenience caused by errors, omissions or changes in regard to information included in this book.

For information regarding permissions, write to:
ThingsAsian Press
3230 Scott Street
San Francisco, California 94123 USA
www.thingsasian.com
Printed in Singapore

ISBN 0-9715940-3-1

Table of Contents

Introduction

Imagine that on the eve of your upcoming trip to Cambodia, Laos, Thailand and Vietnam, you are invited to a party. At this party are fifty guests, all of whom live in or have traveled extensively through these countries. Among this eclectic and well-versed group are authors of acclaimed guidebooks, popular newspaper columnists and pioneering adventurers. As you sit around the table with these connoisseurs, and drift from group to group, they tell you tales from their lives in these exotic places. They whisper the names of their favorite shops and restaurants; they divulge the secret hideaways where they sneak off to for an afternoon (or a weekend) to unwind. Some of these guests make you laugh out loud, and others mesmerize you with their poetry and lyricism. Some are intent on educating, while others just want to entertain. They have accents borne from all over the globe, and their attitudes are as unique as their personalities. But they are united in one thing . . . *their love of the region.* By the time you leave the party, your pockets are filled with slips of paper, dozens upon dozens of recommendations scribbled down by these generous, modern-day nomads.

If you can envision being welcomed at such a party, then you can envision the experience that this guidebook aspires to give you. It was the opportunity to offer the feeling of being confided in, of being entrusted with the kinds of conversation and camaraderie that are usually reserved for the closest of friends, that immediately came to mind when Albert Wen—the driving force behind the fabulous Asia-centric ThingsAsian.com—decided to start publishing books and asked me if I had any projects I wanted to pursue. I was thrilled. I had been thinking about a guidebook in the vein of TO ASIA WITH LOVE for a couple years, and if any company would do it justice, it was ThingsAsian. I have been writing for ThingsAsian (and its beautiful print predecessor DESTINATION: VIETNAM) since 1995. Of all the publications and websites I've contributed to, it is my favorite.

It has always welcomed a passionately written story, and if there is one thing I want this guidebook to convey, it is the passion of its contributors.

I began working on this book by contacting friends I had made during the four years I lived in Vietnam, as well as friends from the States who had settled down in various corners throughout Southeast Asia. I asked them, simply, to recommend their favorite things to see and do in their adopted homes. Word of mouth expanded my group of contributors, as did my pleading with total strangers for morsels to add to the fast-growing feast of suggestions and advice. I have complemented this delicious miscellany with introductions to each chapter, where I take the liberty of waxing sentimental and raving about my own beloved haunts. In addition, I have not only interspersed a few accounts of my own, but I have also provided ample resources to help in planning and getting in the mood for your trip. Enriching the contents even further are the photographs taken by my sister, Julie, during our memorable travels together. United with the insightful essays, Julie's enticing photos seduce with the exotic siren song of Southeast Asia.

In tone and style, the individual contributions are truly diverse; however, this book is very easy to use. Each chapter has its own subject, such as food or sightseeing. Within the chapters are sections for each country, and these country sections are broken down into individual regions and cities, which provide the framework for the essays. While the contributions are grouped by topic and place, each stands on its own, with a corresponding Fact File containing practical information, such as addresses and resources for supplementary research.

I am so pleased with the essays and tidbits that make up this book, but at the same time I am aware that they are just the tip of the iceberg. Unlike the major guidebooks, this one does not claim to be a definitive work. Instead, it joins the growing rank of boutique publications that are meant to supplement your Lonely Planet, Footprint, Moon or Rough Guide. This book is not about maps and train schedules and making sure every decent restaurant in Bangkok gets a mention. It is about inspiring, being inspired, communing, discovering and sharing—a unity of the acts that make traveling in a foreign land (and sometimes stopping to hang your hat there for awhile) one of the most pleasurable experiences on earth.

Kim Fay

MOVEABLE FEASTS

*Musings on exotic gastronomy and where
to go to gratify your taste buds.*

Considering the wealth of exquisite and distinctive dishes and dining establishments on offer in Southeast Asia, it's no wonder that this topic received one of the most enthusiastic responses from the contributors to this book. There are few experiences more memorable than dining in this part of the world. It has something to do with the combination of bruising humidity and crisp lemongrass and the rustle of palm trees and the bite of chili and the scent of jasmine and the tartness of lime and . . . it feels futile to try to capture the experience with mere words. To understand, you must simply take a bite of beef *laap* on a hot equatorial night in a hot equatorial country. It's like falling in love.

Right after moving to Vietnam, I took a weekend trip to Dalat, and my friend and I spent an evening at the Maison Long Hoa restaurant drinking strawberry wine that had been made by the owner's wife from the berries for which the region is famous. When I briefly took a nine-to-five job in Ho Chi Minh City, we would take a taxi to a roadside *banh cuon* stall on Mac Dinh Chi Street and eat breakfast while the taxi idled—the ride always cost at least ten times more than the meal—before racing off to work. One Christmas day in Siem Reap, we asked a café to pack us a meal; armed with bread, cheese, meat, fruit and a bottle of wine, we retreated to the outlying Roluos Temple Group, laid out our picnic on a landing atop a temple, and ate while a group of local children sang and practiced their English and wove flowers into my hair. Papaya salad is always refreshing, but never was it more so than while sitting with my sister on a covered patio at the Jim Thompson house in Bangkok as the rain pattered into a pond in the garden. And on September 11, 2001, I gathered with my sister and a group of friends on pillows around a table at the exotic Indochina Spirit in Luang Prabang and toasted to life and friendship, ignorant of the day's horrific events, protected for a fragile, lingering moment from the tears of the world. If I were allowed to keep

my memories of only one kind of activity, it would be of eating with friends, family and sweethearts around the world.

The recommendations in this chapter have been made by people for whom Southeast Asia has become a physical or spiritual home. They have had time to explore and discover and weed out. A dish that was once mysterious has become a staple, and the most out-of-the-way café, a regular hangout. It is interesting to see that people who have never met recommend the same restaurant—Kafe in Chiang Mai, for example—or the same dish, such as *khao soi*. I loved reading the essay on Vietnam's ubiquitous coffee ritual, although I adore this local brew without sweet milk, the opposite of the way that the writer prefers it.

I would like to comment on two essays that are particularly close to my heart. "Thai Food for Thai Moods" is written by my dear friend, Janet Brown. We were booksellers together at the Elliott Bay Book Company in Seattle, and her life in Thailand overlapped with mine in Vietnam. We spent one great weekend together in Bangkok, drinking beer, listening to diehard expats sing Country Joe and the Fish songs, and eating. Always eating—she is an expert on the mysterious blend of ingredients that make up a perfect dish. The second is Emily Huckson's piece on the Lotus Café in Ho Chi Minh City. After I had checked into the Prince Hotel (a.k.a. brothel), I ate my very first meal as an expatriate at the Lotus Café; it is also where I met Emily. The restaurant continued to provide sustenance and companionship, as did many other wonderful venues, during my four years in Vietnam. May you find your own Lotus Café in the rich collection of restaurants that populate Southeast Asia. *Bon appetit.*

A fact file for the restaurants mentioned in this introduction can be found on page 39.

CAMBODIA ✿ *Phnom Penh*

Nami Nelson loves hunting for dumplings . . .

My introduction into the world of dumplings was at a small, seedy looking shop near the Olympic Market. My friends had discovered the shop on a late evening walk and were keen to introduce the rest of us. We sat down, and as promised, a middle-aged man from Shanghai stood up from his table of friends to greet us with a bottle of whiskey. He didn't speak Khmer or English. We didn't speak any dialect of Chinese. Yet he seemed to know what we wanted. We indicated our preference for two of whatever this might be, and he nodded in agreement while pouring himself another drink.

Minutes later we had bottles of beer open, and two bamboo steamer trays of pork dumplings steaming away in front of us. They didn't last long. We ordered another two trays and before we knew it, the karaoke was on, and our searing renditions of Britney Spears' "Oops, I Did It Again" were getting rounds of appreciative or apologetic (I never can tell) applause.

That was the beginning of my love affair with dumpling shops in Phnom Penh. The little shop on the corner near the Olympic Market may no longer be there, but there are scores of non-Khmer, non-English speaking dumpling shops scattered all over the city. The traditional favorite is on the dumpling shop street near the inter-province bus station at the Central Market. Peking Canteen is by far the most superior in terms of dumpling quality and the ultimate test dish, Braised Eggplant with Whole Cloves of Garlic. The Dumpling Hall on Monivong Boulevard near the turnoff to the Central Market is also a good source of dumplings, and they are one of the few places that serve vegetarian dumplings. If you are lucky enough to get the fresh dumplings they have at the dumpling shop on Monivong Boulevard, south of Sihanouk Boulevard, they are definitely up there with the best. You also get to enjoy watching the making of fresh noodles. The cook stretches out the dough, throws it around in the air and then slams it down on a metal table. It adds an air of excitement to the average dumpling meal when you can witness its creation.

A word of warning, though— don't get too comfortable with any particular shop. There is a rotating management or ownership of the dumpling shops in Phnom Penh, depending on who is having a lucky streak in the private gambling dens. There will always be that day when you turn up with a belly craving for juicy pork dumplings dipped in a vinegar, soy sauce and garlic dipping sauce, and you find that your favorite shop has been handed over to new owners as payment for a badly placed bet. As devastating as it may be at the time, beginning a new search for the ultimate dumpling is half the fun.

Peking Canteen
Located on Street 136 between the Central Market (Psah Thmai, also known as the New Market) and the Asia Hotel (113-119 Monivong Boulevard), Phnom Penh.

Christina Gosnell
weighs in on
the dumpling craze . . .

If you're just looking to get your belly full, there are plenty of options. But if you want a good, hearty meal at rock bottom prices, you absolutely must visit a dumpling shop. There are many of them near the Central Market, including Restaurant China. At the sidewalk cooking area of Restaurant China, you will find dumplings with meat and vegetable fillings—ten for just a dollar. While you're waiting for the dumplings to fry up, why not try some of the other

menu items. Care for frog casserole with mushrooms? You'll find it here, among other exotic menu items.

Restaurant China
81 Street 136, near the Central Market (Psah Thmai, also known as the New Market), Phnom Penh.

Matt McKinney
recommends
local dishes and hangouts,
but warns against
fermented fish paste . . .

Fish and rice make up the staple of the Cambodian diet, and there are just a few things to remember before experimenting with the local fare. First, do not, I repeat, do not, eat *prahok*, the fermented fish paste, unless you have a tall glass of water nearby, a strong stomach and a penchant for unusually strong flavors. It's reminiscent of nothing in the western diet and will turn even an iron gut. *Prahok*, or fish cheese, is what you get by stomping to death millions of minnow-sized fish and then salting and storing the remains. It's a national fascination for most Cambodians, and a thing to be appreciated at a distance for all others. On the other hand, do try *fish amok*, a local delicacy that can be had at Khmer Surin and a variety of other restaurants. Wash it down with a mango smoothie, when in season. Other worthwhile evenings can be enjoyed at places like Young Go Roast Beef, on Street 228 near Norodom Boulevard. It's a grill-it-yourself place with beef and jugs of beer.

❀ ❀ ❀

As everyone in Phnom Penh knows, a cold drink and a view can be had at the Foreign Correspondents' Club of Cambodia, a throwback to the colonial days with slowly turning ceiling fans and large, overstuffed chairs. For a more modern take on the expat scene, wander up north a few blocks to the Riverside Lounge, where DJs spin funky house music to keep you company as you look out over the Tonle Sap River.

Khmer Surin
9 Street 57, near Sihanouk Boulevard, Phnom Penh.

Foreign Correspondents' Club
363 Sisowath Quay, Phnom Penh.

CAMBODIA
❀
Siem Reap & Points Outward

Andy Brouwer wanders into off-the-beaten-path cafés . . .

One eatery that I always enjoy is the Malop Dong (Coconut Tree) in the town of Tbeng Meanchey (pop. 20,000), in northern Cambodia. It's the best restaurant in town by a country mile and considering you're in the back of beyond, the food isn't too bad either. It's packed at breakfast time with a crowd that ranges from moto drivers and the top local policemen, to NGO workers and any foreigners that happen to be filtering through. Everyone in the area heads for the Malop Dong. Over breakfast the TV and video go at full blast, and the last time I was there, the film **Apocalypse Now** was being enjoyed by the packed audience. The owners know my regular moto driver from Kompong Thom, and he's treated like a long-lost brother whenever we arrive. As a result, I get treated with great respect as well. The staff even wastes valuable ice in cooling my cans of Pepsi! I've tried a couple of other places in town, and they don't come up to scratch at all, so it's the Malop Dong whenever I'm in Tbeng Meanchey.

Tbeng Meanchey

is located on the way from Siem Reap to the Preah Vihear temple, which Andy and fellow contributor Janet Brown elaborate on in Chapter Three. See page 62 for directions.

Although an obvious eatery that everyone has heard of or been to in Siem Reap, the Bayon Restaurant deserves a mention nevertheless. Its cheap and tasty fare remains one of the best deals in town, and the recent improvements to the surroundings— as well as the addition of a shadow puppet show—make it a pleasant experience and very affordable for those on a tight budget.

The Bayon Restaurant

Across from The Garden Guesthouse, 99 Wat Bo Road, Siem Reap.

Perhaps the best location I've been to in Cambo for a sunset drink is along the Mekong River at Kratie, where I enjoy watching the flame-red clouds as the sun sets across the river, with a tikalok (or tukalok) in my hand—this shake drink includes fruit, crushed ice, raw egg, sugar and condensed milk whipped up into a froth.

Kratie

is a small town on the Mekong River approximately 5 to 6 hours north by boat from Phnom Penh. It is famous for the freshwater dolphins that can be seen in the area. You can read more about it in articles by **To Asia With Love** writers at:

WEBSITE
www.btinternet.com/~andy.brouwer/kratie.htm

WEBSITE
www.thingsasian.com/goto_article/article.1407.htm

Donald Gilliland enjoys eating authentic Khmer food in tourist cafés . . .

In regard to great food, one dish comes to mind: beef *lork lark*. It is grilled strips of beef that sit on a bed of lettuce along with tomatoes and onions. It is served with rice and a simple but majestic sauce called *duek marit* (lime juice with a salt and pepper mixture). Some places serve this dish with a fried egg on top. Gross! Throw the egg away and enjoy the rest. The best I've had was at the Hawaii No Problem Pizza Restaurant, which, despite its name, had a nice variety of excellent dishes. They also serve a fine breakfast with good coffee. For other good cheap local eats, the Khmer Kitchen has good Khmer and Thai dishes for two to three USD. Huge portions and quite tasty.

Hawaii No Problem Pizza Restaurant
711 Wat Bo Street, Siem Reap.

Khmer Kitchen
Donald writes: This restaurant is in a new location behind the Soup Dragon in Siem Reap. The street it is on does not have a name, but the Soup Dragon is a relatively long-running establishment and the town is small. Happy hunting.

LAOS 🏵 *Luang Prabang*

> *Peter M. Geiser invites you to savor royal dining . . .*

At the restaurant of Villa Santi, sit down at a table made from the trunk of a tree on the first-floor terrace overlooking the main street. Enjoy the delicious Lao food, royal-style, prepared by the daughter of the last king's personal chef. A typical menu could include: *keng phar* (vegetable soup), *phat kin kay* (chicken, ginger and coconut milk), *kao lons mit* (fried

traditional vegetable), *nuat sen lone* (steamed vermicelli), *phar nam* (watercress salad) and seasonal fruit for dessert.

Villa Santi
Sakkarine Road, Luang Prabang, Laos.

THAILAND 🏵 *Bangkok*

> *John Padorr is a fan of duck soup and grilled chicken . . .*

For superb duck soup over freshly made noodles, head for Petchburi Road, Soi 5, about 100 meters from the front of the soi on the right side of the street. Ask for bami phet yahng nam. (Literally, yellow egg noodles - barbecued duck soup). The broth is exquisite. Price: about 75 cents.

For Duck Soup
Ask a taxi to take you to Petchburi Road, Soi 5, or get off the Rajtavee Skytrain stop and walk down Petchburi Road until you reach Soi 5. (Sois are streets that intersect the main road, with odd numbers on one side and even numbers on

continued on next page

THAILAND 🏵 *Bangkok*

the other.) Walk into Soi 5 about 100 meters. Just opposite the first 7-11 you see is the restaurant serving duck soup. John adds: Don't be fooled by the duck soup restaurant on your left before you reach the 7-11. The one you want is on your right.

Knowing the best grilled chicken joint is a matter of local pride in Bangkok. Always at or near the top of everyone's list of favorites is the shop house restaurant on Soi Polo, twenty meters in from the Wireless Road/Lumpini Park intersection. It's open for lunch only.

For Grilled Chicken

This restaurant is on a small street known as Soi Polo, which gets its name because it leads to the entrance of the Polo Club. (Note, though, that the street sign actually reads Soi Prajain). Soi Polo is just opposite Lumpini Park on Wireless Road. You enter the soi from Wireless Road just beside the pedestrian foot bridge near the north end of the park. There is also a semi-outdoor chicken joint on the northwest corner of the park. John notes that it serves fantastic Thai food until midnight.

Robert Power spends his evenings eating Red Pork Noodles with a view . . .

It's not so much the dish as the location. After all, *ba mee moo dang* (egg noodles with red pork) is available on most corners in Bangkok. But when time allows, usually once a week, I hop on at the Northernmost Skytrain Station, Mor Chit, and make my way to Silom Road and exit the Sala Daeng Station. Perhaps what pulls me to this area is its proximity to Bangkok's largest green space, Lumpini Park. Or maybe it's the feeling of comfort I get knowing that the best hospital I have visited anywhere in the world, The Bangkok Nursing Home, is located only minutes away on Convent Road. Or maybe it's the collection of coffee shops (Coffee Society and CafeEase in my opinion being the best) on Silom Road, offering a wide selection of English reading materials and flavorful Americanos.

I suspect I gravitate to this area for a little of all of the above reasons. But certainly what I find most intriguing about it is the nightly transformation from a legal to an illegal commerce district. On the corner of Silom and Convent Roads sits a *ba mee moo dang* noodle stall, open mid-morning until late night. Whatever your reason for coming, arrive during the dinner hour, grab a seat and order a bowl of noodles and a glass of *cha ma now* (lemon tea), sit back and enjoy the show as throngs of smartly dressed office ladies and businessmen exit the scene, and the area is claimed by vacationing *farang* (foreigners), taxi drivers/massage parlor touts, hawkers of pirated goods, as well as male, female and transgendered prostitutes on their way to Silom Soi 3, one of Bangkok's largest gay districts, or to Pat Pong, the world-famous red light district.

If you end up spending any length of time in Thailand, you will understand this nightly transformation is just another example of the many dichotomies that underpin Thai society and make Bangkok a fascinating stop.

For Ba Mee Moo Dang

Robert writes: When you get off at the Sala Daeng Skytrain Station, Convent Road is basically below the station. On one corner of this side of Silom and Convent Roads are usually a bunch of tourists and locals milling about. On the other is the noodle stall. The stall, however, does not have any signs advertising it. None of the street stalls advertise. But Silom is a very prominent street in Bangkok. All anyone has to do is get off the train, look at his or her map, find Convent (which is almost below them) and have a seat at the noodle stall on the corner.

Coffee Society
18 Silom Road, Bangkok.

CafeEase
22 Silom Road, Bangkok.

Roger Crutchley reveals that when it comes to som tam, some like it hot . . .

There is one dish in Thailand that is necessary to sample in order to get a true flavor of the Kingdom. It is *som tam*, a spicy salad based on green papaya with chopped green beans, tomatoes and of course chilies (*prik khee noo*), which give the dish its real bite. *Som tam* comes close to being the unofficial Thai national dish. Certainly in the northeast (Isan), it is an essential ingredient to everyday life. Ask Thais living abroad what they miss most about their homeland, and it's a good bet that *som tam* is lurking near the top of the list.

There are different types of *som tam*, and these days hotels and most restaurants provide a less fiery version for sensitive Western palates. These can be tasty enough in and of themselves, and they're probably the sensible course to take. But if you don't like being sensible, you should try the real thing. Nearly every soi in Bangkok has a *som tam* vendor, and observing him or her hammering away with the pestle while preparing the ingredients in the mortar is an experience in itself. Even better, visit the northeast part of the country and taste this treat in its home territory.

To offset the powerful spiciness of *som tam*, the dish should be accompanied by sticky rice (*khao niaw*), another Isan staple. Sticky rice is fun eating, since you use your hands, rolling the rice into a little ball. Don't feel obliged to eat all the *som tam*. In fact don't even attempt to, since your taste buds will probably be overwhelmed. Thais will love it if you are brave enough just to sample the dish they are rightly proud of.

To illustrate the power of *som tam*, I once hosted an informal beer-tasting "contest" at my Bangkok house in which half a dozen seasoned residents of Thailand had to guess the name of the beer from assorted countries in Southeast Asia. To accompany the drinking, my maid, who hails from the northeast province of Yasothon, provided plentiful supplies of her freshly-made *som tam*. For the first couple of beers, our "experts" were reasonably accurate in guessing the names of the brews. But as the

tasting went on, the accuracy of the assessments declined dramatically. Eventually, one of the team hit the nail on the head. "All the beers taste like bloody *som tam*," he exclaimed, before taking another big mouthful of the fiery dish.

Som tam—an essential part of the Thai experience.

In Search of Som Tam
Roger adds that *som tam* is available at many Thai restaurants in Bangkok but is probably more enjoyable to experience at those with an Isan/Lao theme, such as the following:

Vientiane Kitchen
8 Sukhumvit Road, Soi 36 (about 100 meters from Sukhumvit Road), Bangkok.

Baan Lao
49 Sukhumvit Road, Soi 36 (almost adjacent to the Vientiane Kitchen), Bangkok.

Baan Chiang
Surasak Road, 14 Soi Srivieng, Bangkok.

Café de Laos
16 Silom Road, Soi 19, Bangkok.

THAILAND ✿ *Chiang Mai*

Jason Smith hangs out in a place where everybody knows your name . . .

Do bars like TV's "Cheers" really exist? Sure they do. You just have to know where to find them. Among the myriad drinking establishments in the northern capital of Chiang Mai, there is one such pub. Kafe resides in a quirky old teak house, safely on the fringe of the Tha Pae neighborhood (the traveler's hub of the city). Walk inside and you feel the friendly, casual attitude that is so ingrained in northern Thai culture. It oozes from the dark wooden walls and spills from the soft low-watt glow of the lights. You can read it on the faces of the staff and hear it in the background jazz or blues. Besides its ambiance, what makes Kafe special is its harmonious blend of patrons. Backpackers sitting next to young locals. Expats saddled up at the bar discussing football with Thai old-timers. In a city where most bars have a theme, Kafe remains as it has been for the last 18 years—a true locals' pub. Come back more than

once, and it's likely the waitress will remember your face. They sport the most reasonable happy hour in town, every day from 4-7 p.m., with beer prices barely above cost. Have a snack with your pint. The sun-dried, fried beef with kaffir leaves (*neua dat diaw*) is my favorite. Every night is pleasant in Kafe, but if there's a football game on the TV (that's soccer to North Americans) you can bet the place will be full of cheering fans. Make sure to come early because they close at midnight. Due to its central location along the moat, it is a great place to celebrate Thailand's holidays local-style. Loy Kratong and Songkhran are especially fun. I've had so many great times in Kafe—sometimes just sitting alone watching the people walk by—that I consider its staff a part of my extended family.

Kafe
127-129 Mun Muang (or Moonmuang) Road, between the Tha Pae Gate and Sompet Market, Chiang Mai. Hours: 11 a.m. to midnight.

Loy Kratong
The Festival of Light is held on the full moon night of the twelfth lunar month (usually November). One of its highlights is the setting afloat of candles on bamboo leaves. You can read more about this festival at:

continued on next page

WEBSITE
www.thailand.com/travel/festival/
festivals_loykratong.htm

Songkhran

This annual New Year's Celebration is held on or close to April 13. Contributors Oliver Hargreave and Tara Russell write more about it on pages 159 and 160 in Chapter Seven.

*Candace MacKay
dines on the water
and beneath
green roofed restaurants . . .*

Probably the most popular restaurant in Chiang Mai is The Riverside. It's favored for its very good food, great service, live music and excellent view of the river. During the day you can enjoy a nice, quiet meal. The evenings, however, are quite a different story, with the place usually packed with a colorful assortment of patrons.

When I go to The Riverside, I never sit in the crowded restaurant or at the tables along the river—I sit *on* the river. Every night there is a boat that leaves the restaurant at eight and takes a lazy, hour-long journey down the river a couple of kilometers. It is a wonderful way to spend an evening and enjoy Chiang Mai from the perspective of the water. You can see a lot from here

that you can't see from the road: beautifully manicured back yards, quaint garden restaurants lit with paper lanterns, and shaky shanties that look as if they could fall away with the slightest breeze. Huge, resort-like restaurants dot the riverbank in both directions.

The Riverside

9-11 Charoenrat Road, Chiang Mai. Candace writes: Coming from Tha Pae Road, cross the Narawat Bridge and turn right. The Riverside is the first place on the left. To ensure a seat on the restaurant's tranquil boat outing, you must make a reservation (053-243-239). At only 20 baht a head including food, this is one of the best deals in town. If it inspires you to see the river by day, you can arrange a similar journey at a wooden booth in front of The Riverside. You can have your own boat for 300 baht a person, or you can wait for the scheduled trips, which are about half the cost.

At my house in Chiang Mai, we receive about a dozen non-resident guests a year. On the first day they arrive, we take them, without exception, to what we affectionately call "the green roof restaurant." It offers yummy food, great service and a soothing sunset. It's a little out of the way if you are coming from inside the city, but it's a great getaway where you can indulge for many hours.

The place opens at 5 p.m. and closes at 2 a.m., and there is live music every night, beginning around seven. The owners, husband and wife team Uan and Num, ensure consistently good food and will tailor dishes for vegetarians. My personal favorites are the coconut chicken soup, the fried tabtim fish and the octopus salad, but really, everything is delicious. Prices range from 40 to 120 baht, and drinks are Thai priced.

The Green Roof Restaurant (Lanndoi Roiview)

To get here take Hang Dong Road (the road to the airport) from the south side of the moat. On some maps, the road that leads to the airport is called Wualai Silver Street and then turns into Hang Dong or Hod Road. But if you are on the south side of the moat, there is a sign that points to the turnoff to the airport, and that is the road you take. Go for about 7 km, and when you reach the fourth set of lights from your moat starting point, you will be at a four-way intersection with a tunnel. Take a right. About a kilometer down that road—which has no official name but is now sometimes called New Airport Road—there is a wooden restaurant with a green roof and a sign out front that says "LANNDOI ROIVIEW." Candace adds: This name translates into "a million mountains, a thousand views."

Everyone we have taken there thus far has loved it. My guess is that you will, too.

Kenneth Champeon encourages everyone to drink up . . .

For a people so devoted to Buddhism, which discourages the use of intoxicants, the Thais sure can drink, and Thailand arguably has more bars than temples—no small feat. Favored drinks include whisky-and-soda, Chang Beer and rice moonshine. But amateur tipplers would do well to be wary of these high-octane concoctions.

Given the choice, the funds and a steel-lined stomach, I would drink bottomless carafes of red wine in the following Chiang Mai establishments: Kafe (for the funky atmosphere and canned jazz), The Drunken Flower (for the conversation and moonlight), and Belle Villa (for the unearthly serenity and stunning mountain views). Of course, when I wish to raise and tilt a gin-and-tonic to the departed British Empire, I dream myself into a place called, simply, The Pub.

For me, the view seen while drinking is less important than the views expressed, and Chiang Mai's watering holes tend to foster more varied and smarter views than can be found elsewhere in Thailand.

You can have your insipid Heineken, pool tables and air-conditioned mausoleums. I'll be over in the shabby corner with the journalists, laughing and weeping over the headlines, and blowing my smoke toward the tuk-tuk drivers dozing outside.

Kafe
127-129 Mun Muang (or Moonmuang) Road, Chiang Mai.

The Drunken Flower
Located at the end of Nimmanhaemin (or Nimmanhemin) Road, Soi 1, one block from the Amari Rincome Hotel, Chiang Mai.

Belle Villa Resort
At 19 Hang Dong-Samoeng Road about 30 minutes out of Chiang Mai.

The Pub
189 Huay Kaew Road, Chiang Mai.

Jeff Petry can't get enough khao soi . . .

In a word, or rather, a dish: *khao soi*. Far and away, this is Chiang Mai's most popular fare, and it quickly tops the list of favorites for most folks. Two servings are advised.

Khao soi is a wonderful curry and noodle dish inspired by Thailand's neighbor to its west, Myanmar. *Khao soi gai* (chicken) is recommended over *khao soi neua* (beef), and you can also order vegetarian *khao soi* at most places. This classic treat is made of a creamy, yellow curry spread on boiled egg noodles with fried noodles on top, served with a side of pickled vegetables (*phak dong*), lime wedges and sliced shallots. It also comes with its own special chili paste, called *nam prik khao soi*. (If this doesn't come with your order, ask for it!)

The expert *khao soi* eater will know just how to season this delicacy to taste by adding the requisite amounts of lime juice, chili paste, pickled vegetables and little purple onions. I myself view the first bowl as a starter, to be enjoyed in its own right, of course, but also to be used as the staging ground for the second bowl. That is, you create your own perfectly-seasoned base with the first bowl, and then add it to the second serving for a true gourmet feast.

Order a beer or a nice, cool, sweet juice, such as guava or lime, to complement the taste sensations and to chill the spiciness from the added chili paste. Some people may appreciate knowing that this soup contains many important vitamins and is highly recommended after an indulgent night out.

Seeking Khao Soi
Jeff writes: You can spend several years sampling Chiang Mai's

diverse offerings of *khao soi*, and some of us have, I assure you. For starters, I recommend the following places:

Ratana's Kitchen

320-322 Tha Pae Road. Run by Khun Ratana and her British photo-journalist husband, Ron. Convenient location, excellent food, lovely staff—a comfort zone for the harried hungry, not far from Tha Pae Gate.

Huan Phen

112 Ratchamanka Road near Felix City Inn, which is located at 154 Ratchamanka Road. Join the crowds for the best northern Thai lunch buffet around, or go in the evening for a mellower meal.

Khao Soi Islam

Charoen Prathet Road, Soi 1, at the top of the Night Market area towards the end of the soi near Chang Klan Road and the river (i.e. the eastern end). Order *khao soi gai* (chicken) or *bpaa* (goat) - "*bpaa*" is onomatopoeic, so you can either make a goat-like sound after saying "*khao soi*" or enlist the assistance of the friendly and helpful Khun Chai. Their *khao soi* and other dishes with saffron rice are a wonderful variation on a theme à la Islam.

Aroon (Rai)

45 Kotchasarn Road near Tha Pae Gate. No mention of northern Thai food would be complete without a nod to Aroon (Rai) Restaurant, which has been here, some say, since before the founding of Chiang Mai. Formerly Uncle Rai's, it offers a wide variety of foods, including of course, *khao soi*, which can be had for the usual price of 25 to 30 baht. You can also point to and pick any number of other tasty dishes that are displayed alongside insects, which are à la carte treats you can order to eat with rice and/or drinks. There are even several of the more popular dishes for sale in cans (tins) to eat in your guesthouse or on a trek in the jungle!

Mick Shippen agrees with Jeff Petry, despite spelling kao soi his own way . . .

Of all the wonderfully exotic foods in Thailand, nothing strikes a chord like the mention of *kao soi*. A dish of deceptive simplicity, it is capable of warming the soul when the cool season mornings begin to bite, can lift your spirits when the rains have dampened them, and as the mercury rises and the air grows thick and heavy, it sends out a clear signal that you can handle the heat. To be presented with a large bowl of *kao soi* is indeed a great pleasure. First you are warmed by the golden color and then enticed by the fragrance of Thai and Indian spices blended together and enriched with coconut milk. It is at this point that the diner enters into what is an act of almost ritualistic preparation. To begin with, a generous squeeze of lime juice is added to the soup, followed by a seemingly innocent looking spoonful of *nahm prik pow*— a thick and sticky concoction of fried chilies that fans the coals, adding fire, yet beautifully complementing the flavor. It would be unwise to leave it out. If it is to your taste, a sprinkling of pickled cabbage and a slice of onion completes the dish. Taking up the chopsticks that have been placed across the bowl and mixing the noodles with all the concentration and anticipation of a conductor preparing for a symphony, you are ready to eat. Despite its undeniably spicy kick, *kao soi* delivers a range of flavor that is both as subtle and complex as a grand opus. Although this dish is a deceptively simple mixture of chicken stock, curry powder, shrimp paste, onion and garlic, all ladled over thick, fresh, egg noodles and a piece of chicken, the amber liquid flecked with coconut milk and topped with a tangle of crisp, deep-fried noodles, one bowl never seems enough.

This lovely piece was excerpted from **www.ThingsAsian.com**. To read the full article, go to:

WEBSITE
www.thingsasian.com/goto_article/article.2071.html

Jeff Petry also hides from the madding crowds . . .

I probably shouldn't mention this place, but then again, this isn't the Lonely Planet (sorry, Joe), so here it goes: Khrua Pee Khun Chai. It's a lovely, secret paradise, seldom visited by foreigners, and it's one of Chiang Mai's best and most reasonably-priced restaurants. (If you see a 6'6" foreigner there, it's me—say hi!) Located on the old tree-lined road to Lamphun to the south of Chiang Mai, this place is a gourmet's private oasis and a wonderful place to get away, relax and indulge far from the madding crowds.

I prefer the small outdoor nooks, or *salas*, with tables or floor pillows, but indoor A/C seating is also available. The staff leaves you discreetly alone until you ring a bell in your hidden nook to beckon them. Illustrated English menus are available, and **everything** is superb and generous in my not unsubstantial experience. The selection of *nam prik* (chili paste) dishes is perhaps more of a hit with locals, especially the tamarind one, but westerners should give one a sample. The spare ribs (*see krong moo thawt*) in garlic pepper are to die for, and the green curry (*geng kee-owe waan*) is among the best I've had. Other dishes to sample and savor are *haw mawk thawt* (order it and see!), *khai jeo mom yai* (Grandma's Omelet) and everything else.

As the name suggests in Thai, this place and its food are fit for royalty (*khun chai* is a spoken term for a Thai aristocratic title), and the connotations are certainly proved in the pudding. The owner and chef extraordinaire is the lovely Khun Ming, whose culinary creativity and hospitality are without limit. (To wit, she drove me home one night herself after I had sent off a few guests and found myself stranded alongside the road waiting for a ride!) Tell her what you want and how you want it, and she'll serve it up superbly and swiftly.

Khrua Pee Khun Chai is a seemingly remote garden restaurant to head to when you have (or need to make) a few hours to unwind, relax, escape and recharge. It's a place to "gather ye rosebuds and eat the morning glories while ye may!" Should you find yourself unwilling or unable to leave at closing time, do not despair—rooms are also available here.

Although this was meant to be a recommendation for the "Secret Gardens" chapter of this book, and not a restaurant review, all I can say in my defense is: What good is a Secret Garden on an empty stomach? (You see, I have learned something here in the Kingdom of Thailand.)

Khrua Pee Khun Chai

From the Nong Hoi Superhighway intersection on the southern edge of Chiang Mai, follow the old tree-lined road to Lamphun (Old Lamphun Road) south 3 km to Tree No. 742, which stands guard in front of the restaurant on your left. Jeff notes the following landmarks: after you pass the PTT gas station on your right heading south, watch for the big yellow sign (in Thai) and the gates to the restaurant on your left.

Interesting side note: The restaurant is owned by an elder cousin of Mr. Thanatsri, a well-known intellectual and food guide writer (he rates restaurants for the Shell Guide in Thai). His son, Muk Daeng, also writes about food and does a cooking show on Thai TV.

THAILAND ✤ *General*

Eloise Brown likes raw meat . . .

If you've had your fill of *pad thai*, *tom yum* and the other *farang* favorites that Thai cuisine has to offer, and are after a new kind of tasty morsel from the street stalls of Thailand, then maybe it's time to try something new. Something fresh . . . very fresh. How does raw beef and blood salad sound? There is no need for directions to any particular restaurant. *Larb leuat*, a northeastern specialty, can be whipped up in a matter of minutes at most self-respecting food stalls specializing in northeastern dishes; they are recognizable by loads of chicken on a stick, someone pounding with a pestle in a mortar to make papaya salad and a mountain of sticky rice.

A delicious blend of lime juice, fish sauce, lemongrass, ground rice, chili, kaffir lime leaves, galangal and meat *larb* (minced meat) comes in two versions—raw and cooked. Both types are pretty much the same, although the cooked one is usually made with chicken or pork. The other difference (obviously!) is that the raw one is raw, made with beef, and fairly bloody. Sometimes bits of cow's insides are thrown in too. Yum! Use your sticky rice to swab up the delicious juice. Savor the taste of fresh beef with its oh so spicy flavor.

If you're lucky enough to be invited to a northeastern wedding, you will no doubt be served *larb leuat* (the raw one)—it's the dish traditionally served after the ceremony. As *farang* are not famous for their raw-beef-and-blood-salad eating abilities, you may be served the non-raw-'n-bloody version of *larb*, or something else. However, I totally recommend that you be brave and tuck into the bloody one—the pièce de résistance of northeastern cuisine. Once tried, never forgotten.

Janet Brown reflects on Thai foods for every mood . . .

On leisurely Bangkok mornings, you eat *khao tom*—steaming hot chicken soup with rice, sprinkled generously with fried minced garlic. Paired with a glass of *oleang* (strong sweet black coffee), it's nourishing and you're content. Thai men usually eat this at the end of a long and liquid evening, but you like it as a contemplative start to the day.

Usually, you move too rapidly for breakfast and stop only when blood sugar levels plummet. This is the time for food that yells, "Back into the trenches, soldier," and you look for noodles, fat and chewy, fried with bits of chicken and lots of fiery little chilies, *sen yai pat kee mao* (literally: fried big noodles for drunks), or *khao moo daeng* (red pork served on rice), along with some fresh orange juice that's bittersweet with the tang of salt. This is fast food of the best kind—delicious, restorative and designed to send you straight back to work.

At night when exhaustion has won the battle and you are barely able to totter home, *khao kaa moo* is your drug of choice. This soothing, artery-clogging meal guarantees sleep. Along with slices of pork leg that are edged with fatty skin, rice is put into a foam box with a plastic condiment baggie full of the dark brown broth that the meat was cooked in. You help yourself to the whole chilies and raw garlic cloves that accompany this dish and find the strength to hurry home before it cools.

On those lovely evenings when you have energy to spare, you find friends who feel the same. You walk back down to the beginning of your soi where the dirty canal has been turned by darkness and moonlight into gleaming watered silk. You balance yourselves on precarious chairs next to restless tables on the side of the road, which is also the bank of the canal, and eat *hoy taud*, a flat egg pancake that's studded with mussels and eaten with bamboo sprouts and banana blossoms. You drink *nam manao* (sweet and sour lime juice blended with enough ice to freeze your sinuses), ever careful that the glasses do not slide off the table and roll into the canal. From your instant sidewalk café, at your instant party, you talk and watch the soi, which at night is an open-air food bazaar.

At the end of the month, when you receive your thirty-day lump sum salary, it's time for lots of cold beer in the company of friends. You go to the garden of your favorite restaurant and fill the table with plates of food that all of you love best. You share tender circlets of squid fried with garlic, a huge folded omelet stuffed with pork and vegetables, chicken fried with chilies and cashews, green curry with chicken and pea-sized eggplants that are globes of bitterness in the sweetness of the coconut milk. The ultimate beer food is a coarsely chopped mixture of pork and chilies, guaranteed to send flames from your ears until cooled with some of the accompanying raw vegetables and several gulps of frigid Kloster.

However, you come from a place where you've learned that at times it's simply too hot to eat. In this new world of perpetual heat, there are days when your stomach goes on strike. You learn that a small bag of freshly fried bananas, eaten in the relative coolness of the early morning, will provide a satiety that will last almost all day, and that a milkshake from one of the ubiquitous Dairy Queens provides instant and infantile comfort.

You're a transplant, and occasionally feel dizzyingly rootless in a culture that ordinarily entrances you. In a country that's foreign to you, you are the foreigner, the two-headed elephant who is always out of step. On those off-balance days, you seek out transplanted food whose roots have sunk so deep that they are now Thai. *Poffertje*, the little Dutch pancakes, are *khanom krok*, cooked in dimpled iron pans on food carts—circular, crisp and filled with molten coconut cream and chives or corn. Madeleines are harder to find, but worth the quest. When a street vendor lifts them from their scallop-shaped pans, they're so warm and fragrant, so much of a surprise that they would make Proust weep and write a whole new set of volumes about Bangkok. You also find deep solace in the restaurants near the Sikh temple that have fed the Indian community the food of their homeland for a hundred years or more.

Like seasickness, the loneliness that comes from living far from your family strikes without warning. With it comes misery. Once, when you were immersed in this gloom, a food vendor called to you, beckoning toward a cart laden with grilled chicken beside a large covered basket and a mortar and pestle. She chattered companionably as she made green papaya salad, asking if you wanted it with lots of chili and crab. She offered a taste for your approval before ladling it into a plastic bag. She urged you to choose your piece of chicken and dug enough sticky rice from her basket to feed you for several days. She mashed dried chilies with fish sauce into a dark, blood-like liquid, poured it into a tiny plastic bag, secured the bag with a rubber band and smiled, knowing that you were as warmed by her friendliness as you would soon be by her food.

Then you fall in love with a man who brings you a pot of jasmine that will release its scent into the night. He takes you to have ice cream sandwiches, Thai style. He's delighted by your childish, horrified glee as you watch the vendor split a soft bread roll, add scoops of coconut ice cream, top them with a sugar syrup in which swim little balls of what looks like tapioca, and cover the whole thing with a drizzle of sweetened condensed milk. The squishy bread soaks up most of the melting mixture, but some of it runs down your fingers, and you walk with this man, feeling sticky and silly and happy.

Later, you shop for food and take it home. He shows you how to form a cup from a leaf and fill it with dried shrimp, coconut, minced ginger and shallots, chopped lime and peanuts, and a dark sweet sauce. You feed each other this treat (*miang kam*) and *moo sate* (thin slices of grilled pork skewered on bamboo and dipped in peanut sauce). Later he shows you the way to peel *somo* (polemo), and you eat segments of this papery, juicy grapefruit as you sit outside on your balcony. The sky darkens to violet, the light is golden and together you watch the evening fade, waiting for the jasmine to bloom.

Janet's Favorite Bangkok Restaurants

I love **Hua Plee**, a garden restaurant with a multi-paged English menu and a cocktail bar. The ladies who own it speak English, as do many of their patrons, and the food is addictively wonderful. It's at 16/74 Vibahawadee (or Vipawadee) Rangsit Road, Soi 22, behind the Thai Airways headquarters.

Closer to the city center is **Khrua Khun Kho** (also known as **Khun Kho's Bar and Restaurant**), serving great food with some Dutch influences. Kho and his partner, Cees, both speak English, as does Sunny, the bartender, who makes a mean pitcher of margaritas. The decor is as fabulous as the food, since Cees is a discerning art collector. It's at 112/6 Soi Suwansawas (or Suwansawat), Rama 4 Road, in the Sathorn District.

WEBSITE
www.travelth.com/khunkho/home.htm

Very far afield, but worth the trek, is **Nong Khai**, with wonderful Thai-Vietnamese food in a sparklingly clean, friendly neighborhood place. Few foreigners go this far beyond Bangkapi, but Khun Mart, the owner and a fluent English speaker, welcomes those who do. It's at 7/144 Ramintra Road, Soi Sinpheat, on the outskirts of Bangkok.

Royal India at 392/1 Chakrapet (or Chakraphet) Road in the Pahurat District (look for the English language sign) deserves everything that Lonely Planet says about it. The Sikh temple is near here, on the same road, in the same district. It's hard to find so politely ask a Sikh.

The Greyhound Café on the fourth floor of the Emporium Shopping

continued on next page

Center (on the Skytrain stop, across from Villa Supermarket at 662 Sukhumvit Road, Soi 24) makes a great hamburger—the Elvisburger. Dress up for this one—it's owned by a very chic clothing boutique.

- ❀-

VIETNAM
❀
Phu Quoc Island

*Graham Simmons
is drawn to
island dining . . .*

One of Asia's most surprising food finds is on Vietnam's Phu Quoc Island, in the Gulf of Thailand, nearly on the Vietnam/Cambodia border. I have had the privilege of dining at Phu Quoc's most (deservedly) popular restaurant, Hieu's Place, a family-run establishment right on the beach. Fish is (naturally enough) the specialty of the house—and this is fish like you've never tasted before. Steamed squid the color of lotus flowers and the delicate texture of rice-paper. Blue swimmer crabs cooked in a tangy ginger sauce. King prawns sautéed with lemongrass and chili. Plus stir-fried

vegetables, rice and condiments. For three of us the bill, including ample quantities of beer, came to 170,000 dong (about $11 USD).

❀ ❀ ❀

Every Saturday night the Saigon Phu Quoc Resort has a buffet barbecue around the pool. This is no ordinary barbecue. Dishes range from standard fare—chicken wings, pork ribs, etc.—to snails, pigeon and grasshoppers. This is Vietnamese food at its most earthy, and possibly most authentic.

Hieu's Place
(Mrs. Hieu's Restaurant)
Between the Kim Linh and Tropicana Resorts, just a few km south of Duong Dong on the west coast of Phu Quoc Island.

Saigon Phu Quoc Resort
The island is small. You should have no trouble finding this place.
WEBSITE
www.sgphuquocresort.com.vn

Phu Quoc Island
The island can be reached by air (**www.vietnamair.com.vn/**) or by traveling overland from Ho Chi Minh City through the Mekong Delta to Rach Gia (on the mainland) and catching a ferry (5 to 8 hours, depending on who you ask and the weather conditions) to An Thoi (on

the island). From An Thoi you can take a bus or travel by boat onto the island's main town of Duong Dong. If you're seeking ease and comfort, it's best to take the one hour flight. If you're interested in local color, go for the boat.

VIETNAM
✽
Ho Chi Minh City

Emily Huckson explains why the Lotus Café ain't McDonald's . . .

If you're a backpacker, you will end up on Ho Chi Minh City's Pham Ngu Lao Street, the equivalent of Khao San Road in Bangers (a.k.a. Bangkok). If you're not a backpacker, this is still a worthy area for buying crafts and souvenirs at better prices than in the heart of the city and for feeding on local fare. At the corner of Pham Ngu Lao and De Tham (pronounced "Fam New Lao" and "Day Tam") you'll find the Lotus Café. The staff is very friendly, the lights are extremely bright, the tables are quite lumpy, the chairs are molded plastic, and the toilets are "squat" . . .

and you'll have the best feed, for a few dollars, this side of the Pacific.

When first seated, you're given a sealed package. Inside this pack is a cold fragrant cloth that you use to wipe away the day's sweat and dirt. It is cool, refreshing and costs about 10 cents—go for it. (Most restaurants make them available for about the same price). Try the tamarind shrimp. They're sticky and big and suck-your-fingers, lick-your-lips delicious. Also try the beef or chicken BBQ. A small clay hibachi is brought to your table and you cook the meat yourself. After cooking, roll the meat up in rice paper with cilantro, mint or assorted lettuce leaves and then dip it into the sauce made from a simple chili/garlic/fish sauce mixture. The *banh xeo* ("ban say-oh") is also very delicious. It's a sort of crispy crepe with shrimp, pork and bean sprouts mixed into it. Along with it, you'll be served a basket of assorted herbs and lettuce leaves. First you break off a piece of the banh xeo, place it on a piece of lettuce, add an assortment of leaves and roll it. Dip it into the sauce provided and you're on your way to heaven. Each roll is different, depending on the leaves and herbs used, so each time you roll one you have a different experience. Crunchy, drippy, sweetly scented and delicious—YUM. Don't forget to dump it all down with a HUGE ice-cold Tiger beer.

PLUS . . . whatever you eat, make sure you leave room for the Banana Pancake! Please trust me. I have lived here for more than seven years. I have tasted them all over this country. This one is the best! Order it with chocolate sauce and yogurt for an extra 3,000 dong. It is a totally sharable item 'cuz it's enormous!

As you waddle away from the table, having enjoyed a variety of real Vietnamese food, your pocketbook will hardly give a hiccup to the $5 US spent.

Lotus Café
197 Pham Ngu Lao Street, Ho Chi Minh City.

Emily offers a sample menu: *Banh Xeo* (20,000 dong), Tamarind Shrimp (40,000 dong), BBQ Pork or Chicken (30,000 dong), Banana Pancake (10,000 dong). There are also many vegetarian selections available for similar prices. At the time this article was written, the US dollar was equivalent to 15,000 dong.

Cindy Brown likes people who play with food . . .

When in Hue, be sure to visit Tinh Gia Vien, or as intriguing hostess Madame Ha calls it, "a private villa in the garden of tranquility." And tranquil you feel, dining amidst the 185 species of plants and flowers, in addition to the 400 bonsai trees. Ask for a seat by the fabulous misting waterfall.

Aside from the setting, what is so special about Madame Ha's restaurant? Presentation, presentation, presentation. All of her traditional Hue food is elegantly and colorfully presented, often in the shape of animals. Start with the simple shrimp, already in the shape of shrimp, consisting of four succulent red prawns. Next order Dance of the Phoenix—a plate containing a giant cucumber bird with a pâté plume, resting on a nest of noodles, will appear at your table. Green Papaya with Lemon in the Form of a Dragon comes complete with menacing red pepper eyes and tongue. The more subdued Elephant arrives with carrot ears, cucumber tusks and a pâté head and body properly dressed in a rice paper crêpe. These designs are brilliant, delicious and great fun. Frivolity does not come cheap, however. Expect to pay about $20 US each for the Imperial Meal Set Menu, inclusive of the prawn starter.

Madame Ha will tell you that the first owner of her villa was a princess, and that the grounds house a special Mai plant that is 150 years old, as well as a 200-year-old longevity plant. In fact, her garden is featured in a tourism brochure of royal gardens. As for Madame Ha herself? Well, her full name is Ton Nu Thi Ha, and "Ton Nu" literally translates to "family of the king."

Tinh Gia Vien Restaurant
20/3 Le Thanh Ton Street, Hue.

VIETNAM ❀ *Hanoi*

Samantha Coomber unveils Hanoi's (not so) secret café culture . . .

A legacy from the days of French colonial rule in Indochina, café culture has been embraced by Vietnam in a big way—nowhere more so than in the capital, Hanoi, where I live. (Vietnam is now, in fact, one of the top coffee exporters in the world.) But the ubiquitous, unassuming cafés here aren't just for coffee connoisseurs. They are sanctuaries, where the Vietnamese meet to gossip and pass the time of day . . . and where romantics steal precious moments together.

One of Hanoi's worst kept secrets, Café Pho Co (Secret Garden Café) is justifiably rated by those in the know as one of the best places in town for coffee. Not visible from Hang Gai Street, it requires walking through a souvenir shop at Number 11 and along a passageway before entering a tranquil courtyard garden. Here, and on the mezzanine level above, rain-streaked walls are adorned with traditional artifacts and the owner's oil paintings, while bamboo bird cages and silk lanterns hang from above. Hanoians play chess as chickens run amok around miniscule tables and chairs. Delicate bonsai trees and small stone fish ponds cement the Asian ambience.

You will find no more perfect place to escape the relentless city buzz and try a Vietnamese institution: wickedly strong hot (*ca phe*) or ice coffee (*ca phe da*), served either with a sickly-sweet layer of condensed milk or a frothy egg—the local take on a cappuccino—all for around 50 cents.

Make sure you climb up the narrow spiral staircase in the rear of the café. En route, you'll pass an ancestral family altar. Behind a well-worn gold and black door, framed with ancient wood tablets inscribed with equally ancient Vietnamese character writing, the exquisitely carved, candlelit altar table groans with fruit and incense offerings, overseen by photographic portraits of the deceased. At the very top, you are rewarded with two small open terraces with spectacular views across one of Hanoi's most beloved sites. Sit down and leisurely drink in the shaded beauty of legend-laden Hoan Kiem Lake, at the very heart—literally—of this beauteous city.

Café Pho Co

Located off Hang Gai Street in the Old Quarter, Hanoi. It is reached by walking through the souvenir shop at Number 11.

Dana Sachs
invites you to unwind
in Café Quynh . . .

If it's hard to recommend a favorite pagoda in Vietnam, it's equally hard, in a café society as vibrant as Hanoi's, to pick out a specific café that shouldn't be missed. But Café Quynh, on Bat Dan Street in the Old Quarter, embodies the spirit of contemporary Hanoi like no other café in the city. Like the best of the famous old cafés, Café Quynh is softly lit, relaxed and attentive to the quality of its fare. But, perhaps because it is owned by a famous actress and her husband, a successful photographer, the place also has a cosmopolitan, modern flavor that you don't find in some of the older establishments. It's also rather off the beaten track, and a walk there will take you past parts of the Old Quarter you might otherwise miss.

Café Quynh

46B Bat Dan Street, Old Quarter, Hanoi.

An interesting side note: The café is owned by Nhu Quynh, the beautiful actress from **Cyclo** and **Vertical Ray of the Sun**. Rent the latter to immerse yourself in Hanoi's romantic mood and dramatic hues.

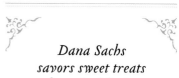

Dana Sachs
savors sweet treats
and tropical fruit . . .

Summer in Hanoi means sugar cane season, and you can spot a juice joint by the long, purple sugar cane stalks piled out on the sidewalks.

Vendors grind the pulpy cane by hand and serve the milky yellow juice, which is sweet but not too sweet, in tall glasses over ice. I like to drink it in sidewalk cafés, sipping the nectar while relaxing in a low-slung wicker chair. On hot afternoons, the taste is so refreshing that the traffic rushing by at the edge of the sidewalk can almost seem to be miles away.

❀ ❀ ❀

Vietnam is not a hothouse culture. Fruits (and, with less fanfare, vegetables) come available during the season in which they are traditionally harvested or—rarely and expensively—when they are imported from abroad. Vietnamese, therefore, are keenly aware of which fruits are in season, and the eating of something like mangosteen, lychee or mango becomes not merely a culinary experience but also a social one. Make sure that you try whatever's in season when you visit, because it's likely to be succulent and delicious. And don't be surprised if you walk into a bank or a travel agency to find all the employees huddled over someone's desk, demolishing a large bunch of lychees. If you're lucky enough to be invited to someone's home, a kilo of whatever is in season will make a lovely gift.

Vietnamese Fruits
The following offers a primer to some common Vietnamese fruits:

WEBSITE
www.vietnamtourism.com/e_page
s/vietnam/culture/foods_fruits/vif.fr
mfruits.htm

Katy Warren deconstructs the ritual of Vietnamese coffee . . .

My first week in Ho Chi Minh City, I followed the recommendations of friends and headed to our neighborhood Trung Nguyen Coffee for a quintessential southern Vietnamese drink—iced coffee. The experience was an utter failure for me, largely because I had no idea what I was doing during the ordering and mixing process, which is an elaborate ritual like many Vietnamese eating and drinking experiences. After applying my analytical skills to the many separate items I was served (one little metal Vietnamese coffee dripping apparatus over a double shot glass, one tall glass of ice with a long spoon, one large metal cup, and one sugar bowl with small spoon), I ignored the metal cup, poured the thick coffee into the ice, added two spoonfuls of sugar, and just about hit the ceiling when I took the first sip. REALLY strong. After seven additional spoonfuls of sugar, I could feel my teeth disintegrating as I sipped.

My critical error was in ordering *ca phe da* rather than *ca phe sua da*, as had been recommended. The *sua* was a very key word—it means they add milk. As I found out, *ca phe da* is iced black coffee and is akin to caffeinated road tar. Vietnamese coffee uses a lot of grounds to make very little liquid, so it resembles espresso, an acquired taste that I had never acquired.

However, I didn't want to give up on the coffee concept altogether since I do love it in general, and I had loads of time to spend lounging about in coffee houses. So for my second attempt I went with the iced milk coffee. The catch is that in Vietnam *sua* (milk) means sweetened condensed milk, which just sounded a bit icky to me with my western tastes. Of course, now I realize that was just my irrational, sweetened-condensed-milk-prejudice talking. *Ca phe sua da* made the traditional Vietnamese way is fabulous. After my first taste, not a day went by without at least one rich, refreshing glass, relaxing in the air-conditioned comfort of a local coffee house or just sitting on a tiny stool on the sidewalk watching life in Ho Chi Minh City pass by. The really good ones taste like a chocolaty dessert,

and they have so much caffeine that you're wired for an hour—the perfect drink to prepare a traveler for more sightseeing.

Katy's recipe for making the perfect iced coffee at home.

Ingredients:
- 1-3 Tablespoons finely ground coffee (to taste)
- Hot water
- 3-10 Tablespoons sweetened condensed milk (optional, to taste)
- 1 glassful of ice

Equipment:
- 1 coffee cup or small glass
- 1 Vietnamese coffee filter (easily purchased in most markets)
- 1 drinking glass filled with ice
- 1 metal cup (optional – this is used in some coffee houses, since by the time your coffee is finished dripping, the ice in the glass has melted somewhat; you can use the metal cup to drain out the excess water before you pour the coffee/milk combination onto the ice. Personally, I just drink the melted ice.

Directions:
Into the coffee cup pour the sweetened condensed milk. The more you use, the more like

dessert the final product will be. Put the grounds into the filter and screw down the press, place it over the coffee cup, and pour hot water to near the top of the filter (this part is usually done for you in Vietnamese coffee shops). After a few minutes, lift the lid of the filter to make sure all the water has gone through. When finished, remove the filter, stir the coffee and milk together in the cup (the milk will remain at the bottom of the cup if not stirred) and pour the mixture over the glass of ice. Drink up!

Cindy Brown eats her way through the country & history of Vietnam . . .

Bittet
French-Vietnamese Cuisine
in Hanoi

When you see the sign for Bittet, turn into the narrow, poorly lit doorway and just keep going and going and going. This place gives you your first taste of the old French system of property tax—based on width, it meant that houses were built extremely narrow and ridiculously long. Seemingly hours later, still in the corridor of the house, you arrive at the kitchen. As the smells of oil and garlic pleasantly assault your senses you think, aah, the expedition was worth it. Simply decorated and densely packed, this place is the haunt of many a happy Vietnamese family. Try the *bittet*, a nice slice of beefsteak and a deal at 15,000 dong. Where else can you get a steak for one dollar? Chicken dinner arrives with a generously sized portion of leg and thigh, nicely roasted and accompanied by *pomme frites*, also introduced by the French. It's a good value at 30,000 dong, but the real treasure here is the seafood. Your choice of blue crab or giant shrimp is served deep-fried and topped with heaps of scrumptious garlic. Both cost under five dollars. All meals come with French bread. Hey, what is it with the French theme!

Hotel Saigon Morin
(Morin Hotel)
Garden Dining in Hue

Several centuries ago, the capital of Vietnam was relocated to Hue. The emperors felt that the more dishes that were created during their reign, the more power and sophistication they would exude. They hand-picked Vietnam's finest chefs and transferred them to Hue. These culinary transplants were ordered to whip up hundreds of new creations, causing the chefs to introduce numerous new flavors and textures to traditional Hue dishes. During this time, commoners were forbidden from eating these creations that were reserved solely for Vietnamese royalty.

To begin a love affair with Hue food, reserve a table for two at the oldest hotel in central Vietnam. Rice puddings, pancakes, seafood and delicate sauces figure prominently. Watch as the crêpe-cook quite literally dips her hands into the batter and drizzles it into a saucepan, imparting a bird nest texture to the spring rolls. All of the 30-plus dishes on the buffet are prepared under the watchful eye of the chef, a Hue local who has been with the hotel for five years. My personal favorites include the rice pudding with sugar cane in banana leaf, papaya and shrimp salad, and special rice cake Hue-style with mashed shrimp. The buffet dinner costs 100,000 dong ($7 US) per person and includes live traditional Vietnamese music, as well as a two-person dragon dance. Wander the hotel grounds after dinner, as this place is quite a historical landmark, having survived the Dragon Year Typhoon of 1904 (though its roof blew off) and the French and American Wars.

Cua Dai Restaurant
Eating on the Beach
in Hoi An

Chinese port traders descended upon Hoi An in the 1700s and introduced Chinese delicacies to the local community, making such elements as rice dumplings and noodles a staple. Limited in scope compared to the food of Hue, Hoi An fare centers around three main dishes: White Rose, *Won Ton* and *Cao Lau*. This cuisine also uses hot chili paste, much more so than in the rest of Vietnam.

White Rose, consisting of rice dumplings steamed with pork and shrimp inside, is similar to Chinese dim sum. At Cua Dai, where Chef Tu presides, the White Rose is served with a delicious homemade squid-fish sauce. The *won ton* here is light, fluffy, melt-in-your-mouth delicious, accompanied by a sweet and sour sauce that is a cross between a salsa and a chutney. The *cao lau*, (noodles with pork slices, bean sprouts and herbs) is perhaps the most special, since only the well water in Hoi An can create the high quality of these noodles. In addition, the pork here is marinated and simmered during an intense six-hour process. This is Hoi An cuisine at its finest. It should come as no surprise that Chef Tu's parents are also chefs. Each Hoi An specialty here costs a very reasonable $1 to $1.50 US.

Hoi An Restaurant Urban Interpretations in Ho Chi Minh City

Built to resemble an Imperial Dining House, this up-market restaurant offers both Hoi An and Hue cuisines. Inside, the decor is a study in simplicity and dark wood. Chairs are individually carved from solid (in other words, extremely heavy) ironwood. Bonsai trees that grow in caves also thrive here. For a starter, sample the Hoi An Spring Rolls—the substantive shrimp and pork paste filling offers a tasty contrast to the light and crispy black sesame, cassava flour and rice flour roll that enrobes it. Tiny Rice Custard With Crumbled Shrimp is a veritable palette of orange (shrimp), yellow (pork rind) and green (buttery chives), set atop a white translucent custard. Though not made with authentic Hoi An noodles, the Cau Lau is still luscious, with lean pork, fresh shrimp and a crunchy fried onion/sesame/ crouton topping, served with a separate clear-beef-bone broth. The Vietnamese green tea is delivered in an elegant wood box, and the service is first-class, with staff standing at-the-ready to assist . . . no need to ask for help with pulling out your weighty chair. Prices are first-class, as well. Including a glass of wine, dinner for two will set you back about $25 US each.

Bittet
51 Hang Buom Street, Hoan Kiem District, Hanoi.

Hotel Saigon Morin
30 Le Loi Boulevard, Hue.
WEBSITE
www.morinhotel.com.vn

Cua Dai Restaurant
Located in the Hoi An Beach Resort, Hoi An.

Hoi An Restaurant
11 Le Thanh Ton Street, District One, Ho Chi Minh City.

This essay was excerpted from **www.ThingsAsian.com**. To read the full article, go to:
WEBSITE
www.thingsasian.com/goto_article/ tell_story.1702.html.

Kim Fay's fact files from the chapter introduction . . .

Maison Long Hoa
#6 Ba Thang Hai Street (3 Thang 2 Street), Dalat, Vietnam.

Indochina Spirit
Ban Vat That 50-51, Luang Prabang, Laos.
EMAIL
Indochina1@yahoo.com

A primer for serious shoppers and other treasure hunters.

It is interesting how an object can evoke a sense of place even when it is far removed from the landscape where it was purchased. My apartment is filled with keepsakes from my travels that feel more like variations on my diary entries than mere inanimate objects. When I look at a small, plump, blue and white ceramic teapot, I recall the warm hospitality I encountered in Hoi An. Each time I set my table with a beautiful, sage-colored, hand-embroidered linen tablecloth, I think about my dear friend Loan—the sister of the embroidery shop's owner—and the many hours she and I spent in the back of the family's Ho Chi Minh City store talking about our childhoods, taking painting lessons and eating whatever fruit happened to be in season on the day I visited. A few days after September 11, 2001, my sister and I were in Hanoi. No longer able to bear watching the news, we went to a traditional water puppet show. Afterward, we stopped in a shop on the street outside the theater to buy puppets. The girl who ran the shop, Hanh, was very concerned when she learned that we were from America. She wanted to know if our parents and friends were all safe. After my sister and I bought four of her lovely puppets, she gave us a small, carved stone pagoda (worth at least the value of our purchases) to take to our mother—a gesture of friendship and a symbol of peace. My puppets now sit in my living room. They are both adornment and a reminder of the power of the kindness of strangers.

In this chapter, when Eloise Brown raves about the luxury of having an item of clothing made by a tailor, she is talking about the experience as much as the purchase. Every time I visited the popular-with-expats Tuyet Lan Tailor Shop in Ho Chi Minh City, it took at least three fittings with the exuberant Chin before my weekday work blouse or weekend sundress was ready. The ritual was always as important as the resulting purchase, which is often the case in Southeast Asia no matter what you are buying—Emily Huckson's essay on bargaining in

Vietnam is proof of this. Those who like to make an event of their shopping excursions will love Lori Ashton's fabulous walking tour of Phuket, which includes history, culture and good food along the way. And those who value quality and social responsibility will appreciate learning about Carol Cassidy's textile shop in Vientiane, while hard-core shopaholics will find Nancy and Nima Chandler's informative article worth the price of this book. Nancy and her daughter are *the* gurus when it comes to shopping in Thailand; their shopping maps are considered bibles. In fact, during my last trip to Bangkok, I discarded my general guidebook in favor of one of their maps. It was easy to use and filled with insider tips; needless to say, it provided inspiration for To Asia With Love.

A fact file for the shops mentioned in this introduction can be found on page 56.

CAMBODIA ❀ *Phnom Penh*

Matt McKinney does his gift shopping at the Russian Market and in a silver village outside of town . . .

The Russian Market is a favorite stop for most tourists. Walk in with an empty backpack and do all of your Christmas shopping at once. Silver, wood and clothing are popular purchases. Or buy 32 of the small Hindu and Buddhist figures for a chessboard. Or stock up on silks, there are dozens to choose from, to decorate your dream bedroom. If you buy a hand rice harvester, remember that the blade is unlikely to make it through airport security!

Also, if you take a day trip up to Oodong, stop by the silver village nearby and watch local craftspeople hammer figurines out of silver plate.

Russian Market (*Psah Toul Tom Poung*)
On Street 182.

Directions to Oodong
See page 112.

CAMBODIA ❀ *Siem Reap*

Donald Gilliland befriends the owner of a souvenir stall . . .

A girl named Sophea runs a small souvenir stall in the Old Market (Psah Chas). She's a charming young lady and she speaks excellent English—a pure delight to meet and to know. Her shop is located on the first row of stalls behind the group of booksellers that are located across the street from The Only One Restaurant near the river.

(Editor's note: if you can't find the stall, drop in at Donald's Lazy Mango Bookshop and ask for directions.)

LAOS ❀ *Vientiane*

Liza Linklater admires Carol Cassidy's commitment to weaving Laotian treasures . . .

As a child, Carol Cassidy loved to rummage through "all of those old clothes" in her grandmother's attic. Her grandmother was a tailor who lived in an old Woodbury, Connecticut, home built in the 18th century. One wonders if, back then, Carol ever imagined that as an adult she would be creating intricate textiles for London art collectors, New York designers, museum curators and Thai royalty. Today her showroom/studio is located in an early 20th century, French colonial home juxtaposed by a white picket fence on a partially paved, pot-hole ridden street halfway around the world in dusty, downtown Vientiane, Lao PDR.

Laotian silk weaving thrived from the 1300s until the start of the First World War. In the 1980s, when Carol and her husband reached Laos—she was a UN Development Program textile specialist sent to assist women to revive and develop their traditional weaving skills—some of the rich past had survived the years of French colonialism, Japanese occupation and American bombing. She savored the impeccable woven silk she found and was certain collectors from around the world would cherish the lush fabric. When her UN tour finished, she decided to go into business for herself. She and her husband, a former UN rural development specialist she had met in Africa, invested their life savings of $200,000 US and became the first Americans to own and incorporate a company in Laos after the country opened its doors to foreign investment in 1986. The Lao Textiles Company now employs about fifty weavers, dyers and bobbin-winders who carry out her designs on looms that she designed herself.

Because many of the old techniques were disappearing, Carol first had to identify weavers who still retained the knowledge and skills. She found some in Vientiane and others came from all over the country. She located rural families raising silkworms, encouraged mulberry production, persuaded villagers to spin the thread, trained the weavers for 18 months, designed, modified and built specialized looms, researched and recreated the designs, and in 1990, persuaded the Laotian government to provide her with one of the first business

licenses given to a foreigner. The company finally had some work to sell in 1992 and made its first reasonable profit in 1995. That same year Carol also held a major exhibition at the Fashion Institute of Technology (FIT) in New York and no longer felt like she was operating "in a cocoon."

Carol admits that in the beginning "lots of psychological issues" were raised, particularly a resistance to the idea of a Westerner wanting to create contemporary interpretations of the traditional designs—all of her work bears her own modern stamp. However, she eventually persuaded her weavers that they could maintain the integrity of a 150-year-old tapestry design by using color and motifs in different ways. The company's weaving techniques utilize tapestry, brocade and ikat. The complicated process uses selective dyeing before the pattern is woven. The silk is colored by chemical dyes from Germany that are computer matched to the colors of traditional dyes such as saffron and indigo. Carol dyed the silk herself for the first three years, just one aspect of her artistic journey that has been enhanced by "watching the staff realize that everything is possible and we can do anything." Furthermore, she stresses that her weavers are "part of the dream because we shared an idea and watched it emerge and grow into a strong viable product."

Carol does not have to worry about losing her talented weavers. In a country where an average government worker makes about $20 US a month and where the average annual income is $350 per year, Carol pays her professional weavers of art between $80 and $220 a month. They also receive an unprecedented (for Laos) three months of paid maternity leave, a pension, and health benefits. Carol contends that "as one of the first businesspeople in Laos, I wanted to set a good example," and she certainly has established a laudable standard. Aout Chansouck, Carol's principal—and only male— weaver, was making $20-$30 per month and his only possession before he connected with Carol was a bicycle. Now he has an air-conditioned house and a truck, and he supports numerous family members. His life has improved significantly, and he continues to thrive as an artist.

In regard to Carol's customers, most are foreign—80 percent of the work is exported and commissions generate approximately 60 percent of sales. In fact, Lao Textiles has just designed a spring/summer collection for Barney's (New York). As for the process, an order for curtains will take up to two looms for nine months as the weavers can only finish a few centimeters a day on a complex pattern with four-color inlays. The workshop produces no more than 30 to 50 pieces a month. It can take weeks to weave a scarf or shawl, and months to weave some of the complex wall hangings. Some of these pieces can even be found in the collections of international museums, and Carol still manages to have at least one major international exhibit of her wall hangings every year. She believes that "each exhibit gives me the chance to step back and look at the elements which later enable me to push on to the next level."

Carol's dedication and integrity have earned her numerous accolades. In January 2001, she was the first recipient of the Preservation of Craft Award presented by Aid to Artisans, a US-based non-profit group working globally to promote traditional artisans. In 2002, Lao Textiles received a Certificate of Excellency from UNESCO for quality, workmanship, color and overall design. Over the past three years, Carol has also been active advising numerous other weavers in the region on how to help revive and renew their traditions. Among her many endeavors, she has led the team at Lao Textiles in conducting training for the Cham weavers of Vietnam and working with rural and urban weavers in Laos, and since 1999, she has been advising a group of disabled weavers in Cambodia who recently launched a new label of hand-woven silks (using her designs and colors). Carol markets these mostly overseas, but has some stock in her Vientiane showroom. In April 2003, she was invited to Bhutan to look at potential there. As she says, "Many places to go and much work to be done. Preserving weaving traditions is a full-time job!"

Carol is often compared to Jim Thompson, the American who built a silk empire in Thailand. She takes issue with this association because she is herself an artist and a weaver who has always focused on collector's pieces and not on mass production. Posters for her exhibitions state that she "has fused Western design ideals with centuries-old weaving skills from Asia to create beautiful works that are both practical and collectible." But most of all, Carol Cassidy has contributed to a renewed appreciation for Laotian textiles by the people themselves. This truly is one of her greatest achievements. Many Laotians are now creating high-quality work, as well. It is hoped that the revitalization of this intricate cultural art form will thrive long into the future.

This article was published in a different form in Bangkok's **Metro** magazine.

Lao Textiles
Ban Mixai, P.O. Box 5088, Vientiane, Laos. You can find the Vientiane showroom by asking directions at any of the hotels, restaurants, or just about anywhere else in town.

WEBSITE
www.laotextiles.com

Carol writes: "I especially like *BoO village* along the banks of the Mekong south of Vientiane. You can still see skilled weavers hand-weaving both brocade and Ikat skirts." Ask Carol about this village when you visit her shop, which offers both scheduled and impromptu tours. For tours, she prefers it if you contact her in advance, especially if you're bringing a group. This way the shop will be open, and she will try to be in town.

Items from the Carol Cassidy Cambodia collection are currently on sale at the Asia Society in New York City.

WEBSITE
www.asiasociety.org

THAILAND 🏵 *Phuket Town*

Lori Ashton embarks on a walking tour of Phuket Town . . .

You've come to paradise on Phuket surely for the crystal azure waters and some of the best silky sand seen anywhere. Regardless of the time of year, Phuket's scenery is breathtaking. However, during the months of April to October, the southwest monsoon winds are prevalent, and with them come some overcast days and rain, not always conducive to sunbathing. But fear not. Off the beach, Phuket offers a rich cultural history. Historical architecture and shops filled with beautifully crafted Thai products (not to mention the personalities behind them) are all within walking distance in Phuket Town. Take a walk, a cultural walk, one that encompasses treasures easily missed from the back seat of a taxi and that isn't overly strenuous.

Start at Phuket Reminder, on the north side of Rasada Road, near the corner of Phuket Road. Owner Pat Tiengthong has seen many changes in Phuket over the past 18 years of operation. It's a nice place—not fancy, but then neither are the prices. The selection includes varieties of chopsticks, coconut cutlery and scarves. Both her new and antique hand-woven textiles are among the most reasonably priced in the city, and Pat can tell you the history of most. In addition, you can sign up for Pat's Home Thai Cooking Classes. She has taught the secrets of authentic Thai cuisine to amateurs and professional chefs alike.

Walking on the same side of the road, heading west (from Pat's, go out the door and turn right) toward Yaowarat Road, you will find Soul of Asia: Master Paintings & Antique Gallery in the next block. Billed as ". . . almost a museum," its two aging Chinese shophouses have been renovated into a magnificent gallery by Eric Smulders. Combining his love of Phuket with his Dutch family tradition of fine art collecting, he offers a truly distinctive collection. Asian art, Chinese furniture and hill tribe jewelry complement the original Chagall, Dali and Picasso assemblage.

Supaporn Tannapai said, "My father promised me that one day, with my degree in Fine Arts from Chulalongkorn University, I could eventually pursue my love of textiles with my own shop." That dream has come true at Radsada Souvenir and

Hand Made, located two shops further on. The shop includes a large array of old and new textiles from Thailand, Laos, Cambodia and Indonesia, diminutive spiritual figurines and numerous other collectables.

Continuing on, and turning right just before the roundabout, will take you to Yaowarat Road. But before you reach the corner, if you are feeling a bit peckish, you will want to detour into one of the best eateries on the island. Salvatore's, voted the "Best Italian Restaurant in Thailand 2003" by **Thailand Tatler**, is a perfect lunch or dinner stop. Meet Salvatore and his family, who will personally prepare something special for you.

Directly across the street from the restaurant are two more finds. Azur specializes in fabulous bedcovers, cushions and table accessories. Designed by Sophie and constructed in her Phuket workshop, the signature pieces in Thai silk and natural fabrics can be bought by the piece or exported in quantity. Go into Touchwood next door for carved wooden décor and furniture.

Now it's time to move onto Yaowarat Road—a thoroughfare that is constantly changing—home to fascinating owners and funky merchandise. Before venturing far down this road, however, you may want to divert onto Phang Nga Road, the first main street to the right. Walk down the right side of the street, where you will pass a few trinket shops. In the third block you will find Antique Arts. Established in 1980, this Phuket-family-run shop features historical curios and Chinese furniture. The father and son display their intricate traditional Thai style paintings. These special treasures are painted on animal bone or handmade paper. Continue down towards the cross street, Phuket Road, and make a U-turn and come back up the other side of Phang Nga Road. Just a half block from the corner is Sarasil Art Gallery, which houses an array of original work by five Thai artists. Some paintings are based on the near extinct Sakai people of the deep southern provinces.

Proceed walking up the street. Look carefully on the north side within the last block of Phang Nga Road, near the T-junction at Yaowarat Road. You should spot a small archway indicating a Chinese temple—some Thais have lived here all their lives and missed this treasure. Walk up the narrow soi (alley) and behold the Shrine of Serene Light, believed to be about 120 years old. The garden in front provides a calm sanctuary from the hustle and bustle in the street.

When leaving the small soi, turn right en route again to Yaowarat Road. At the junction, cross the street to the west side of Yaowarat Road and walk to the right. Just a few doors further on from here is China House (*Baan Jeen* in Thai), revamped by Ms. Supat Promchan and enhanced at every turn with Chinese and Thai accents. Vintage Asian items and original clothing are on display on two levels. A few shops on from here is Ban Boran Textiles, specializing in ready-made, hand-woven cotton clothing, jewelry and bags. The owner frequently travels, searching for special, hard-to-find items for his collection.

At the crossroad, turn right onto Thalang Road. (You will be walking on the south side in the opposite direction to the one-way traffic.) Within the first few shops, you will see—or perhaps sniff—Guan Choon Tong, a Chinese herbal medicine shop. For the past 70 years the same family has been skillfully combining natural remedies to treat a wide range of ailments, carrying on traditions that date back in this region over 200 years, when Hokkien Chinese immigrants began arriving in Phuket. Most were following new opportunities. Phuket was an important trade center for Indian, Malay, Arab and European traders who exchanged goods from the rest of the world for tin and rubber. Land leases were granted to many of the Chinese in Phuket, and fortunes were made. It is estimated that by the early 1900s, over 30,000 Chinese were working in the Phuket mines

and as merchants. To display their newfound wealth, large mansions were built, blending Chinese and European architectural styles. It is more commonly known as Sino-Portuguese style, as the Portuguese were amongst the first successful European traders in the region. Fabulous examples of this style, dating back more than 150 years, can be found in this area, so as you pass along Thalang Road, take a moment to appreciate the flavor of old Phuket.

All of these houses are typically long and narrow. Carved teak louvers on the windows and wooden inlaid doors marked with Chinese characteristics are combined with European designs of Corinthian columns or Doric decoration. In the center of each expansive narrow home is an open-air garden, which adds natural light and beauty, and also circulates a cooling breeze. A further glimpse at this middle class lifestyle of bygone days can be seen on nearby Krabi and Dibuk Roads and on the small Soi Romanee. On the corner of Yaoworat and Dibuk roads is an example with Doric columns on the lower level and Corinthian styling on the upper level.

Phuket has over 150 Sino-Portuguese buildings listed for preservation by the Fine Arts Department. Although this history has all but disappeared from the

THAILAND ❀ General

island, a walk in Old Phuket Town reflects the rich and diverse past of its multicultural heritage. There are also many other areas for touring Phuket's history or simply experiencing the culture, people, shops and places of fascination. Travel by car from Phuket Town along the Bypass Road to the Boat Lagoon. En route, stop at Ceramics of Phuket in Kathu, the only stoneware studio in Phuket (take a left at the Tesco-Lotus junction). Return to the junction and continue north—on your left you will see Phuket Creative Furniture, for all your home décor needs, and Chan's Antiques and Art, for one of the largest selections of antiques on the island. Lastly, find your way to the Boat Lagoon. (It's all the way up to the T-junction, where you bear left and take your first U-turn. Look for the boat at the entrance). Here you can savor Australian fusion food and good music at the stylish Watermark, while enjoying views at the water's edge amongst the yachts. Along your travels, you will find numerous Thai food vendors. Try some of the signature dishes like *sa-taw* beans sautéed with shrimp and red chilies or masala-based, Indian-type food.

Even if you take home only a richer understanding of Phuket's fascinating culture and a few tangible treasures, you will find that Phuket can offer much more than just beautiful beaches.

Lori's fabulous Art & Culture website provides extensive listings (with great descriptions) of shops, restaurants, spas and much more in northern and southern Thailand (with Bangkok on the way soon.) For more about most of the places written about in this article, visit this website and click the Art & Culture South section. On the left, click "List by Shops." You can click on the name of each individual shop for more information.

WEBSITE
www.ArtAndCultureAsia.com

THAILAND ❀ General

John Padorr shops for Thai silk and practices the art of gentle bargaining . . .

For Thai silks go to Roi's Shop at Bangkok's Chatuchak Weekend Market, Soi 3, Section 25. Vasana Lemthong is the proprietor. The shop has some of the best selections of scarves, tapestries, clothes and trinkets.

❀ ❀ ❀

When bargaining for quality items, Thais in general do not start with an absurd figure. You can often get 15-20% off the first figure given, but not much more. Don't expect an enormous discount. Exceptions abound, of course, but usually for cheap street vendor stuff, not fine crafts.

Chatuchak Weekend Market is easily reached by the Skytrain. Get off at Mochit—the end of the line. With around 15,000 stalls along Phahonyothin Road, it's hard to miss.

Eloise Brown indulges in tailor-made clothing . . .

Attention ladies . . . you want to get some clothes made while you're in Bangkok, and you want to do it on a budget? Where to start? There are plenty of tailors on Khao San, Sukhumvit and Silom Roads displaying tacky photos in their windows of satisfied customers in their newly made outfits. But perhaps they seem too expensive? Don't despair. Bangkok is full of Thai women wearing great tailor-made clothes, and they didn't get them from one of these overpriced shops. I suggest that you search out a small local tailor shop for some bargain fashions and a bit of fun to boot.

Having a local tailor is a woman's dream come true. Tailors can be found in most market areas, residential areas or town centers. Keep your eyes peeled . . . and not for the glossy Armani ads in the windows, but most likely for a small shop front, a mannequin or two on display and a middle-aged woman at the sewing machine. Take in your material, a picture or rough sketch of what you want and see what they can do. Anything from a simple pair of trousers to a fantasy outfit of orange silk—you name it, you got it.

Nima and Nancy Chandler like to shop 'til they drop . . .

Shopaholics unite at:
www.nancychandler.net

PLAN YOUR SHOPPING BEFORE YOU ARRIVE

Treasures & Pleasures of Thailand

Prior to your visit, pick up this insightful guide—**The Treasures and Pleasures of Thailand** by Ron and Caryl Krannich, each of whom have a Ph.D. For serious shoppers, it explains the how-to of shopping in Thailand. From how to bargain and how to select Thai silk that suits you, to what to ask for when buying lacquer and what to look for at the tailor, no other guide goes to such great lengths to make sure you return home with a few items you will treasure forever, instead of a suitcase full of kitsch. Visit **www.ishoparoundtheworld .com** for ordering information. (The September 2003 edition also includes Myanmar and can be ordered from **www.amazon.com**.)

One Tambon, One Product

Under a recent government initiative, "tambon"—or village— products have been regrouped under this official campaign, with goods now available at select exhibitions around the country and online at **www.thaitambon.com**. (For information in English, visit **www.thaitambon.com /English/AboutTTB.htm**). The site contains over 1,400 listings for producers of gift, decor and craft items. It includes addresses and contact details, and is worth browsing if you have specific interests, and wish to make sure you visit certain outlets.

DON'T MISS OUT ON BANGKOK'S BEST BARGAINS

Bangkok International Gift & Houseware Fairs

If you are interested in innovative quality handicrafts and decor, time your visit to coincide with Thailand's biggest gift fair, so popular with overseas buyers that it's now held twice a year in March/April and again in October. Plan two days at "BIG." When the event opens to the public on the second to the last day, browse the displays and identify what you want and where it is. Return on the last day of the exhibition ready to dart past the crowds to your favorite booths and pick up some great bargains—exhibitors begin selling off their displays in order to avoid lugging them home! A warning: prices drop later in the day, but if you've seen something you absolutely love, go early to make sure someone else does not snap it up! For dates of the next fair, click on the Event Calendar at the Exhibition Center website at **www.impact.co.th**.

Thai Craft Sales

Support charity when you shop these craft fairs that bring together village products from around the nation once a month for a one-day only sale at Bangkok's Imperial Tara Hotel. The Thai Craft Association is a non-profit organization that provides training and marketing support for artisans in order to keep traditional crafts alive. For more information and sale dates, visit the Thai Craft website at **www.thaicraft.org**. (The hotel is located at 18/1 Sukhumvit, Soi 26. **www.imperialhotels.com/tara**.)

Chatuchak Market, Sections 2 and 8

This huge market may be the first listed in every guide to shopping in Bangkok, but what few guides mention is the fact that you can visit one weekend, then return four weekends later to find a whole new range of products, particularly in sections 2 and 8. Many shops in these areas were small-time ventures that have suddenly gone big-time, with major exporters and copyright pirates forcing them to release new products on a monthly basis. (For directions to the market, go to page 51.)

Phra Arthit and Khao San's Growing Student Art Market

Think of community art fairs back home and this is the closest you'll get to the same in Thailand. On the back streets of Phra Arthit and Khao San Roads near the Grand Palace and Sanam Luang, every weekend sees more students setting up pavement stalls selling their own creative designs. Products range from street-side art and handmade hemp and leather sandals one day, to hand-painted t-shirts and unique candles the next.

Newspaper Listings

Keen shoppers will also want to check listings of current events in **The Nation** or the **Bangkok Post**. These reports usually include a few events in Bangkok that don't get the publicity they should. For example, a recent art show featured works from Thailand, Vietnam, Laos and Cambodia—all paintings were priced at less than 10,000 baht (approximately $250 US). Other sites that list current exhibitions include **www.thaitradefair.com** which mentions all major trade shows and **www.nancychandler.net/cityevent.asp** which covers shopping opportunities nationwide and also lists several small expatriate-oriented shopping fairs in support of charity.

INCLUDE CHIANG MAI ON YOUR ITINERARY

Chiang Mai's Handicraft Village Artisans

Chiang Mai is a treasure trove for the keen shopper. Surrounded by handicraft villages, this northern city boasts some of the best bargains for quality products in the region. The key is to avoid the air-conditioned showrooms that line the "Shopping Highways" on the way to San Kamphaeng (Highway 1006) and Hang Dong (Highway 108), focusing instead on the smaller open-air shop houses and small factory outlets hidden behind these big showrooms and actually run by artisans. You will find it hard to bargain, though, as your conscience simply won't let you, with opening prices so low you'll feel you're cheating the artisans that work there! A quick guide to the main handicraft villages in the area: On the Shopper's Highway 1006 (San Kamphaeng Road), visit Ban Ton Pao for saa paper products, Bo Sang for umbrellas and San Kamphaeng for silk. Additionally, Hang Dong is for rattan-ware, Saraphi for baskets, Ban Tawai (or Thawai) for woodcarvings, Lampang for blue and white ceramics and Pasang for cotton. Nima adds: The best roadside shopping is now en route to Ban Tawai (3 km from Hang Dong), where top designers have set up unique home décor showrooms.

Editor's note: San Kamphaeng is approximately 35 km from Chiang Mai and is home to camping and hot springs. Read more about its attractions at **www.thailand.com/ travel/natural/natural_chiangmai_sa nkamphaeng.htm**.

Chiang Mai's Guide to Innovative Designer Outlets

For the best guide to top quality boutiques, many of which are in fact factory outlets, pick up a free copy of **Art & Culture Lanna: The Definitive Northern Thailand Guide to Studios, Shops and Special Places**. It is available at the Tourism Authority of Thailand's bureau, the Thai International Airways' office and many hotels and guesthouses. You can also visit **www.ArtandCulture Asia.com**. If the economic crisis of 1997 had any positive effect, this was it: creative minds made redundant from big jobs in Bangkok were let loose only to move to Chiang Mai to start their own companies, resulting in refreshing new products of high quality. (Art and Culture Asia also publishes a similar guide to Thailand's southern provinces, and a Bangkok guide is scheduled for the future.)

OTHER

Shipping Agencies Aren't Just for Professional Exporters

Don't ever let the size of an item deter you from following your heart. Where there is a will there is a way. Most shops selling large items can arrange shipping to your home country on your behalf. Alternatively, in cities like Chiang Mai, all you need is a free tourist magazine to source agents who can consolidate your purchases and arrange for shipping. In Chatuchak Weekend Market, UPS has actually opened a branch to provide services to those who would rather not (or physically can't) lug home their new woodcarvings, antiques, furniture, etc.

VIETNAM 🏵 Hanoi

Dana Sachs lingers at Salon Natasha . . .

Whenever I have a chance, I recommend that travelers visiting Hanoi make a stop by Salon Natasha in the center of the Old Quarter. Natasha Kraevaskaia came to Hanoi from the Soviet Union in the 1980s to teach Russian, but when she fell in love with Vietnamese art and a Vietnamese artist named Vu Dan Tan, she decided to stay. Tan and Natasha's gallery is easily the most vibrant, creatively inspired center for contemporary art in Hanoi. While much of Vietnamese art returns again and again to the tired motifs of national stereotype—conical hats and water buffalos, for example— the artwork on display at Salon Natasha (particularly that done by Tan himself) defies stereotype and manages to capture the spirit of Vietnam in utterly original, often breathtaking ways.

Salon Natasha
30 Hang Bong Street, Old Quarter, Hanoi.

WEBSITE
www.artsalonnatasha.com

VIETNAM 🏵 General

Emily Huckson explains the pitfalls and benefits of wheeling and dealing . . .

Bargaining is a fact of life in Vietnam. It is conducted, with relish, between vendors and people in all walks of life. It is a chance to experience true human interaction, yet at times seems far too exhausting for the foreigner furiously shopping in this country. How sad. If approached with the same spirit of adventure that brought you in the first place, you'll walk away with *face* and a great tale to tell. If you merely pay the price that is asked, you walk away without any face at all and are "marked" as yet another stupid tourist. This information, by the way, can spread faster than an urban legend on the Internet!

Case in point: my friends had to stop at a roadside stand to have their motorbike fixed. Flat tire. Having had ample experience in bargaining, they spent the time to set the price— which ended up to be considerably less than the initial one. Everything being settled, the vendor found that he didn't have the necessary inner tube, and he set out to another spot to purchase one. He returned in a very short time explaining that the other vendor did not have inner tubes in stock. My friend, a patient woman, asked him to go to another vendor. He did so posthaste, and returned with the inner tube. He proceeded to install it and put the tire back together. All was well. As my friend doled out the agreed upon amount, the vendor began his theatrics. The amount owed had risen due to the fact that he had to go to two places and spend more time to find the inner tube. My girlfriend stood fast and said that this was the amount agreed upon and this was the amount she would pay. The vendor then enacted the famous **MacBeth** scene . . . everyone dying in his family, no money, so poor, etc., and refused to take the money. As the bartering between the two continued, my friend said, "enough is enough" and lay the money on the street (as the vendor was not willing to touch it, because, *my gawd* he was so insulted!). As both of my friends did a U-turn to drive away, a competing vendor gave her the "thumbs up" . . . and so did the vendor who had fixed her tire. She not only saved face, but she would always know she had a reliable person to go to should her motorbike break down again.

Kim Fay's
fact files from the
chapter introduction . . .

Kim Phuong
Hand Embroidery

The main shop is located at 39B Ngo Duc Ke Street, Ho Chi Minh City. Many travelers prefer the sophisticated look of the Bao Nghi showroom at 127 Dong Khoi Street. Because of my friendship with the owner's sister, Loan, I like the 125 Le Thanh Ton Street shop, which she manages. All of the shops are within easy walking distance of one another.

WEBSITE
www.kimphuong.net

Tuyet Lan Tailor

75 Nguyen Hue Boulevard, Ho Chi Minh City. Phone: 84 0903 926286 or 84 08 8225616.

EMAIL
tuyet_lan@hcm.vnn.vn

My Nge Hoang Nam

(Hanh's shop where we bought the water puppets)
25 Ho Hoan Kiem Street, Old Quarter, Hanoi.

Some Final Advice on Shopping in Paradise

In Southeast Asia inventory overload can daunt even the most exuberant shopper. As you round a street corner, you are suddenly confronted by an entire boulevard of shops all carrying the same celadon pottery, embroidered tablecloths or paper lanterns; and there are entire villages devoted to a single craft. The problem with this is that it can make even the most beautiful object seem like a knick-knack. The following is a selective list of such items that will feel one-of-a-kind once you separate them from their kin and get them back home.

Rubbings from the Angkor Temples:
These are made by laying a piece of paper over a bas relief and rubbing charcoal over the paper. Elegantly framed, they are works of art, and they offer the mystique of having touched the real thing.

Sticky Rice Baskets:
These small, lidded baskets—which range from simple to elaborate—are staples in markets throughout Southeast Asia. In Laos it is said that if you eat enough sticky rice, you will eventually speak fluent Lao.

Jewelry:
Shopping for gems in Thailand can be a risky, expensive business. Silver, on the other hand, is reasonably priced and can be judged at face value. Exquisite craftsmanship is the norm, particularly in the north.

Pillows:
I adore the triangular pillows that unfold to make floor chairs and mattresses. They look great strewn around a family room or patio. You can buy them cheap in the markets of Thailand. The only drawback: you'll need to ship them home.

Lacquerware:
This ancient Vietnamese art has taken on some wonderfully functional modern forms: salad bowls, jewelry boxes and serving trays, to name a few. This is also a perfect gift for those back home.

Spices:
While not *objets d'art* in the traditional sense, these are a must for those who consider cooking a fine art. What better way to bring the flavors of a country home than with a bag of saffron, cinnamon or cardamom from a local market? ❧

*Fresh perspectives on old standbys and insights
into under-appreciated attractions.*

When it comes to the countries celebrated on these pages, there is a list of must sees that almost every major guidebook mentions. Angkor Wat, the Tuol Sleng Museum and the Killing Fields in Cambodia. All of Luang Prabang in Laos. The Grand Palace, the beach resorts of Phuket and the markets of Chiang Mai in Thailand. The War Crimes Museum and Ho Chi Minh Mausoleum in Vietnam. Tourists almost constantly overrun these attractions, but at the same time, all are well worth visiting. There are few apparitions more mesmerizing (and disturbing) than Ho Chi Minh's embalmed, waxy body at rest in its cold mausoleum (such a dramatic contrast to the heat outside), no matter how many people you have to stand in line with or how quickly you're ushered through the building. The majority of the expats I've talked to agree—sights can be overrun and still be worthwhile. In this chapter, contributors offer a few new ways of looking at the same old sights, as well as recommendations for some lesser known attractions. A few top guidebook authors also weigh in. Both Joe Cummings of LONELY PLANET and Jan Dodd of the ROUGH GUIDES have compiled lists of their favorite things to see and do in Laos and Vietnam, respectively. Some of their choices are enhanced by the writings of contributors to this book. For example, Cummings recommends the Boat Landing Guest House, and in Chapter Six, one of the Boat Landing's founders has written about the Luang Namtha region where the guest house is located.

Arguably the most intriguing destination described in this chapter is Preah Vihear (according to contributor Andy Brouwer) or Khao Prah Viharn (according to contributor—and close friend—Janet Brown). The temple is located in Cambodia on the Thai border; Andy came at it from Siem Reap, while Janet arrived from Bangkok—thus the variation on its names. When I received Andy's piece, I had no idea that he was talking about the same temple that Janet had written to me about when she was living in Thailand and I was living in Vietnam. Her letter was so evocative that I recalled it the moment I decided to put this guidebook together. I dug it out,

reread it and knew that Janet had to write about her journey. She did, and the result is a wonderful piece that exemplifies the spirit of this guidebook.

While the recommendations for off-the-beaten track sights are invaluable, the bottom line of this chapter is that no matter how popular or well-known an attraction is, perspective is everything. How you look at something can be as important as what you see; for example, Donald Gilliland suggests walking around the Angkor Wat temple rather than through it. And when I visited the gorgeous Banteay Srei temple in Cambodia, I was accompanied by the ghosts of Andre and Clara Malraux, who attempted to loot it in the 1920s. No matter what, I would have found the temple beautiful, but knowing its colorful background infused my visit with adventure and mystery. (For background reading on the Malraux heist, see page 204). No matter where you go and what you tour in the region, it's always possible to view a place from a fresh angle and to find an experience that you can call your own.

A fact file for the attractions mentioned in this introduction can be found on page 90.

CAMBODIA
❁
Siem Reap & Points Outward

Donald Gilliland prefers walking around Angkor Wat . . .

When it comes to seeing an old sight in a new way, Angkor Wat is ideal. More specifically, I am suggesting walking around it, as opposed to through it. Between the outer wall and the moat/water that surrounds Angkor Wat, there is a nice shady path you can navigate. Take a leisurely walk around the great temple for a totally different perspective. See kids swimming, locals gathering wood, water buffalo out for a stroll and all sorts of typical Khmer sights. You can still enter Angkor Wat from the other three gates (as opposed to the main gate) and avoid being trampled by hordes of tour groups. A definite must.

Andy Brouwer discusses friendship, trust and a mountaintop temple . . .

(Editor's Note: In response to a chapter topic that was deleted from the final draft of this book, Andy wrote about his favorite moto-driver. Because the people we meet along the way can so often make or break our travels, and can turn a simple sightseeing excursion into an unforgettable experience, I felt it was appropriate to include his piece in this section.)

❀ ❀ ❀

There are too many people to mention in a short article, so I'll select just one and that's Im Sokhom. He's my moto-driver (and best friend) from Kompong Thom. I mention him in my web articles repeatedly whenever I write about visiting that part of the country. Okay, so I hire his services as a moto-driver, but he goes beyond what you'd normally expect. And that's why our friendship has blossomed over the last few years. He first took me to visit Sambor Prei Kuk. Since then, we have gone deeper and deeper into the northern parts of Cambodia and are usually away for days on end.

He's the only English-speaking motodub in Kompong Thom, and as you can imagine that comes in very handy for me when we're "up north." I could say every nice word in the dictionary about him 'cause they all apply. I trust him, literally, with my life, and I always make sure I spend time with him and his family once our long trips are over. He has dreams of becoming a farmer, (after spending time in the border camps), but all of his spare cash goes toward getting the best education for his daughter that he can afford. She is an absolute credit to him and his wife. I could go on and on, but perhaps you should just read more about him in my online stories.

❀ ❀ ❀

As for "don't miss" sites, I would recommend staying overnight at the mountain-top temple of Preah Vihear. Bring a hammock and some food and water; witness the sunset at the end of the day and then the sunrise the next morning. It's all about the location and the sheer quality of the temple itself, overlooking the whole of northern Cambodia.

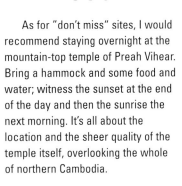

Getting in touch with Sokhom

He can be reached at 012 691 527, 012987722@mobitel.com.kh or chaopich@hotmail.com. (If these don't work, contact Andy at his website). For more of Andy's recommendations for reliable moto-drivers, log onto:

WEBSITE
http://cambodia.e-files.dk/moto.html

You can read about reaching Preah Vihear through Thailand in Janet Brown's article in this chapter. There is also more from Andy about this temple on page 96 in Chapter Four.

Many thanks to Andy for helping with the information in this Fact File. You can read more about his trips to Preah Vihear and the route there at the following URLs:

http://cambodia.e-files.dk/2002.html

www.btinternet.com/~andy.brouwer/pvihear.htm

www.btinternet.com/~andy.brouwer/route6.htm

www.btinternet.com/~andy.brouwer/kthom.htm

Directions for Reaching Preah Vihear from Siem Reap

Route	Time/KM	Notes
Siem Reap to Kompong Thom	4 hrs (150 kms)	Mode of transport: share taxi or truck.
Kompong Thom to Tbeng Meanchey Town (See page 13 in Chapter One for a great restaurant recommendation here.)	3-4 hrs (137 kms)	Mode of transport: share taxi or truck. Andy hooks up with his moto-driver, Sokhom, in Kompong Thom. In Tbeng Meanchey Town, Andy and Sokhom stay overnight at the Mlop Trosek Guesthouse.
Tbeng Meanchey Town to the base of the mountain below Preah Vihear.	6 hrs by moto.	There is now a good direct road to the mountain. It took Andy and Sokhom six hours by moto; a truck or share taxi would be much quicker.
Hiking from the base of the mountain to Preah Vihear at the top.	2 hrs	A new road to the top of the mountain was opened in January 2003, but it's only good for 4WDs and dirt bikes. If hiking, you can stop at the midway point village of Bram Makara for something to drink. The views of Cambodia and Thailand from the top are fantastic. Feel free to stay overnight. Andy stayed at the hut of the temple ticket official. He took his own hammock, but there was no need for a mosquito net as it's cool up there.

*John Hoskin takes
a stroll through daily life
in the Angkor kingdom . . .*

They built wondrous temples in stone, rivals to the glories of classical Greece and Rome. They commanded a vast empire under the auspices of an all-powerful god-king. And they sustained a civilization of unparalleled achievement in peninsular Southeast Asia. But just what was daily life like for the ancient Khmer?

So often with the world's most magnificent monuments, we are left in awe at their scale, their architectural genius and the magnitude of the power and prestige of the monarchs in whose honor they were built. But rarely is there any indication of who the ordinary people were—traders, farmers, fishermen, soldiers, craftsmen, market sellers and the myriad others whose efforts, however minor, ultimately sustained the empire or the kingdom.

What appreciation of the past we generally have mostly relies on the chronicles of kings, which rarely touch on everyday life. With the Khmer of Angkor, however, we are fortunate in possessing a pictorial record carved in stone and extraordinarily rich in its details of the common man. This living history is found in the bas-reliefs carved on the walls that enclose the Bayon, itself arguably the most evocative, most haunting of Angkor's temple ruins, famous for its fifty-four towers each with huge stone heads facing the four cardinal points. Although everyone looks up in wonder at these enigmatic carvings, few bother to trace the bas-reliefs below, which in their own way are equally intriguing.

Less famous and less artistically accomplished than the reliefs adorning the galleries of the site's biggest temple, Angkor Wat, the Bayon's carvings hold perhaps more interest. Whereas Angkor Wat's superbly drawn and finely finished reliefs depict mythological and courtly themes, those on the outer walls of the Bayon, although somewhat crudely executed by comparison, and in some cases unfinished, show daily life in vivid detail.

Clearly, life wasn't always peaceful, and one of the most graphic of the Bayon reliefs contains scenes of war between the Khmer and Chams, the latter recognized by their tiered headdresses, while the Khmer sport little chignons. The carvings are extremely lively and full of movement; in one cameo, an aggressive looking Khmer, armed with a lance held in his right hand and a shield in the left, is thrusting forward as his foot stomps on a fallen Cham soldier. The mêlée of battle is indeed well captured, and you can almost hear the clash of arms.

The best way to view the Bayon murals is to take a clockwise path around the monument, starting in the middle of the East Gallery. This tour begins with a military procession, detailed in its showing of dress and weapons, but also contains images fascinating for their persistence today. The wooden baggage carts bringing up the rear of the procession are of similar design to those still seen in Cambodia's rural landscape. Also, the woman shown huddled over a cooking fire is a timeless figure.

The South Gallery displays what are perhaps the most finely worked reliefs at the Bayon. They begin magnificently with scenes of the 1177 naval battle against the Chams, who had invaded up the Mekong River and on into the Great Lake near Angkor. Again the ferocity of war is well depicted—some unfortunates are shown being thrown to the crocodiles. The struggle against the Chams continues on land and concludes with the king and his subjects celebrating victory, with cooks tending fires in preparation of a feast. More peaceful scenes of daily life are depicted among the lower rows of reliefs along this southern section: fishermen on the Great Lake, hurling a net in the manner still employed today, a hunter

with bow and arrow, and even chess players. There is also a scene of a hospital showing a patient reclining against some sort of cushion, looking rather sorry for himself while an attendant rubs his brow.

Many of the reliefs on the West Gallery are unfinished, but one section is of note. This has been labeled "Civil War" and whether that is the case or not, it shows a crowd of armed men and women readying to fight, and later, warriors and war elephants enter the scene.

The North Gallery, on which only the lower part of the wall is carved, has two sections of particular interest. One displays a circus, with jugglers, acrobats and wrestlers, and the other, a lively procession of various kind of animals and fish, among the most notable a rhinoceros, a puffer fish and a lobster.

Such a brief description of the Bayon bas-reliefs as is possible here merely highlights some of the more memorable scenes, but time taken in carefully perusing the carvings is richly rewarding in bringing Angkor to life and showing how the ordinary people lived in times of peace and war. The most remarkable aspect of the sculptures is that they depict facets of an ancient lifestyle that exist today. Market women, for example, laying out their wares on mats spread on the ground, appear in much the same manner in

Cambodian villages now as in panels of the Bayon reliefs.

Another example, rather more striking, was the experience I encountered a few years ago. I was traveling with a photographer, and after spending the morning at the Bayon, we were touring the countryside around Angkor. First we saw a young boy wading in a pond harvesting lotus flowers, one arm holding the long-stemmed blooms above his head. We had seen the same picture just hours earlier on the walls of the Bayon. As if one similarity wasn't sufficient, we later came across a man grilling fish over an open fire. The man's squatting posture and his manner of pinning the fish between a split stick were both identical to one of the carvings at the Bayon.

Sometimes art does truly replicate life. In this case, it most certainly gave a whole new dimension to exploring ancient monuments, where the life they had once supported has not totally vanished.

The Bayon
The temple site is located in the center of Angkor Thom, which is about 1.5 km north of Angkor Wat. Most travelers visit the temple with a moto-driver or in a car, with the driver acting as a guide. Needless to say, your guide will know the way. And if you're on

your own, there are plenty of people around who can point you in the right direction.

Editor's note: While most of the major guidebooks offer decent overviews of the Angkor temples, they can't—with their limited amount of space—do these magnificent structures justice. I recommend picking up a copy of Dawn Rooney's **Angkor**, published by Odyssey. It is in-depth, fascinating and essential for those who want to do more than simply "tour" Angkor.

LAOS ✿ *Vientiane*

Christina Gosnell recommends climbing the Victory Gate . . .

Laos is the Asia of many years ago. While China and Thailand grow at amazing speeds, Laos remains slow-paced, honoring the old as well as the new. Its symbol, Prutaxai Monument—an Asianized version of the Arc de Triomphe in Paris— represents the country and its purpose in the world. The structure is at the center of the capital city of Vientiane. While its decorations, such as its mythical half-female half-bird figures, can leave visitors puzzled, it is awe-inspiring nonetheless. It is sometimes called the Victory Gate, although, ironically, it is in the middle of a country that has won so few battles. It is also called the Vertical Runway because it was completed with diverted U.S. concrete that was supplied as military aid to upgrade the city's airport. Some visitors choose to climb the monument for a breathtaking view of the city. From up high, you will see a metropolis of almost half a million people, quietly on their way from here to there on bicycles and motor scooters, with few cars or trucks in sight. Some of the girls carry colorful parasols to block the sun while they pedal, while smaller families of three or four pile onto a single motor scooter for a trip across town.

Because of the difficulty of romanizing the Lao language, there are numerous spellings of the name of this monument. Patuxai, Patuxay, Patousay and Pratuxai are among them. As for the monument's location, it is fixed at the northeastern end of Lane Xang Boulevard.

Joe Cummings selects his Best of Laos, based on his years of experience authoring "Lonely Planet Laos" . . .

Nang Khambang
97 Khun Bulom Road, Vientiane

Offering dishes for a dollar or less, this is just about the only restaurant in the capital serving real Lao food. House specialties include stuffed frogs, roast quail and roast fish. It's open for dinner only.

Xieng Khuan (Buddha Park)
24 km south of Vientiane
off Tha Deua Road

Built in 1958 by a wacky yogi-priest-shaman named Bunleua Sulilat, the concrete sculptures at Xieng Khuan include statues of Shiva, Vishnu, Arjuna, Avalokitesvara, Buddha and every other Hindu or Buddhist deity imaginable, as well as a few secular figures, all supposedly cast by unskilled artists under the guru's direction. They're bizarre, but compelling in their naïve confidence, and remarkably uniform in style.

Wat Xieng Thong
Luang Prabang

Luang Prabang's most magnificent temple dates to 1560 and represents classic Lan Xang-Lanna temple architecture, with rooflines that sweep low to the ground. Don't miss the "tree of life" mosaic at the back of the main chapel, and the smaller "Red Chapel," which contains an especially rare reclining Buddha. Instead of merely supporting the head, the unique right-hand position extends away from the head in a simple but graceful gesture. In 1931, the image was taken to Paris and displayed at the Paris Exhibition, after which it was kept in Vientiane until its return to Luang Prabang in 1964.

The Boat Landing Guest House
Luang Namtha
www.theboatlanding.laopdr.com

This eco-friendly guest house sits on the Namtha River in the northern Lao town of Luang Namtha. Spacious wooden bungalows come with verandahs overlooking the river and solar-heated showers, while the restaurant serves delicious traditional Lao food. The staff can arrange rafting or tubing excursions on the Namtha and fishing trips, as well as birding and trekking to nearby villages or to the Nam Ha National Biodiversity Conservation Area.

Is Pham Don, Southern Laos

The "four thousand islands" of Is Pham Don occupy a scenic 50 km-long section of the Mekong River just north of the Cambodian border. Here the Mekong reaches a breadth of 14 km, the river's widest girth along its 4,350 km journey from the Tibetan Plateau to the South China Sea. During the dry months between monsoons, the river recedes and leaves behind hundreds (or thousands, if you count every sand bar) of islands and islets. The largest of the permanent islands, Don Khong, is inhabited year-round and offers fascinating glimpses of tranquil, river-oriented village life. The French left behind a defunct short railway (the only railway ever built in Laos), a couple of river piers and a few colonial villas on the adjacent islands of Don Det and Don Khon. Other attractions include some impressive rapids and waterfalls, where the Mekong suddenly drops in elevation at the Cambodian border, and a rare species of freshwater dolphin.

Xieng Khuan
(a.k.a. Buddha Park)

Drive 24 km south from Vientiane toward the Laos/Thailand Friendship Bridge. The park is 3 km east of the bridge. The park can also be reached by bus from the main station in Vientiane. The station is located on Mahasot Street by the Morning Market/

continued on next page

Talad Sao. (For more on this park, continue on to the following piece by Joshua Samuel Brown.)

Wat Xieng Thong

This temple complex is located almost at the end of the peninsula where the Mekong meets the Khan River in Luang Prabang. It is between Khaem Khong and Xieng Thong Roads.

The Boat Landing
Guest House

Bill Tuffin, General Director of the guest house, has written a wonderful piece on the Luang Namtha region on page 130. His essay is followed by information on traveling to the area.

Joshua Samuel Brown searches for gods and monsters on the Mekong . . .

My travels have taken me to many weird and wonderful places throughout the world, but few have struck me as so purposely eccentric as the twin Mekong statue parks—which the locals call "Buddha parks"—products of the twisted vision and dogged perseverance of holy man, Luang Puu Bunleua Sulilat. It is not known from what divine beings this prophetic yogi received

his directives. However, in 1958, near the Mekong River in Laos, something inspired the monk to begin building statues to honor the gods—not merely the gods who hold sway over the area, but deities, heroes and legends drawn from theologies worldwide, arranged in no discernable order. Sword-wielding Hindu divinities peacefully share turf with the Buddha, deep in meditation. A sculpture of two skeletal lovers locked in an embrace sits on a park bench, watched over for eternity by primitive bestial totem deities.

Whoever imparted these sacred building orders upon the monk never told him to stop. After the communist victory of 1975, he and his sect were forced to leave Laos. A lesser man might have given it up, but not Luang Puu Bunleua Sulilat. Undaunted, he crossed the Mekong into Thailand and began building what would eventually become an even larger sculpture park, just a few miles from the first one. Today, the Thai Park has a carnival-like atmosphere complete with piped-in Thai pop music and a visitors' center selling the late master's paintings and other spiritually uplifting knick-knacks. The Laotian Park is smaller and quieter, with neither pop music nor souvenirs to distract you from appreciating the statues. Both parks stand as bizarre testaments to the power of spiritual artistry and high weirdness.

The Buddha Parks

Joshua adds: Should you find yourself on either side of the Mekong close to the Thai-Lao Friendship Bridge, both parks are easy to find. The Thai Park is on the outskirts of the border town of Nong Khai, and the Lao Park is on the banks of the Mekong just a few miles south of the Friendship Bridge.

For further directions to the Lao Park, see the Fact File that precedes this piece. The Thai Park is known as Wat Khaek and Sala Kaew Ku. It is 4.5 km east of Nong Khai on Route 212. From Nong Khai, you can take a song thaew, or you can rent a bike and pedal out.

Peter Geiser ponders an ancient wat, weaving villages and talking to monks . . .

Wat Phu, Champassak

Even in our modern times, the spirit of sacred peacefulness lingers on in the empty vastness of the ruins of the 10th century temple of Wat Phu. Once connected by road with the Khmer capital of Angkor Wat, it is now rather out of the way of the main traffic lines and usually receives few visitors or tourists. But some monks still live in its Buddhist monastery, and several annual festivals draw masses of worshippers. Some of these events have Hindu origins, and at the full moon of the 7th lunar month, a water buffalo is sacrificed. During this festival, there is also a pagoda market and people compete in games. At other times, the wat is virtually deserted, producing quite an eerie feeling.

Banpo Village (a.k.a. Ban Phanom Village), outside Luang Prabang

Luang Prabang is a very small town, and getting out into the country and visiting the villages is no big deal. Banpo Village has become especially famous due to easy accessibility and outstanding beauty. People there still live very traditionally in huts raised on stilts. Only the first floor is used for living, while the ground floor, open on all sides, is used for manufacturing all kinds of goods (e.g. pottery), weaving beautiful sarongs, or embroidering clothes, bags, rucksacks and pouches.

Talking to Monks

If you take the time, you will learn more about the culture of Laos from talking to monks than from any other source. The monks are usually grateful for the opportunity to practice their English, and novices will cluster around you, eager to catch a word from that strange foreigner. If you are lucky, the monks may invite you to tea. They are always grateful for any book that you may spare, and a good idea is to take a picture of them with you—don't forget to get their address so you can send them prints!

Wat Phu, Champassak

Champassak is located in the south of Laos on the Mekong River, about an hour and a half boat ride south of Pakse. Travelers can fly to Pakse from Vientiane or reach it by boat. To get to the temple of Wat Phu you can charter a boat from Pakse to Champassak and then hire a tuk-tuk to the temple, which is about 8 km away. This will be a full day trip, and you'll want to leave time for hiking to the top of the temple site. Check out the following for more information:

WEBSITE
www.visit-laos.com/where/champassak/

Banpo (or Ban Phanom)

The village is located 3 km southeast of Luang Prabang.

THAILAND 🏵 *Bangkok*

Tara Russell loves visiting Chinatown, Thai style . . .

Having previously lived in China, I had to know what Bangkok's Chinatown was like. I took the Skytrain to Saphan Taksin (the last stop on the Silom line) and then rode the Chao Phraya River Express north to the Tha Ratchawong stop where I could walk into Chinatown. I walked straight off the ferry dock, following the people and the pungent aromas into the heart of the activity. I knew I was nearly there when I took in the smells—sweet meets sewage, dried fish meets dried fruit. I had arrived. Food vendor after food vendor lined the streets selling everything from char-grilled fish and squid to dumplings, chestnuts and skewers of barbecued meat. From moist rice squares filled with veggies or sesame paste, to fruit, watermelon seeds, heaps of colorful, jelly-like worms and dried fish. My gaze drifted from the food to the background of GOLD (you'll understand when you go!) shops with their bright red interiors. I continued walking and came face to face with what instantly took me back to China: a pig—snout, ears, and all—looking back at me. I turned down Sampeng Lane and began weaving through mobs of people in the narrow alley. Every once in a while, a giant pushcart rolled through, consuming the entire lane and forcing me aside. Specialized stalls stretched as far as I could see. One man sold buttons; another sold beads. One woman hawked women's underwear, while another vended neon cell phone cases. Plastic baggies of all shapes and sizes, belts, shoes, purses—the list goes on; however, the majority of the vendors sold fabric. Rolls and rolls of fabric. All varieties of colors, styles and weights. This was the place to buy in bulk! But I couldn't get away from the smell of dried fish. Hadn't I passed that area? Where was this coming from? Oh, I spotted the source—more dried fish, and . . . even more GOLD stores. Food surrounded me; I was getting hungry. I made my way to Yaowarat Road and had dim sum (very good) at the Shangarila Restaurant. On my way back toward the river, I saw a Chinese pharmacy and several tea shops, a requisite in Chinatown. I continued dodging people and never ever escaped the smell of dried fish or lost sight of the easily identifiable GOLD stores. This area is definitely worth the trip!

Shangarila Restaurant
306 Yaowarat Street, Bangkok, Thailand. Phone: 02-235-7439. Open from 11 a.m. to 10 p.m.

Tara explains: Tha Ratchawong is a river express stop. The piers at the river express stops are all labeled (i.e. Tha Si Phraya, Tha Oriental, Tha Ratchawong, etc.). There are river express maps at each of the piers, so it's fairly simple to see where the boats will be stopping.

John Padorr unwinds by boating in Bangkok . . .

Few excursions around Bangkok are as easy to arrange or as exotic, serene and stress-free as a river trip winding around the Chao Phraya and Thonburi klongs. Boats are for hire at the pier beside the Oriental Hotel. The best pier is the one less traveled—behind the hotel parking lot. For 400-500 baht per hour, you can hire a 7-meter long "Rua Yon" boat, an older, once-commercially driven, wooden motor boat, seating up to 12 passengers comfortably. They are much quieter than the long-tail boats. Go with friends, stock up on refreshments or stop for snacks along the way. The boatmen are agreeable to whatever you want to see for any length of time—generally two to five hours. My favorite boat captain is an old Chinese-Thai whose boat horn imitates the sound of a rooster crowing. His name is Mr. Tai and last time I checked, his number was 02-476-3225.

The Oriental Hotel
48 Oriental Avenue, Bangkok.

WEBSITE
www.mandarin-oriental.com/bangkok

*Jim Algie
takes you to a little
park of horrors . . .*

Schoolgirls play badminton here; teenagers shoot hoops on the concrete basketball court; people of all ages work out at the outdoor gym, go through the slow motions of tai chi, and jog around the flower-brightened park. But then you notice a row of vacant prison cells on the north side, and guard towers standing like big stone sentinels. Welcome to Romanee Lart Park, once the site of Maha Chai Prison, Bangkok's most draconian penitentiary. Built by the French some 100 years ago, most of it was torn down back in 1990.

In his cult autobiography, **The Damage Done: Twelve Years of Hell in a Bangkok Prison** (1998), convicted heroin trafficker Warren Fellows recounts some of his hellish

experiences in Maha Chai, such as being locked in a "darkroom" for 23 hours and 55 minutes a day. The cell was so cramped there was not even enough room to lie down, and some of the prisoners, left there for months at a time, ate flattened cockroaches mixed with fish sauce in order to survive. If that wasn't enough, the sadism of the guards goes far, far beyond anything in **Midnight Express**. In one particularly nauseating episode, Fellows (who was imprisoned there in the late '70s) writes how a guard forced a bunch of the prisoners to stand in a septic tank, chin-deep in excrement for many hours, because they'd been playing a dice game in their cell.

To check out Maha Chai's legacy of barbarity and the harshest penal tortures from Siam of yesteryear, as well as the old machine gun used to execute prisoners at Bang Kwan Prison in Bangkok, head over to the Corrections Museum in the southeast corner of the park, which is just down the street from the Golden Mount, but on the opposite side of the street. Sommai, a pleasant young Thai man, will be happy to show you around and explain some of the exhibits. On the ground floor, there's a big rattan ball with long, sharp nails on the inside. A prisoner—curled up—was placed inside it and then an elephant would kick it around. King Rama V outlawed this form of punishment a century ago.

Also on display are knives and syringes made by the former inmates. But upstairs is the real *coup de grâce*: a wax-dummy depiction of two machete-wielding executioners dressed up in red outfits, ready to lop the head off a condemned man who sits on the ground blindfolded, clutching three lotus blossoms, a yellow candle and incense. The hands of the condemned man are tied together with the sacred white thread monks use to bless people and ward off evil.

Because the museum has never appeared in any big travel guides, it receives only about ten foreign visitors a month. So please don't tell any Lonely Planeteers about it and, as always, happy horror-mongering.

This essay was originally published in **Farang** magazine. (**www.farangonline.com**.)

Romanee Lart Park
Jim writes: The park is on Mahachai Road, across from Thanon Luang (Luang Street) and is open from 5 a.m. to 8 p.m. The Corrections Museum entertains morbid souls from 8.30 a.m. to 4 p.m. Admission is free, but you should make a donation.

For more on this park and other parks around Bangkok:
WEBSITE
http://thailandforvisitors.com/central/bangkok/bkk-parks.html

The following wonderful website also describes in detail a walking tour that includes the park:
WEBSITE
http://thailandforvisitors.com/central/bangkok/gold-tour.html

To read a review of Warren Fellow's book, go to contributor Kenneth Champeon's article:
WEBSITE
www.thingsasian.com/goto_article/article.1535.html

The book can be ordered from all the usual online resources, but don't forget to try your local, independently owned bookstore first.

For those interested in visiting a Thai prison, go to the following website and click "Visit a Prisoner" in the "Other Stuff" section on the left hand side of the page.
WEBSITE
www.khaosanroad.com

At the following website, the "Letter from the Inside" column is a must read—very eye-opening!
WEBSITE
www.farangonline.com

Kat Tosi mingles with ghosts and the macabre . . .

Do you believe in ghosts? People from all over the country bring dresses, cosmetics, toys, flowers, shoes, refrigerators, closets, motorbikes and television sets to honor one in Bangkok. Her name is Nang Naak. She lived over 100 years ago and died during childbirth while her husband was off at war. He later returned and was found sitting in his house chatting with the ghosts of his dead wife and child. The temple Abbott was called, and an exorcism was performed, during which Nang Naak is said to have risen from the grave. The Mae Naak shrine was later built on her burial place. Inside the shrine, you will find a statue of Nang Naak—it is watching television and is surrounded by gifts, while dozens of people line up to bring her more. Outside there is a bustle of fortune tellers and a "magic" tree that reveals winning lottery numbers when rubbed correctly. Vendors will let you set eels, turtles, birds and frogs free, for a fee, a gesture that is said to bring you good luck in the future. You can add even more adventure and photo opportunities to this outing by hiring a long tail boat to take you to this temple.

Not for the weak at heart! The Museum of Forensic Medicine, located on the premises of the massive Siriraj Hospital, will shock the most macabre loving of visitors. Skeletons, mummified bodies, the bloody shirts of stab wound victims, ropes used in hangings, preserved body parts and deformed children, autopsy kits, amputated legs, bones, teeth, preserved skin with tattoos, bullet casings, gruesome photographs, a variety of ruptured organs, plus the preserved body of Thailand's notorious executed child abductor (Si Quey) who believed that eating children's organs would grant him eternal life—all are here. Don't eat lunch before you visit.

Temple of Nang Naak
The temple is located within the Wat Mahabute compound in On Nut, Sukhumvit Soi 77, Bangkok. Admission is free. It's best to go during the daylight hours.

Kat's directions to the shrine: Take the ferry from Sukhumvit Soi 71 (near the Phra Khanong Skytrain station) in the northern direction. Get off at the Wat Mahabute stop.

Museum of Forensic Medicine
Siriraj Hospital is located at 2 Prannok Road, at the intersection of Arunamarin and Prannok Roads, in Thonburi in Bangkok. The museum is officially known as Songkran

Niyomsane Forensic Medicine Museum. Admission is free. For more information, check out:

WEBSITE
www.si.mahidol.ac.th/eng/

THAILAND 🏵 *Lopburi*

XXXXXXXXXXXXXXXXXXXXXXXXXXXX
◦◦◦◦◦◦◦◦◦◦◦◦◦◦◦◦◦◦◦◦◦◦◦◦◦◦◦◦

John Hoskin hunts down the ghosts of Lopburi . . .

I've always reckoned Lopburi to be one of Thailand's ugliest towns. In my idiosyncratic list of the Kingdom's superlatives, however, I also rate it amongst the most historic. Ignore the pretentious traffic circle, the railway tracks, the monotonous shop houses, and, most especially, avoid the notoriously malicious monkeys at the Kala Shrine, and you will discover an extraordinary window onto the past. It's a window easy to access; Lopburi is about 150 kilometers north of Bangkok.

Once arrived, pay no attention to first impressions and explore selectively. You'll soon discover within the heart of the concrete sprawl a number of ancient ruins that are clear indications that the town has seen better days. Indeed, it was once

briefly the center of the Thai world, where international diplomacy was played out at the height of Siamese power in the 17th century. Although Lopburi achieved early distinction—most especially as an important outpost of the Khmer Empire during the 10th to late 13th centuries, from which monuments survive—it was King Narai (1656-88) who put the place, then known as Louvo, on the map. Indeed, if Lopburi belongs historically to anyone, it is properly the domain of King Narai and his chief advisor, the wily Greek, Constantine Phaulkon. To any visitor even only slightly receptive to echoes of the past, the town is haunted by the shades of these two very remarkable men, both of whom lived their most exciting years—and met their deaths—there.

Narai made Lopburi Thailand's second capital when he elected to move his court there for part of each year, turning the city into a sort of Versailles to Ayutthaya's Paris. In so doing, he set the stage on which one of the most intriguing episodes of Thai history was enacted. But while the monarch played the lead, the star performer was the foreigner Phaulkon.

The 17th century saw the first big wave of European interest in Siam. Foreign powers, such as the Dutch, English and French, were anxious to establish lucrative trade links, while adventurous individuals sought to amass private fortunes as they ostensibly served the royal monopoly on trade. Of them all, none rose so high as the remarkable Phaulkon. A British seaman of Greek origin, he arrived in Siam in 1678, and in a meteoric career spanning just ten years, he rose from trader to become the second most powerful man in the land, and was Narai's first minister in all but name. Never before or since has a foreigner held such influence in Siam.

As the King's favored advisor, Phaulkon attempted to walk an impossible diplomatic tightrope, trying to win French support to further achieve Narai's diplomatic goals while, at the same time, appeasing conservative elements at court wary of a growing foreign presence. He was doomed to failure. On his rise to power he had made numerous enemies, partly through his own arrogance and partly through others' envy of his wealth and position. In 1688, when Narai lay on his death bed, Phaulkon was arrested during a palace revolution and charged with treason. Without the protection of his ailing benefactor, he was imprisoned, tortured and finally executed.

Following the Revolution of 1688, the French were expelled from Siam, effectively closing the door on international relations for the next 200 years. Ayutthaya once again became the sole capital and Lopburi declined into obscurity. But while France had failed in her 17th century attempt at political and commercial links with Thailand, she had a lasting impact in other respects. Lopburi was left with an indelible Gallic stamp.

Firstly there are the ruins of Narai's palace, a grandiose affair that was partially designed by French architects and comprised of courtyards set within courtyards, the whole surrounded by huge crenellated walls pierced at intervals by tall imposing gateways. What remains of the interior buildings is mostly in ruins, but the walls and gates (at one of which Phaulkon was ambushed and captured) are as imposing as ever. Not far away is Phaulkon's house, also known as the "Ambassadors' Residence," since French delegates stayed there. It again shows a strong European influence in design. Only the exterior walls have survived, but the architectural borrowings are clear. Between these two important 17th century ruins, is Wat Sao Tong Thong. Its preaching hall was used in Narai's time as a Christian chapel. Once more, the stylistic departures of the period are noticeable.

In addition to these notable structures, Lopburi's single most imposing religious ruin is Wat Phra Si Ratana Mahathat; located

3. Seeing the Sights

opposite the railway station, it is an example of the modern town's uncanny habit of blending the venerable with the mean. It is an extensive site dominated by a large laterite *Khmer prang* (tower), though the temple is most fascinating for its overall construction, which spans the Khmer period and the 17th century. Most likely first erected in the 12th century and remodeled in the 14th, it was considerably expanded by King Narai.

In all, in spite of its modern overlay, Lopburi remains a lasting monument to an intriguing past. Guidebooks perhaps rightly promote Ayutthaya as the window onto old Siam, but it is overlooked Lopburi that most loudly echoes with the 17th century ring.

Lopburi

is approximately 150 km north of Bangkok. Trains going to Lopburi leave from Bangkok's Hualamphong Station on Phra Rama IV Road. Buses (both sweltering and air-conditioned) leave from Bangkok's Northern Bus Terminal—aka Mo Chit—at Kamphaeng Phet 2 Road near the Chatuchak Weekend Market. Information on taking the train can be found at:

WEBSITE
www.railway.co.th/httpEng/

Narai's Palace, Phaulkon's House, Wat Sao Tong Thong and Wat Phra

Si Ratana Mahathat all reside within walking distance from one another in the Old City of Lopburi. Many guidebooks, such as the **Eyewitness Travel Guide: Thailand**, offer good maps identifying all four locations.

For more information on Lopburi, go to the following URLs:

WEBSITE
www.tat.or.th/province/central/lopburi/

WEBSITE
www.thingsasian.com/goto_article/article.1873.html (written by contributor Donald Gilliland.)

THAILAND
❀
From the Malay Border to Bangkok

Stephen Engle goes for Bangkok or bust(ed) . . .

It's midnight on the Sorry-You-Went Express. My earlier dinner of instant noodles and Chang beer is getting a wake-up call, as we rumble up the Ismuth of Kra. A Canadian girl down the carriage shrieks after finding her Walkman has been stolen from under her head while she slept. There are nine hours to go before Bangkok.

THAILAND ❀ *From the Malay Border to Bangkok*

Singapore seems a faint memory.

This is not the Eastern and Oriental Express, mind you, which whisks the well-heeled up the Malay Peninsula in colonial-era-like opulence. There are no rosewood-paneled compartments or marbled baths on the "rapid" state-run trains of Thailand and Malaysia. Here, afternoon tea is served in fine Styrofoam—one bump or two?

There's no resident pianist either, and the chefs are known neither internationally nor locally. If you're looking for "spicy snow fish" or "delectable dim sum," you're on the wrong train. But you know what? The view from the window is the same. The 2,030-kilometer journey is a moving feast for the eyes—offering glistening green rice paddies, small villages and orchards of tamarind and mango—regardless of the price printed on one's ticket.

One-way Singapore to Bangkok aboard the E&O Express will set you back between $1,500-$3,000 US—an extravagance some might call ostentatious. Personally, I have no such qualms—I just don't have the clams. So I ended up traveling basically the same stretch of rail by more modest means for the equivalent of $42 US plus noodle and beverage expenses. If all connections worked as planned, I would roll into the Thai capital not having showered or shaved in more

than 40 hours. You could say I was ripe for the challenge.

In Singapore I boarded the overnight Express Timuran bound for Pasir Mas (near the Malay-Thai border). I crawled into my clean 2nd class upper berth ($27 US) and pulled the curtain closed, knowing that in the morning I would be but a short taxi ride from Thailand. Malaysia's KTM rail network has two main lines: one up the west coast through Kuala Lumpur, and the other up the gut—the so-called jungle line, which I chose. Had I gone west, I would have had to change trains twice instead of once.

Unfortunately, for my route, most of Malaysia passed in the dark—a price I had to pay for expediency. But hurtling through a strange and darkened world is in itself a journey of exotic intrigue. The sway of the carriage and unvaried clack of wheel against rail lulled me into a half-hypnotic state, as I gazed at the dancing windowpane. Lonely platforms, thick with shadow, jumped from the moist night as we rattled past—a choreography that would last until first light.

From Pasir Mas, Mohamed, a quiet man with a leaden foot, drove me by dilapidated taxi to the border—about a 20-minute ride. I crossed into Thailand by foot over a small bridge spanning a brownish-green river. I set my watch back an hour, which gave me plenty of time to catch the next "rapid" train (21 hours!) to Bangkok ($13 US).

Thai sleeper compartments differ slightly from their Malaysian counterparts in that the top bunks fold down like large overhead bins on airplanes, leaving no windows for the travelers up top. The most noticeable similarity, though, is the tiny toilets. Aiming over a moving squat pot while getting knocked around like a piñata is simply no fun. Don't even think about going in there in bare feet.

Beyond that, I do believe in the old adage that the journey is half the fun. And it doesn't have to cost an arm and a leg—just perhaps a Walkman and a good night's sleep.

Taking the Train
Steve offers the following advice on booking your tickets:

Malaysia
WEBSITE
www.ktmb.com.my

You can easily book and buy e-tickets at this site. Just make sure you print out a copy of the purchase page. Not all stations in Malaysia (including Pasir Mas) have ever dealt with online bookings. The station manager at Pasir Mas approved my booking but tried to charge me again. And remember!! When doing this trip north to south, Malaysia is one

hour later than Thailand. Don't do what I almost did on my return trip and miss the train to Singapore because I hadn't taken into account the time difference.

Thailand
WEBSITE
www.railway.co.th/httpEng/

Click on English Version on the right of the screen. Here you can check availability up to one month in advance, but no e-ticketing is available. Be warned that Thai trains fill up fast during holidays, especially during the New Year's celebration.

CAMBODIA
❈
From Bangkok to Si Saket to Khao Prah Viharn

Janet Brown wants to know, "Today where do you go?" . . .

Visiting Khao Prah Viharn, a distant mountain temple that had belonged alternately to Cambodia and Thailand until the World Court ceded it to the Khmer in 1962, had been my dream for years. One of the last strongholds of Pol Pot, it was a frequent battleground until after his

CAMBODIA ❀ *From Bangkok to Si Saket to Khao Prah Viharn*

death in the late 1990s. The only recommended route from Bangkok was overland through the country's northeastern region. That, I reminded myself, was why I was miserably waiting for dawn in a filthy room with blood smeared walls and a bed full of ravenous insects at Hotel Si Saket in the town of the same name.

A large, brightly lit alternative hotel had beckoned as the train wheezed into town, but I wanted character, not comfort, and I was paying for it now as I curled up on a plastic loveseat and listened to calls and shouts from the bus station across the street. As I killed mosquitoes that found me through holes in the window screens, I wondered whether the local water was clean enough to breed malaria carrying insects, and if I'd be allowed across the border into Cambodia without a re-entry permit back into Thailand.

My boss in Bangkok had told me that my visa and work permit would be invalidated without a re-entry form; our secretary had called Immigration and was under the impression that the form wasn't required. Everyone I knew had a different opinion, so I had climbed onto the train hoping I had enough cash for an acceptable bribe, if necessary.

By the time the morning sky lightened to a milky gray my first morning in Si Saket, I was on a motorcycle taxi fleeing to the brightly lit hotel that I had rejected the night before. "Today where do you go?" the driver asked me.

"Khao Prah Viharn," I said. "Will you take me?"

"Two hundred kilometers." His eyebrows shot up. "Take the bus."

"I hate buses. On motorcycles you can see everything. How much?"

And we agreed on 1,000 baht.

Ponsak dropped me off at the new hotel, and then returned at ten to pick me up, looking dubious. "Don't you have jeans?" he asked.

"I don't like them. It's okay. I can ride like this." I tucked my skirt under my side-saddled legs, as I'd been taught in Bangkok.

He looked back, nodded, and we were on the highway.

The sky and flat open fields were a waterless ocean. Grassland held huge, haystack-like wasp nests, small temples that were simple and Grecianly chaste, trees that looked as though they'd been put in exactly the right spot by a landscape architect. Rice paddies were contained by borders as precise as picture frames, and a huge pond filled with lotus blossoms touched the horizon.

The road began to climb, winding through outcroppings of rock and clumps of pine trees. Sunlight broke through the pewter clouds, and the sky cleared. We approached the Thai checkpoint near the Thailand/Cambodia border, where a line of trucks waited for inspection. I clutched my bag with my passport and money, mentally rehearsing persuasive phrases that would let me pass the gates, but an officer impatiently waved us through without stopping.

"They don't think you're a tourist." Ponsak grinned as we sailed past what could have been a bureaucratic nightmare.

A dusty parking lot crowned a hilltop, and Ponsak stopped near a cluster of other drivers whose glances were less than cordial. "Don't tell them that you're paying me," he muttered as the men drew closer. I watched as they asked where we were from, and saw how they sneered when Ponsak told them we were friends on an outing.

"Three thousand baht," one of them said, when asked what they charged to make the trip from Si Saket.

"She has no money," Ponsak said, and held their eyes steadily until they turned back to their own motorcycles.

I exhaled, and he nodded briefly as we walked away from men whom I realized could be convinced to cut my throat for the thousand baht I had paid Ponsak. We waited for the vehicle that drove from the parking lot to the border entrance. "Do you want to come?" I asked.

"No, I'll stay here and sleep." And then, "Are you afraid?"

"No," I replied, "but I don't think I can go," worried that the border sentries would turn me back without an official receipt from the Thai checkpoint.

Another ride ended less than five minutes later at the edge of a forest. A path through the trees was studded with signs that warned of landmines beyond the sanctioned route. A clearing and stream marked the entry into Cambodia, and smiling Khmer soldiers beckoned me toward a ticket booth.

Two hundred baht let me cross the border into a place that only a god could have imagined. Giant cobras flanked the entry, and slabs of quarried stone cobbled the stairs that were carved into the cliff. Meadow grass (sprinkled with aspen-like trees) waved against signs cautioning that landmines were still a distinct possibility.

Five buildings broke the climb at regular intervals, and entering their roofless walls gave the feeling that I was in the heart of the mountain. Their massive doorways were crowned with intricate, fading pictures carved into the rock. Halfway up, there was a small building in a meadow with a smashed plane lying in pieces beside it. Beyond that reminder of recent death and war, the cliff and sky lured me away from the buildings. The rustling of leaves and grass was all that could be heard as I walked over ground that could harbor mines and felt nothing but benediction.

The final structure at the top led to a temple, a tiny room that held a statue of the Buddha and a monk from Phnom Penh, who blessed visitors in Pali, with sprinklings of water and three light blows on prostrate backs. Covered stone passageways beside the temple led me down a geometrically straight hall to the edge of the world. Cambodia stretched below the cliff, brilliantly green, with Angkor Wat only 100 kilometers away. Surrounded by the windblown grass and the infinite stretch of sky, I knew I had reached sacred ground.

Later, back in my hotel room in Si Saket, listening to a Wagnerian thunderstorm that Ponsak had outrun like a hell-spawned bat, I pictured lightning flashes on the walls of Khao Prah Viharn and knew that part of me had stayed behind.

Traveling to Khao Prah Viharn

Information on taking the train from Bangkok to Si Saket can be found at:

WEBSITE
www.railway.co.th/httpEng/

Regarding how to get to Khao Prah Viharn, Janet writes: It is a 200 km round trip from the city of Si Saket to the temple. If a motorcycle doesn't appeal to you, you can take the bus or a *song thaew* (pickup truck with two long benches in the canopied back). Or if you want the motorcycle experience, but just not 200 km of it, you can also take a bus or *song thaew* to Kantharalak (64 km) and then pick up a motorcycle from there. In 2000, when I went, there was a barrier across the road and a Thai checkpoint sentry box about 35 km out from Kantharalak. Here I paid a 200 baht admission fee and left my passport (no entry/exit visa was required). About one km along the road up the hill from that point was a parking lot, a logical place for it since it's clear and barren and spacious, and there's no room at the end of the road near the forest and the border stream. It's an easily walkable half km (about) to the end of the road, but I took the tractor train—several little canopied cars pulled by a tractor-like vehicle, costing five or ten baht and taking less than five minutes. Once they dropped me off, it was a two or three minute walk through the forest and across the stream, which brought me to a clearing at the foot of the 525 meter hill which holds Khao Prah Viharn. There were little stalls selling water and souvenirs; a Khmer sentry collected another 200 baht admission fee. I then began the climb up the very dilapidated staircase . . . don't wear heels, as I did.

For more about visiting this temple from the Cambodian side, see Andy Brouwer's piece in this chapter on page 61.

THAILAND 🏵 *Chiang Mai*

XXXXXXXXXXXXXXXXXXXXXXXXXXXXX
ooooooooooooooooooooooooooooo

Oliver Hargreave encourages you to explore Ban Tha Chang . . .

A lone footbridge crosses the River Ping in the middle of the city to the district of Ban Tha Chang on the east bank. It goes directly to Wat Ketkaram, a charming old temple at the center of the neighborhood. If you walk round the temple (don't forget to look in its small museum), you may observe that the stupa is askew—apparently its builders were too shy to have it pointing straight to heaven.

In the late 19th and early 20th centuries, elephants once hauled logs down the banks of the river at Ban Tha Chang during the floating seasons—hence its name, which translates as "Elephant Landing Village." Safely across the river from the seat of northern royalty in the old city to the west, this was where the first overseas Chinese merchants were allowed to set up shop forty years before the railway came to Chiang Mai in 1921. Later on, when the commercial heart of the city developed on the west bank between the old city and the river, Ban Tha Chang and its wooden architecture were largely overlooked.

Chiang Mai chic is now defined in the quaint buildings of Bang Tha Chang. Here you can find stylish local cottons (Paothong), exquisite adaptations of Karen home-weaves and basketry (Sop Moei Arts), "Lanna décor" and Euro-Thai cuisine (Oriental Style), teak furniture and Thai cuisine (Khampan), and Northern art and Thai cuisine (The Gallery.) The area has become a cluster of restaurants, boutiques and even a spa (Padma Aroma). Pub-restaurants—including the Riverside, the Good View and Brasserie—have terraces that look out over the river towards the city and Doi Suthep-Pui mountain to the west. This is the place to cool out with a sundowner and let the good times roll on into the night.

Ban Tha Chang

The footbridge that crosses the River Ping to Ban Tha Chang is on Praisani Road near the junction of Praisani and Chang Moi Kao Roads, Chiang Mai.

continued on next page

Shops
Paothong
Local cottons. 66 Charoenrat Road.

EMAIL
paothong@hotmail.com

Sop Moei Arts
Home-weaves and basketry.
Located at The Elephant Quay
House at 31-35 Charoenrat Road.

WEBSITE
www.sopmoeiarts.com

Oriental Style
Lanna décor and Euro-Thai
cuisine. 36 Charoenrat Road.

Khampan
Teak furniture. 9 Charoenrat Road.

EMAIL
khampan_chiangmai@hotmail.com

The Gallery
Northern Art. 25,27,29 Charoenrat
Road.

WEBSITE
www.mydestiny.net/~asiasoft/
gallery.html

Spa
Padma Aroma Spa
204-206 Charoenrat Road.

WEBSITE
www.chiangmainews.com/padma/

Restaurants/Bars
The Riverside
9-11 Charoenrat Road.

The Good View
13 Charoenrat Road.

Brasserie
37 Charoenrat Road.

VIETNAM ✿ *General*

*Dana Sachs
recommends visiting
an imperial tomb,
watching a water puppet show,
taking the train and touring
the Red River Delta . . .*

On a quick run through Hue,
travelers mostly focus on the
Imperial Forbidden City and the Tomb
of the Emperor Tu Duc (neither of
which should be missed), but many of
the other imperial tombs are worth a
visit. The Tomb of Minh Mang (1820 to
1840), 12 kms down the Perfume River
from Hue, beautifully incorporates
its architecture into the natural
surroundings of hills, streams and
forest. These days, the 160-year-old
monument has become overgrown
and somewhat spooky, and feels a
little like a secret garden.

The Tomb of Minh Mang
is located on the Perfume River
approximately 14 kms from Hue.
You can hire a boat to take you
there from Hue. You can also rent

a bicycle and pedal out to the village of Ban Lang, where you can hire a boat to take you across the river to the temple. More information about the temple can be found at:

WEBSITE
www.chiengfa.com/otherplaces/vietnam/tombs.html

All the guidebooks urge you to catch a performance of a Water Puppet show, but come on, do you really have to see one? Yes, you do. You'll spend the first half of the performance marveling at the sight of brightly colored wooden puppets dancing across, diving through and bobbing in the water. And you'll spend the second half trying to figure out how the puppet masters do it. The feat is astonishing, both in terms of technology and artistry, but perhaps that's not surprising, given that the Vietnamese have been perfecting it for a thousand years.

Water Puppet Shows
Hanoi
Kim Dong Water Puppetry Theater
57 Dinh Tien Hoang Street.

Ho Chi Minh City
In the History Museum at the Zoological Gardens
2 Nguyen Binh Khiem Street.
Hourly until late afternoon.

It's become so easy to hire a car with a driver, or to get together with friends to rent a van, or to fly, that many people skip the Vietnamese trains entirely. That's a shame. Nothing can give you a clearer feel for the expanse of the country, and nothing can bring a traveler closer to local people, than sitting among them on a train. In some strange and miraculous way, a train ride can make friends out of people who don't share a single common word, and an astonishing amount of information can actually be communicated during card games, over shared food, and through mime. If you don't have much time, buy a ticket between Hue and Danang (the fast train is about three hours). Though you'll miss the spectacular heights of a drive over the famous Hai Van Pass, you'll still see gorgeous scenery and you'll get to share it with the Vietnamese. For more intrepid travelers, consider making an all day, or all night excursion, say, from Hue to Hanoi. By day, you get to see the view. By night, you save on hotels and get to sleep in motion.

Taking the Train
Comprehensive information on train stations and schedules can be found at:

WEBSITE
www.vietnamtourism.com

continued on next page

VIETNAM ✸ General

The Hue Train Station is at the junction of Le Loi (west end) and Bui Thi Xuan Streets, one km from the city center.

The Danang Train Station is at 122 Hai Phong Street at the corner of Hai Phong and Hoang Hao Tham Streets.

The ancient villages surrounding Hanoi seem almost unchanged from how they looked a hundred years ago, or more. And if the occasional motorbike didn't whiz by, or if you didn't hear the rumble of someone's television, or see a young girl walk past in bell bottoms, you might be able to imagine that you had, indeed, stepped back in time. The traditional family homes in these villages are actually a series of small, airy buildings constructed around a central courtyard. In addition to these compounds, most villages also have a local meeting hall, a village well (often a lotus pond with a wall around it), a pagoda or temple, and various other public spaces. You're likely to find such villages if you head out of Hanoi in any direction, but some of the most beautiful are the ones that contain the area's revered pagodas, such as Thay, Mia and Tay Pagodas.

The four preceding pieces were originally published at:
www.vietnamuniverse.com.

For a beautiful description of this area and its temples, go to Dana's **ThingsAsian** article:

WEBSITE
www.thingsasian.com/goto_article/article.642.html

For more about the Red River hamlet of Mong Phu, read on.

Han Thuy Giang discovers a beacon of village beauty . . .

About 40 kilometers beyond the old streets, ancient citadels and shady trees of Hanoi, travelers will arrive at a cluster of small, beautiful towns at the foot of Tan Mountain. Duong Lam Village—the homeland of two national heroes, King Phung Hung and General Ngo Quyen—embraces six hamlets whose houses and walls are made of unprocessed blocks of laterite, the stone that creates the unique beauty of the area.

This long-standing community has a dense population, and houses nestle cozily next to one another. One can tramp down quiet country lanes where on each side moss-grown laterite walls and closed gates create a thoughtful, poetic atmosphere. After the many changes of time and history, only one village gate remains—the gate of Mong Phu hamlet. This simply designed and typical family gate is the size of a village gate; built in a traditional style, its wooden parts are hewn from four kinds of precious wood: bassia, ironwood, teak and dinh. Round panels engraved with Chinese characters held aloft by two rafters create the two symmetrical roofs; its principal pillars stand on round stone blocks reminiscent of four overturned millstones.

Another structure of note is the Mong Phu hamlet temple, standing on a low hill. This large building, belonging to the system of Doai temples, is not very old, but its Viet-Muong architectural style is quite unique. In front of the temple's door is a vast yard which is really a six-way crossroad spreading like fan blades to the hamlets of Sui, Xay, Trung Hau, Sai and Dinh. There is a secret about this pattern that is not widely known: the paths to and from the temple have been designed so that no matter which direction you are walking, you never turn your back on the temple's main gate. Because Mong Phu, like many Vietnamese hamlets, is communal, during festivals local residents travel these lanes to gather in the temple yard. The Mong Phu Festival still takes place from the 4th-10th of lunar January. The festival is an agricultural rite with offerings of food and wishes for good weather.

It would be a shortcoming to write about these hamlets without mentioning some of their other distinctive features, such as their system of watch-posts that may be used as places to worship the Soil God of hamlets, or the individual hamlet wells, each with its own unique history; the well in Sui Hamlet even has a stele engraved with the four words *nhat phien bang tam*, meaning, "a clean mind." In addition, the area is also home to many famous scholars. Giang Van Minh earned the Tham Hoa degree, the third highest academic title in the ancient educational system, and Nguyen Khac Nguyen was Prime Minister under the Nguyen Dynasty. In particular, the locals are proud of provincial chief Phan Ke Tien, a famous scholar born in Duong Lam. With their history and old-world charm, Mong Phu and the hamlets surrounding it embody many factors that add to the history and unique beauty of Duong Lam Village.

This article was originally published in a slightly different form at Vietnamnet (**www.vnn.vn/english/**).

Duong Lam
is approximately 40 km west of Hanoi. It can be reached along National Highway 32.

To find out more about *Mong*

continued on next page

Phu's Mia Pagoda (not to be confused with the hamlet temple), go to the reference to Dana Sach's **ThingsAsian** article in the preceding Fact File.

VIETNAM
❀
Mekong Delta

Christina Gosnell travels on delta time . . .

While buses are the main mode of transportation between Ho Chi Minh City and the Mekong Delta, a relaxing alternative to such cramped and hectic travel is the passenger ferry. It departs from Ho Chi Minh City daily from the pier on Ton Duc Thang Street at the end of Ham Nghi Boulevard. The boat reaches My Tho in 6-8 hours, Can Tho in 15-18 hours and Chau Doc on the Cambodian border in 30-36 hours. It provides a way to reflect on the nuances of Asia, relax with a great book or meet fellow travelers and share experiences.

Cruising the Delta

The Ho Chi Minh City passenger ferry departs from Bach Dang Station at 1 Ham Nghi Street, District One. Also, there is a Green Line Hydrofoil to Can Tho via My Tho that takes only four hours, but it doesn't offer the same experience.

VIETNAM
❀
The Best of . . .

Jan Dodd chooses her favorites, based on her experiences as the co-author of *The Rough Guide to Vietnam* . . .

The Old Quarter of Hanoi

Hanoi has changed enormously since my first visit in 1994, but I still find it a beguiling city. The Old Quarter is as captivating as ever, while some of the revamped French colonial buildings are just stunning. I love wandering the intoxicating tangle of streets that make up Hanoi's commercial heart. Many streets are still dedicated to one particular craft; my favorites are the bright red prayer banners of Hang Quat Street, Lan On Street's piles of fragrant medicines and Hang Ma Street, full of tinsel, votive objects and all kinds of paper products.

Street Food

Perhaps it's because I like snacking, but my favorite occupation in Vietnam is cruising the street kitchens for interesting tidbits. Not only is the food usually excellent, it's also cheap, and you can see it being cooked in front of you. The quintessential Vietnamese breakfast is *pho*, a wholesome noodle soup to which you add a squeeze of lime and a dash of eye-watering chili sauce. Later in the day, there's *bun cha*—pork-and-herb patties grilled on tiny roadside braziers, then served on a bed of cold rice noodles with a sweet dipping sauce and a side dish of salad greens. Afterwards, it's time to search out a quiet café and watch the world go by. Vietnamese coffee has a real kick.

Bia Hoi Bars

In the north of Vietnam, early evening is the time to join a few friends for some *bia hoi*—local draught beer. Everyone sits on pint-size stools or plastic chairs, often set up on the pavement or in the garden of an old villa, to quaff glasses of weak tasting (in fact, *bia hoi* measures in at a respectable four percent) but still flavorful beer drawn straight from the barrel. In Hanoi, I've spent some particularly happy evenings in the *bia hoi* bars just north of the Opera on Tong Dan Street. To soak up the beer, order plates of chips, peanuts or dried squid. It's cheap, convivial and fun.

Hue

Hue is an easygoing, peaceful city with lakes and canals, tree-lined boulevards and a certain refinement, thanks to its imperial past. It also has great cuisine and wonderful restaurants. Nothing beats an early morning bowl of *bun bo hue*, the regional version of noodle soup, flavored with lemongrass, shrimp and basil; locals swear by the bowls served at 11b Ly Thuong Kiet. Or slip behind the banyan tree at 2 Nguyen Tri Phuong for the best *banh khoai* in town. This crispy pancake is topped with shrimp, pork and bean sprouts, and is accompanied by a peanut and sesame sauce. Hue is also no slouch when it comes to historical sights, of which my favorite is the Mausoleum of Tu Duc, the finest of Hue's seven royal mausoleums. Rather than dealing with the affairs of state, Tu Duc preferred to hide in his lyrical pleasure garden, composing poems, drinking lotus blossom tea and being entertained by his 104 wives and countless concubines. A busy man!

The Northern Mountains

Sapa, a mountain resort in the most magnificent location close to the Chinese border, is well-established on the tourist trail. While relatively few people venture deeper into the mountains, it's well worth the effort—and a spot of discomfort—to visit ethnic minority villages in which the way of life has changed little over the centuries. Stumbling across a traditional weekly market, with the women dressed in all their finery, is an unforgettable experience.

Hanoi's Old Quarter
For more on the streets of Hanoi's Old Quarter, see Barbara Cohen's article at:

WEBSITE
www.thingsasian.com/goto_article/article.586.html

More on *bia hoi* can be found at:

WEBSITE
www.thingsasian.com/goto_article/article.778.html

Banh khoai
is a lighter version of *banh xeo*, which is found in Ho Chi Minh City. The use of the word *khoai* comes from the type of pan in which the dish is cooked.

Sapa
is located approximately 325 km from Hanoi. Usually, travelers take the train from Hanoi to Lao Cai, and then catch a mini bus right at the Lao Cai Train Station for the 35 km trip to Sapa. Hanoi has a main train station, but the train for Lao Cai leaves from a smaller station just north of the main station at Tran Quy Cap Street. (Editor's note: While the night train can save you travel time, I've heard it's best to take the day train for the views.)

Kim Fay's fact files from the chapter introduction . . .

Tuol Sleng Museum
On Street 113 near Street 350 on the southern side of Phnom Penh, Cambodia.

Grand Palace
This place is pretty difficult not to find. It sits surrounded by Na Phra Lan, Sanamchai, Thai Wang and Maharat Streets, near the Tha Tien riverboat stop, Bangkok.

War Crimes Museum
28 Vo Van Tan Street, Ho Chi Minh City, Vietnam.

Ho Chi Minh Mausoleum
5 Ngoc Ha Street, Hanoi, Vietnam. This museum is not open year-round. It's said that the body is

removed annually for maintenance. When we visited in September— one of the months it's listed as being shut down—we were told the mausoleum was closed, but when we went there, it was open. Also, we were told that foreigners are put into their own line and ushered through in groups. My sister and I found ourselves in the "locals" line, and it was fascinating. We followed a cluster of old women dressed in black communist/peasant clothing. One of them wept as she passed Uncle Ho, transforming the atmosphere from sterile and circus-like to intimate and revelatory.

A Few Last Words on Expert Advice

Footprint. Lonely Planet. Moon. Rough Guide. They are but a few of the illustrious names that have paved the way for thousands of travelers throughout Southeast Asia. Each is a reputable publisher of guidebooks, and therein is the dilemma. Which one should you choose? Following are a few suggestions to help you out.

Check the Publication Date:
Many guidebooks are not updated every year. In fact, some are only updated every three or four years. No matter how trustworthy a guide is, you don't want one that's four years old (not counting the year it took to get the book to press).

Set Aside an Hour or So to Compare and Contrast:
Select an attraction or restaurant category, and then read about it in a handful of guides. Do you like the way a museum is described in one book more than in the others? Does one book include more of the type of cafés you enjoy than the others? In essence, you're choosing a traveling companion, so take the time to find a viewpoint that's compatible with yours.

Go Local:
When you finally hit the road with your trusty guidebook in hand, set aside a twenty just in case you happen upon any specialized publications along the way. Self-published books that are only sold in-country can be gems, filled with invaluable recommendations. They make excellent complements to a well-chosen guidebook. ❧

Secret Gardens

*Where to hide away when you need to retreat
from the madding, tropical crowds*

For the purpose of this chapter, "secret gardens" describes both places and activities used to escape from the chaos that is life in a Southeast Asian country. Some expats actually live in their own secret gardens, such as Stuart Cavaliero who, along with his wife, runs the Chiang Dao Nest outside Chiang Mai (see page 185) and Bill Tuffin who works with the Boat Landing Guest House in Luang Namtha, Laos (see page 130). But most live among revving motorbikes and cawing street vendors who start hawking their wares at dawn; often, this local color is exciting, but on occasion it can necessitate seeking out a corner where you can find peace for an hour or two.

For almost a year, one of my favorite retreats was the rooftop swimming pool at the Rex Hotel in Ho Chi Minh City. My friend, Huong, and I would pay the guy in charge of the towels a couple bucks to let us laze up there on Saturday mornings and pretend we were far away from the city's frenetic streets. I'm not sure if visiting this swimming pool retreat is still allowed, but the hotel's rooftop restaurant/bar is an equally pleasant place to while away an afternoon drinking *so da chanh* (lemon soda) and reading the newspaper. Not only is the noise from the streets muffled, the enormous open-air patio catches the occasional breeze, even during the hottest months. The rooftop bar at the Majestic Hotel is also nice; no matter what your budget, you can stake out a table—the one up in the "crow's nest" is the best, with its 360 degree views that include the river—and have a cup of tea for a dollar or two. While I can't speak for Cambodia, Laos and Thailand, I do know that the city parks in Vietnam offer a distinctive, escapist experience during the early morning hours. Mine was Le Van Tam Park in Ho Chi Minh City, where my friend, Duyen, and I went three mornings a week to power walk two laps around its perimeter. On the grass, groups of old women did Tai Chi and old men and teenagers played badminton. After we finished exercising, we bought homemade yoghurt for 10 cents from a stall at the

center of the park. It was the best yoghurt I've ever tasted. Along with providing reprieve, the park has historical interest. When I first started walking there, one of the corners looked like an unfinished construction site that had been only partially excavated. After a year and absolutely no progress on this section of the park, I finally asked what had happened. Duyen told me that the city had planned a swimming pool for that corner, but when they started digging, they found bones. It turned out that the park had once been a European cemetery. The bones were removed to their home countries, but superstition kept the pool from being completed. The last time I went back to this park, the pool area had been filled in, and the entire grounds had been updated with kiddie rides and better exercise equipment. The Tai Chi-ers and badminton players were still there, though, as was the yoghurt, which was as wonderful as ever. As both an expat and a traveler, I have always had days when I felt overwhelmed and in need of a holiday from my holiday. I would have given anything for the following list of places where I could go to be recharged, and ready, after an hour or two, to face the next big adventure, or motorcycle, coming my way.

A fact file for the secret gardens mentioned in this introduction can be found on page 107.

CAMBODIA
❀
Angkor Temples

*Donald Gilliland
hunts for swimming holes
and remote temples . . .*

The West Baray Reservoir is an ancient man-made lake that is still used for swimming and fishing. There is even a small island in the middle that has some Angkor-era ruins. Unless it's a Khmer Holiday, there are usually no crowds. This is a relaxing place for a swim or to take in a sunset.

❀ ❀ ❀

Around the Angkor Park, most temples get visited by hordes of tourists, but there is one that is close by but seldom gets visited; Banteay Thom is located northwest of the popular Preah Khan temple, but is tucked away in a village, accessible only by narrow dirt roads. Paths, really. Anything larger than a motorcycle probably won't make it. There are a few carvings and such to be seen at Banteay Thom, but nothing that will take your breath away. Instead, it's the isolated atmosphere of the place that is so appealing. I've gone four times with a friend or two, and we were the only people there. Another more remote spot, but quite awesome in size and appearance, is Beng Mealea. It's a true Jungle Temple in the Indiana Jones sense. Absolutely no restoration has been done to it. It's about a 2-3 hour drive east of Angkor and not an easy trip, but well worth the effort.

The West Baray

is located (naturally) west of Siem Reap and can be reached from the road to the airport.

Banteay Thom

is located northwest of Preah Khan. Preah Khan is north of Angkor Thom and can be reached on the Grand Circuit road. Contributor Andy Brouwer writes about Banteay Thom at:

WEBSITE
www.btinternet.com/~andy.brouwer/gems.htm

Beng Melea

is approximately 40 km east of the Bayon (60 km east of Siem Reap). Plan on a full day trip if you're basing yourself out of Siem Reap. You can read more about Beng Melea at:

WEBSITE
www.btinternet.com/~andy.brouwer/bmealea.htm

WEBSITE
www.time.com/asia/magazine/article/0,13673,501030519-451012,00.html

Donald goes into further detail in his article "Jungle Vines and Khmer Finds" at:

WEBSITE
www.thingsasian.com/goto_article/article.2292.html

Andy Brouwer offers his expertise on Khmer temples . . .

The most obvious secret gardens would be the country's ancient temples, which I use as targets when I visit Cambodia. That is, a temple may be the destination, but it's the experience getting to and returning from it that makes up the

CAMBODIA ❀ *Angkor Temples*

most pleasurable experiences on my trips. However, if asked to pick just a few choice temples, they would include ones like Ta Nei—in the Angkor Park, but tucked away out of sight and visited by very few of the Angkor hordes. I keep going back to this temple. It can be accessed from the front, through a winding and leafy lane, or from the rear by clambering over a dam. It is tucked away in the forest, which produces its own atmosphere with the sound of crickets, frogs and cicadas. It's sometimes closed to visitors and not on the main temple "A" list; as a result it's overlooked by most, so whenever I've been there, I've always been on my own. It's also a place where the Angkor authorities are teaching their conservationists how to preserve and reconstruct a temple. From the reign of Jayavarman VII, it has apsaras carved into its walls, and some fine lintels and pediments to discover. Also, it's a ruined temple, which means there's lots of climbing and clambering over the fallen blocks of stone. Since the temple is surrounded by forest, sometimes the light is good, sometimes not so good, so it's best visited in the morning.

Other temples that I'd pick are Preah Vihear and the Sambor Prei Kuk group. Visit each of these distinctive sites in the very early morning. Preah Vihear is in an incredible location on the edge of the Dangkrek Mountains overlooking northern Cambodia. The temple can be covered completely in mist so you can't see anything, or the sun will burn that off and reveal a great view for many miles. You can see the plumes of smoke from small cooking fires on the plains below as Cambodia wakes. I've been to the Sambor Prei Kuk temple group in the very early morning; with the tree cover surrounding the many small temples, and the sun shining in shafts through the trees, it is fantastic, especially since it is accompanied by the sounds of the forest and the sight of butterflies fluttering in the shafts. The mist hanging in the forest adds a magical element to the scene. And in my experience, you'll be alone, which is even better.

Finally, I'd recommend the pyramid temple of Prasat Thom at either sunrise or sunset. You'd have to stay overnight at the site to witness it, as you would at Preah Vihear. The climb to the top is risky, and the access ladders aren't particularly safe. On top, there's not much room to move about either, but the view is tremendous. You are so far above the tree-line that you can see for many kilometers. The setting sun, which I witnessed, was a great occasion, so I'd imagine the sunrise would be equally affecting. The only concern is climbing up to the top in the darkness/gloom. It's also in an ancient capital city that very few visitors have been to, so again, you are very likely to be there completely alone.

Ta Nei

is located in the Angkor complex on the west side of the East Baray. You can read more of Andy's observations on this out-of-the-way temple at:

WEBSITE
www.btinternet.com/~andy.brouwer/gems.htm

For directions to Preah Vihear, go to page 62.

The Sambor Prei Kuk Temple Group

is on a side road off National Route 12, north of Kompong Thom. Kompong Thom is approximately 150 km southeast of Siem Reap and 165 km north of Phnom Penh. Traveling to this temple group is best done as a day trip out of Kompong Thom. Read more about Andy's trips to Kompong Thom and the temples at:

WEBSITE
www.btinternet.com/~andy.brouwer/kthom.htm

Prasat Thom

is part of the Koh Ker temple group. This group is best reached as a day trip out of Tbeng

Meanchey (See page 62). The 70 km stretch of road from Tbeng Meanchey to Koh Ker is pretty rough in spots.

CAMBODIA ✸ Phnom Penh

Matt McKinney escapes to an urban oasis . . .

Stop by Wat Svay Pope, across the street from the Russian Embassy, for a bit of solitude in otherwise congested Phnom Penh.

Russian Embassy
Samdech Sothearos Boulevard at Street 312.

THAILAND 🏵 *Bangkok*

Tara Russell knows THE place to watch the sunset and a pretty park to hang out in . . .

Finding a spot to see the sunset in Bangkok is harder than you might think. High-rise offices, hotels and apartment buildings block this colorful evening show. Some friends invited us to Vertigo, an open-aired restaurant atop the Westin Banyan Tree, and claimed that seeing the sunset would be no problem from there. They didn't mention, however, that finding the Westin was a bit tricky! Once you pass the Sukkothai Hotel on Sathorn Road, you're nearly there—its slim physique is tucked behind another high-rise.

Once inside the hotel, even the journey to Vertigo is dramatic. First, you're escorted to an express elevator that whisks you to the 59th floor. From there, you climb three sets of stairs—the last beautifully lined with candles and infused with soothing piano music. You reach the open-air top and immediately your eyes are drawn to the stunning panorama. You can eat while taking in the view or head to the bar for a drink (I'd recommend the bar first). The bar sits slightly higher than the restaurant (elevated by another small staircase), allowing for an even better viewing spot. The décor is simple, modern and tasteful, and doesn't detract from the surroundings. Off to one side you can see the Chao Phraya River winding through Bangkok, Lumpini Park, the heart of the Sathorn business district and much more. But the BEST part of the evening is the sunset. The clouds painted across the sky partner with the smog to produce brilliant hues of orange, pink and red, and sitting atop the Westin, you're able to observe the full scattering of rays—no other buildings ruin the show! Not only do you get a great show, you're served drinks in vertically challenged glasses (leaning like the Tower of Pisa) by Thais who speak perfect English. Surrounding you seem to be all the beautiful people in Bangkok . . . and, in addition to seeing a fantastic sunset, the unique aspect of the restaurant is the high level of static in the air that causes women's long hair to stand straight up (you'll have to go see for yourself!) This is a place you'll want to hit, and if you live in town, it's a place you'll want to take visitors. It's the only interference-free sunset show I've seen to date!

✵ ✵ ✵

When in need of a quiet break from the afternoon traffic and mad rush of people on the streets, I love to duck into Benjasiri Park. As I enter, I pass a playground full of children. Their glee-filled giggles drown out the sounds of horns, motorbikes and screeching tires in the streets, immediately releasing the tension I carry throughout the day when busily moving to and fro. As I walk deeper into the park and nearer to the pond, I see families picnicking on the grass, men feeding the pigeons and my empty bench awaiting me. Sometimes when I reach the shady bench, I pull out my journal or a book to read. Other days, I buy a drink at the park snack bar and sit back to be entertained by the water fountain in the pond, the constant circling of birds or the curious kids running and playing throughout the park. If I get antsy, I wander around gazing at the myriad tropical flowers, bushes and trees or walk toward the back to watch locals play basketball, skateboard in the skate park or play takrat, a fast-paced, fascinating game—using a small, thinly-woven wooden ball—that blends volleyball and soccer skills. While activities here never become dull, you can always find a quiet area to escape to if you're craving time alone. Mostly I love the change of scenery and spending time unnoticed and undisturbed, forgetting briefly that I live in one of the biggest, busiest cities in the world.

Vertigo
At the top of the Westin Banyan Tree Hotel, 21/100 South Sathon Road, Thai Wah Tower II Building, Bangkok.
WEBSITE
www.banyantree.com/bangkok/

Benjasiri Park
is located next to Emporium Mall, 662 Sukhumvit, Soi 24.

Kat Tosi unwinds at The Oriental Hotel . . .

The 125-year old Oriental Hotel has a worldwide reputation for good reason. Even though you might not be able to afford the $300-$2,200 US a night rooms, keep in mind that you can visit this spectacular hotel regardless of whether or not you are checking in. Pleasure and relaxation are guaranteed! Sit on the grand patio, watch the Chao Phraya River go floating by, order one of those oh-so-tempting cocktails, kick back, relax and enjoy the sunset. If you really want to spoil yourself, go for the all-you-can eat buffet, presented every evening. It's not often that you can stuff yourself on lobster, prime rib, sushi and fine cheese in a setting such as this one for the price of 1,200 baht ($30 US). After dinner, head over to the legendary Bamboo Bar to listen to some jazz or trio singers and let the jungle décor, along with the music, sweep you away.

The Oriental Hotel
48 Oriental Avenue, Bangkok.

WEBSITE
www.mandarin-oriental.com/bangkok

THAILAND ✿ *Chiang Mai*

Candace MacKay
relaxes on temple grounds and at the zoo . . .

"With each day passing What have you been doing?"
- Lord Buddha

There are oodles of temples one can visit in Thailand. They all have similarities, and they also all have unique qualities that set them apart. The most famous temple in northern Thailand is Chiang Mai's Wat Prathat Doi Suthep. This incredibly beautiful temple is set on the top of a mountain on incredibly beautiful grounds. These grounds house dozens of large bells, which are continually being rung by visitors. It offers a great view over the city and is home to monks who are ready to bless both devout Buddhists and curious tourists. I always take our guests there and have still not tired of it.

Although it is hard to beat the beauty of Doi Suthep, it can be very crowded, and it is quite a distance from my house. So I have an alternative temple that my daughter and I enjoy visiting on a regular basis. For a more relaxing outing, we go to Wat U Mong. There are dozens of buildings here, although none of which I have entered—I feel that this temple is about the grounds, not the buildings. Walking the grounds can take some time if you stop to read the trees that have Buddhist messages attached to them. Everywhere you look, there is something to see, from ancient statues to "dogs playing cards" posters.

Whenever we visit, we spend most of our time at the far end of the grounds where there is a large pond. One can find pigeons, ducks, geese, turtles and fish. It's an excellent place to relax on a bench and feed the birds. Among other highlights is a very peaceful walking meditation circle around an ancient *chedi* at the top of the stairs, near the center of the grounds. One of the buildings is a library that houses Buddhist literature in English, and there are also regularly scheduled, informal

Dhamma discussions about life's problems and their solutions.

I highly recommend visiting both of these temples, each for a very different reason. And make sure your mood matches the temple—it's much more enjoyable that way.

Wat Prathat Doi Suthep

Follow Huay Kaew Road from Chiang Mai (the base of the mountain) to the top of the mountain—about 16 km. You can hire a car or motorcycle, or catch a ride in a *song thaew* (a small pickup whose covered bed has seats in it) near the front gate of Chiang Mai University. Be prepared for the 300 steps you'll have to climb to reach the temple. For more information, go to:

WEBSITE
www.thailandforvisitors.com/north/chiangmai/suthep

Wat U Mong

Starting at the moat, travel west on Suthep Road for about two km. Then turn left at the Canal Road and follow the signs another two km. Transportation options are the same as for those to Wat Prathat Doi Suthep. You can read more background information on this temple at:

WEBSITE
www.thailandforvisitors.com/north/chiangmai/umong/index.html

Candace writes that the Dhamma discussions at Wat U Mong are held Mondays, Wednesdays and Fridays from 1-3 p.m. and on Sundays from 3-5 p.m.

WEBSITE
http://meditationthailand.com/N/umong.html for more information on meditation in Thailand.

When my family has only a small amount of time and a desire to go far away, we simply head for the Chiang Mai Zoo. It's not that the zoo is far away—it's at the top of Huay Kaew Road—but it seems as if you are very far away when you find the right habitat. A few years ago I would never have recommended visiting this zoo, but there have been a lot of changes recently, and although there are still animals that are suffering, there are many living in improved or new environments.

Our first stop is at Gibbon Island. This is a relatively new habitat, consisting of four islands. Gibbons can be seen swinging high up in the trees or feeding their babies in little wooden hutches. There are nine different kinds of gibbons, and all of them are endangered. Some people claim that there are still wild gibbons on Doi Suthep Mountain. In any case, this is an excellent place to watch these amazing animals.

The next stop is my daughter's favorite destination: the aviary. The birds have a huge habitat, which can be accessed through many different

THAILAND ❀ Chiang Mai

entrances. There is every color of bird imaginable, and you're right in the middle of the action. This is a great place to sit and have a snack with the myriad hues flying around you.

We usually head home after this, but there are lots of other things worth seeing. Here are our honorable mentions:

1. The finch den: a small structure that houses many different kinds of finches.

2. The giraffe and zebra habitat: the giraffes come so close that you can count their eyelashes.

3. The big cats during feeding time: they are fed between 10 and 11 a.m.

4. The new animal show held at the amphitheater: it costs 10 baht for adults and 5 baht for children. Times are posted at the zoo.

Chiang Mai Zoo

The entrance to the zoo is located just past the front gate of Chiang Mai University, at the base of the mountain, at 100 Huay Kaew Road, Chiang Mai.

WEBSITE

www.zoothailand.org/chiangmai/

Candace adds: The zoo is enormous and situated on the side of a mountain, so if you plan on visiting, bring good walking shoes. Motorbikes are not allowed, but if you have your own car, you can drive from habitat to habitat. Electric trolleys are now available for tours.

Jason Smith hides away in an outlying coffee village . . .

The late morning air hovers cool and fresh here at the top of Doi Suthep, the mountain that rises invitingly above the busy city of Chiang Mai. I'm already thinking about the cup of velvety coffee that's waiting for me at the end of my walk through the forest. I give a casual nod to the forest service guy in his bungalow as my feet pass from pavement onto dirt and rock.

The high mountain road to the Hmong coffee village is a bit rough for driving, but just right on foot or bike. Other than the occasional old-timer puttering by on a beat-up Honda Dream, I've got the hills to myself. My mind wanders away from the teeming world that lies in the valley below. Butterflies and birdsong keep me company. A couple of clear streams give me an excuse to pause and admire the multi-hued flowers that dot the hills.

Around a bend, two Hmong women emerge from the curtain of jungle. The colors of their clothes splash against the green. Their arms are full of herbs and vegetables. When they spot me, their conversation stops, they smile shyly, and disappear back into the jungle.

Below me sprawls the metropolis of Chiang Mai, but up here I'm still a stranger in a strange land. After just the right amount of walking, the welcoming sign announcing "Fresh Coffee" appears. I grab a seat on the deck, sip my coffee and disappear into the terraces of coffee plants sprinkled across the valley.

The Coffee Village

Jason explains: Starting at the zoo at the western end of Huay Kaew Road, drive 16 km up the mountain—passing Doi Suthep Temple and the Summer Palace—to a small hilltribe market. Continue through this area another 1 km and you'll come to a fork in the road. To the left is Meo Doi Pui Village, but you want to turn right and head toward Kun Chang Khian Village, which is 8 km away. You won't go all the way to Kun Chang Khian—you'll only drive 3.5 km from the fork. At this point the narrow paved road turns to dirt. You will see a small Forest Service shack and a parking area. Leave your motorbike and enjoy a leisurely walk along the 4WD road. After 4 km, you'll come upon fields of dark green coffee plants. Stop at the tiny coffee shop (there's a sign) on the edge of a large field and enjoy a fresh cup of coffee. Another half km up the road is the actual village of Kun Chang Khian. There is nothing at all to see or do in this village, but dropping off to

the right is another rough dirt road leading down the mountain to Tung Ting Lake. This is best done as a self tour; you can rent a Honda Dream motorcycle in town and easily motor yourself up the mountain to the end of the pavement. Walk the remaining 4 km to the coffee shack, sit and have a cup of coffee overlooking the fields and then turn around and walk back. The leisurely walking part of this tour takes about an hour and a half each way.

VIETNAM
✿
Ho Chi Minh City

XXXXXXXXXXXXXXXXXXXXXXXXXXXXXXXX
ooooooooooooooooooooooooooooooo

*Richard Craik
gets back to nature at the
Saigon Botanical Garden . . .*

The botanical gardens are an oasis of green and calm in the midst of the cacophony of downtown Ho Chi Minh City—a must for all lovers of nature, culture and coconut juice. They were planted in 1864, shortly after Cochinchina, the southern most part of what is now Vietnam, became a French colony. Escape the city's hawkers and Hondas to stroll along the leafy pathways and sip refreshing coconut juice under towering tropical trees. Spare half an hour to look around the fine collection of artifacts in the History Museum, housed in a splendid colonial era building just inside the main entrance gates. The small zoo has perhaps seen better days; you should instead cast your eyes skyward to search the treetops for some of the more fortunate (and liberated) inhabitants of the gardens. Here with a little luck you may catch sight of some of Asia's avian gems. A flash of red could be a brilliant Scarlet Minivet or a diminutive Scarlet-backed Flowerpecker. A yellow bird may be the more soberly attired female Minivet or perhaps the larger and more boisterous Black-naped Oriole. A beautiful deep green bird foraging among the smaller trees or bushes might be a Blue-winged Leafbird or higher up, a Coppersmith Barbet tonk, tonk, tonking in the upper branches. Jewels of the rainforest exist right in the center of the city.

Saigon Botanical Garden and Zoo
At the eastern end of Le Duan Street at 2 Nguyen Binh Khiem Street, Ho Chi Minh City.

VIETNAM 🏵 *Hanoi*

*Dana Sachs
visits a tiny temple
and an alternative to
Hoan Kiem Lake . . .*

Not far from Hanoi's Hang Da Market, on a tiny lane in the Old Quarter, The Temple of Y Lan seems hidden behind an enormous and ancient banyan tree. You can't get there by car since the little lane is too narrow; therefore, it's one of the quietest spots in the city. Try visiting on the occasion of a full or new moon festival, when worshippers will be slipping off their shoes and stepping inside to arrange offerings at the altars there.

🏵 🏵 🏵

Most travelers know about Hoan Kiem Lake in the center of Hanoi, but not many people make it to the much larger Lenin Park, which also has a lovely lake at its center. I love to take a stroll along its tree-lined paths on summer mornings, when the mist rests on the lake and the green of the grass and the trees seems particularly luminous. At that time of day, you can see Hanoians busily completing their morning calisthenics. If you have children, they can ride the kiddy rides or take a tiny train that circles the lake. Late afternoons and evenings in Lenin Park take on a different mood altogether, as lovers congregate in the semi-privacy of the park's many quiet corners.

The Temple of Y Lan
is reached on crooked Tam Thuong Street off Hang Gai Street.

Lenin Park is also called Thong Nhat Park
It is surrounded by Tran Nhan Tong, Le Duan, Dai Co Viet and Nguyen Dinh Chieu Streets.

SOUTHEAST ASIA
❀
General

Kim Fay loves the fine art of good pain . . .

On my last trip to Bangkok, the budget hotel my sister and I stayed in boasted one notable asset—it was within walking distance to Wat Po, a temple where the majority of the city's (legitimate) masseuses are trained. Architecturally, Wat Po is a unique

experience in and of itself. Imagine if Gaudi decorated cakes for Siddhartha: these large temple confections would be the result. The fact that it has a massage school on its grounds only adds to the attraction.

The school is located in a far corner of the temple compound where, impossible as it seems, the noise of street traffic is muffled beneath a prevailing calm. It is a single room, with three of its walls made of mesh to let in the breeze. This room is filled with beds, and the scent of eucalyptus drifts through the air. There's something about the setup that's reminiscent of a hospital ward, except that this is a place of wellness rather than infirmity.

I was given a pair of loose trousers and a loose blouse to change into. Then I was led to a bed where I lay down on my back and closed my eyes. The first thing I felt was the ruffle of air as the fan rotated slowly above my head. The fan hung from a high timber ceiling that had been painted autumn yellow, bathing the room in a comforting, late afternoon glow. When the masseuse began with my right leg, I could only wonder how the pressure of someone else's thumb pushed into my skin could feel so good. Another woman was being massaged on the next bed, and the two masseuses talked softy to one another, their voices clinging to the languid air. As always, I found it comforting to be surrounded by a language that was not my own.

As I sank into the luxury of human touch, my mind wandered . . . *I wonder how many more of these I can get before this holiday is over . . . where'd my headache go . . . ow, she's going to rip my leg off . . . oh, that feels good . . . I wish I could figure out this crazy exchange rate . . . hey, she's going to sink her finger right through my stomach . . . I wonder what kind of massages they give in Laos . . . yikes, this woman is climbing up my back like a monkey, do I look like a palm tree?* My musings were interspersed with pockets of pure relaxation.

I went back the next day for the foot massage. This time I sat near the door, and I could see out into the temple grounds. Across the path, a guard rested on a bench in the shade beneath a tree, his hat perched on the head of the stone dragon beside him. I was tucked into a little alcove. The masseuse offered to turn on a fan, but the heat was a cocoon, a humid harbor between each passing breeze. This kind of heat is organic, it becomes part of your body, and each breeze then offers a tiny glimpse of paradise. You wait for it, and when it arrives, it's impossible to be disappointed.

The hands of my masseuse were so beautiful, fragile and strong at the same time. Her fingernails were smooth, and her fingers had a thin elegance. Sunlight wove a pattern through a bamboo shade. An ant crawled slowly up the wall. The masseuse used a small, smooth wooden dowel to search the sole of my foot for sorrow, fear and stress. She found it all. She cured me of it all, if only for that short while. She knew just how much pain I could bear, and just when to release me. Was she in any way related to God?

A French tour group approached, and their guide ushered them in. As they filed past, each one looked at me as a part of the whole. Briefly, I became a scene from their holiday. They won't remember me, or the details of my face, but I will be there, in a corner of their memories, a vague sketch in that bigger picture, preserved. Just as they are there for me, walking through the background while I rested back in my chair, closed my eyes and savored the fine art of good pain.

Wat Po
South of the entrance to the Grand Palace, near the Tha Tien express boat pier. You can also take massage courses through the school. For more about the statues, shrines and famous Reclining Buddha in the temple compound, go to:

WEBSITE
http://thailandforvisitors.com/centr al/bangkok/watpo.html

Massages come and go, but you never forget the truly good ones.

Following are a few of my most memorable:

Juliana Hotel

Thai massage can be quite brutal. I've come away from some feeling as if I'd barely escaped a back alley brawl. But one time, at the Juliana Hotel in Phnom Penh, I experienced the perfect unity of strength and gentleness in a quiet, not-too-hot-not-too-cold room. It was one of the more expensive massages I've had in Asia (over $10 US!), but it was worth it. Address: 16 Street 152.

WEBSITE
http://indochina-services.com/html/Juliana-Hotel/

Red Cross

I'd read in a guidebook that you could get a massage at the Red Cross for a few dollars. Early in the afternoon, my sister and I sought out the building up from the Nam Khan River. No one was there. The boy in the internet café downstairs finally summoned an older woman who showed us a blackboard beside a door where we wrote our "reservation." We chose the cool hour of 8 p.m. When we came back, the masseuses were waiting for us. We were shown into a shabby room with mattresses on the floor, separated from each other by hanging sheets. Despite this first impression and the soft-spoken, English 101 questions from my masseuse, the hour was quiet,

the fan was a relief and her touch was firm and slow, seeking out each needy muscle and working it back to health. Address: On Visounnalath (or Visounalat or Wisunalat) Road, across from Wat Visunnarat. There is also an excellent herbal sauna; bring a sarong if you plan to use it.

Resources

Tom Aikins comprehensive "Spas in Thailand" article can be found online at:

WEBSITE
www.thingsasian.com/goto_article article.1603.html

Kim Fay's fact files from the chapter introduction . . .

The Rex Hotel

141 Nguyen Hue Street, Ho Chi Minh City.

WEBSITE
www.rexhotelvietnam.com

Majestic Hotel

1 Dong Khoi Street, Ho Chi Minh City, Vietnam.

WEBSITE
www.majestic-saigon.com

Le Van Tam Park

On Hai Ba Trung Street between Dien Bien Phu and Vo Thi Sau Streets, Ho Chi Minh City, Vietnam.

Short, But Oh So Sweet

Unique weekend escapes to hidden beaches,
lost jungles and other idyllic destinations.

One of the best things about being an expatriate is that every day is an adventure . . . at least in the beginning. The first months abroad are exquisite as you seek out new cafés, unravel unfamiliar customs and bask in being a foreigner in a foreign land. But there comes a time—the turning point is often difficult to pinpoint—when you find yourself *living* in that land. You wash your dishes there, you grocery shop there and you pay phone and electricity bills there. Depending on your situation and inclination, you even pay taxes there. Your new and exciting home goes from being a place you'd like to take a holiday to (perhaps you did and chose to stay), to one you need to take a holiday from. This is where being an expat comes in handy. Your choices for brief and easy retreats are excellent. Since I live in Los Angeles, it would be ridiculous for me to dream of flying off to the Ana Mandara Resort in the Vietnamese beach town of Nha Trang for the weekend, but in Ho Chi Minh City, a jaunt to Nha Trang is as easy as a trip from L.A. to San Francisco. The same goes for Dalat, Phan Thiet and even the Thai islands. One month I escaped to Phuket twice! In Southeast Asia, the flights are cheap, luxurious accommodation can be had for a song (the Dalat Palace is one of my favorites), and—if you're an expat—your mini-holiday is both familiar and exotic at the same time. Sometimes, even a traveler needs to get away from the bustle and frantic pace of his or her itinerary, and the recommendations in this chapter provide a thoughtful selection of tried and true places where you can go to kick back, unwind and recharge before getting back on the road.

A fact file for the escapes mentioned in this introduction can be found on page 125

CAMBODIA ❀ *Sihanoukville*

Graham Simmons suggests a beach holiday . . .

For a quick getaway from Cambodia's chaotic capital Phnom Penh, there could be no better choice than the beach-side town of Sihanoukville.

Sihanoukville's beaches stretch like a string of pearls along the coast to the southwest and southeast of the town, from Victory Beach through to Ochheuteal Beach. The further east you go, the finer the beaches become, with Sokha and Ochheuteal being probably the pick of what is on offer. At the farthest (northwest) end of Ochheuteal, a sand strip recently dubbed "Serendipity Beach" now boasts half-a-dozen bar/restaurants, several guest bungalows and a handful of small guesthouses (The Beach, Moha Chai, Sokha Linda, etc.). All except one of these facilities have sprung up since 2001. Such is the fast pace of change around Sihanoukville. East again of Ochheuteal are the completely undeveloped Otres Beach and the National Park-contained Ream Beach (with a couple of rustic bungalows).

Sihanoukville

Graham explains: Getting to Sihanoukville is easy. From Phnom Penh, air-con buses leave at 6:55 a.m., 7:30 a.m., 8:30 a.m., 12:30 p.m. and 1:30 p.m., taking three to four hours for the trip, including a meal stop. The one-way fare is 10,000 riel (about $2 US). The Phnom Penh Station is on Charles de Gaulle Street by the Central Market, and the Sihanoukville Station is located in town on Ekareach Street.

For comprehensive travel information on Sihanoukville (as well as other Cambodian destinations), visit:

WEBSITE
www.canbypublications.com

CAMBODIA ❀ *Koh Kong*

Nami Nelson flees to a not-so-quiet border town . . .

Koh Kong is generally described by guide books as a place no tourist should have to stop at, except to use as a transit point when traveling through from Thailand to Phnom

Penh. Located on the Thai-Cambodian border along the coastline, it has much more to offer than first meets the eye. As a border town, traditionally it has been the center for all things seedy and illegal—not a quality that would entice most tourists to stay there for long periods of time. However, Koh Kong is a seaside town that is nestled at the foot of the Cardamom Mountains. This location provides more than enough pristine wildlife, islands, floating villages and jungle to explore.

Just outside of town, along the newly opened dirt highway to Phnom Penh, is a set of rapids where local Koh Kong-ites like to go on weekends with bags of BBQ chicken and sticky rice; however, those visiting during the week are left to themselves to explore the jungle paths and enjoy the serenity of the area. Once arriving at the rapids, don't restrict yourself to the area around the main entrance—follow the pathway along the river. The path crosses the river at a point where the water is often a little more than knee deep. Follow this path for another 10-15 minutes. Eventually, you'll see a sidetrack that leads you to the best part of the rapids: a water hole with a waterfall only about three meters high, but with sections deep enough to jump off the top into the pool below.

Now, picturing myself swimming around in the water—alone and

watching the wind in the bamboo trees hanging over the edges of the river as the sound of water crashes down behind me—is enough to make me wish I had never left Koh Kong.

If you are more interested in exploring other areas of Koh Kong, boats are available to take people upriver along any of the rivers crossed by the highway. I have taken one boat up for about an hour's ride, and camped out next to some rapids under the light of the full moon. Although it was an amazing experience, it is wise not to venture too far away from the riverbank, as illegal loggers/land clearers and hunters do not welcome strangers.

Koh Kong

is the counterpart of the Thai border town, Hat Lek. Inside Cambodia, it can be reached by road from Phnom Penh and by sea (ferry) from Sihanoukville.

The best website for Koh Kong is:

WEBSITE
www.kohkong.com/kohkong/

To get to the water hole, Nami writes: The rapids are about 15 minutes out of town by motorbike, along the newly opened dirt highway to Phnom Penh, at the bottom of a steep hill. You turn right just before you get to the bridge at the bottom of the hill.

continued on next page

This leads into the parking area. You can swim at this point, and there are boiled "fetus" eggs and other snacks available here. Staying on the parking side of the river, the path follows the rapids upstream. At one point the path does cross the rapids, but the water is usually only about knee deep and not flowing too strongly. Keep following the path upstream.

CAMBODIA
✤
Out of Phnom Penh

Matt McKinney recommends Oodong and Kep . . .

I always enjoyed a trip up to Oodong on the weekends. It's an easy one hour drive out of Phnom Penh, and the destination is nothing less than the burial site of some of Cambodia's greatest Kings. It's not that hidden away, but few people get up there, despite the easy drive.

I also recommend Kep, south of Phnom Penh; it sits along the ocean and is a beautiful escape. Full of collapsed, abandoned homes left behind by the French colonialists, Kep is now undergoing a renovation as expats move in and fix up the old places. A sea wall and a large beach in the center of town make it a good place for a swim. Restaurants serving crab, fish and prawns cater to seafood lovers. Spend the afternoons exploring the once-majestic homes of this seaside resort.

Oodong (or Udong)
is located 35 km north of Phnom Penh. Take National Highway 5 to the Prek Kdam Ferry. Go approximately 4.5 km past the ferry. Turn left at the archway and follow the road to Oodong. Buses from the Ho Wah Genting Company depart for Oodong southwest of the Central Market in Phnom Penh at regular intervals daily. Comprehensive information about travel in and around Phnom Penh can be found at:

WEBSITE
www.canbypublications.com/phnompenh/pptransp.htm

Kep
is located 172 km from Phnom Penh (26 km beyond Kampot). Kampot is reached by traveling south on National Route 3. A great introduction to lodging, dining and attractions in Kep (and Kampot on the same website) can be found at:

WEBSITE
www.canbypublications.com/sihnoukville/kepintro.htm

CAMBODIA
❁

Into the Wilds of the Northwest

*Ray Zepp
helps you find your own
lost temples . . .*

Let's say you are in Siem Reap with a couple of days on your hands. Within a few hours, you may discover a lost temple or Angkor-era ruin that has not been visited in over a century. This opportunity is due to a recent translation (published by White Lotus Books—see page 202) of a remarkable book written back in 1901 by the Frenchman, Etienne Aymonier. He explored the entire northwest of Cambodia looking for ancient ruins, and not only did he describe them in detail in his book, **Khmer Heritage in the Old Siamese Provinces of Cambodia**, he also drew maps showing how to reach them. Now, you can also follow these maps to find what remains of the ruins he described.

In most cases, looters have totally destroyed the temples described by Aymonier, but even finding a few stones, a section of a wall or a moat and reservoir system is a real thrill. And sometimes you can strike it lucky and discover a relatively intact ruin. Since the area immediately surrounding Siem Reap has been thoroughly researched, it is best to take a share-taxi out to a base town and go by moto taxi from there into the bush to the villages named by Aymonier. The following is an example of a lucky weekend that I spent in Kralanh, the crossroads town halfway along Highway 6 west, between Siem Reap and Sisophon.

I first went to the northwest of Kralanh to what Aymonier's map calls Toeuk Chou. The ancient temple (*prasat*) called Prasat Sang Keah is easy to find along a good road beyond Toeuk Chou. It is in pretty good shape, although, as always, the statues have been stolen. I was extremely fortunate to visit on January first, when the nearby villagers hold a peace vigil at the temple. The monks from the local wat keep many carvings and statues hidden from looters, and only bring them out this one day of the year.

I carried on along the road to the site of an ancient bridge, called Spean Sreng by Aymonier. Its impressive photograph is included in the new translation, but I was able to locate only a few stones and a naga head from the entrance to this bridge. It turns out, though, that the bridge is still there, only hidden! The

Khmer Rouge covered it with earth to form a large dam for their irrigation system. In theory, it would be possible to unearth this huge structure and to create an impressive tourist attraction.

The following day, I took another moto up the road north from Kralanh to find more bridges along an Angkor-era road just south of the district capital of Chongkal, near a village called Choeung Tien. The bridge crossing the main river has been destroyed, but you can see some of the stones surrounding a shed just to the west of the modern bridge. However, a couple hundred meters further, you cross the main ancient bridge, perhaps without realizing that you are crossing a bridge at all. If you walk down the sides of the embankment, you will see the immense stone pillars of Spean Toeup (Divine Bridge). You will be amazed that such a huge structure can remain hidden and in fact be a part of the main road. Less than a kilometer to the west is a rather large and fairly well-preserved temple. Finally, back on the south side of the river, there is another smaller bridge, but in good condition. It is located in a peaceful setting to the east and a bit south of the new bridge.

I have never met a foreigner who has known about these bridges and temples, since the road north of Kralanh is not usually traveled by tourists. There are several other ruins in the area, in worse shape and more difficult to access, but it is fun to try to find them from Aymonier's maps and descriptions. One word of caution: keep on the main paths and don't go off into the bush, as there may be landmines.

I have just described only one example of a possible weekend adventure. There are many more—for instance, from Sisophon or in the area of Banteay Chhmar. To lay eyes on lost ruins that have not been visited in over a century is a rare treat, and northwest Cambodia is one of the few places in the world where you can experience such an adventure.

Kralanh

Ray explains: Kralanh is the crossroads town halfway along Highway 6 west, between Siem Reap and Sisophon. I took the share taxi from the Siem Reap taxi park on Highway 6 east, out past the new market. It takes two hours to reach Kralanh, where there are restaurants and a guesthouse right at the crossroads. From there you can hire a moto taxi for the rest of the day.

LAOS 🏵 *Mekong River*

*Kim Fay thinks
the entire world should live
on Mekong time . . .*

According to many a seasoned traveler, you can't truly say you've been to Laos until you've traveled a portion of the mighty Mekong through it. From the northeast border town of Huay Xai to the ancient royal capital of Luang Prabang, you can take the notorious fast boat, whose passengers wear helmets and whose drivers are rumored to be hopped up on amphetamines. You can take the slow boat, which offers hard wooden benches, leg cramps and toilets designed solely to strike fear into the hearts of *farang*. Or you can take the *Pak Ou*.

The slender hardwood *Pak Ou* is more than just two days of floating paradise. It's a journey into the heart and history of Laos, an unforgettable encounter with the country's vibrant ethnic traditions, its unspoiled landscape and the graceful remnants of its colonial past. You board in the morning in Huay Xai, and pass the following hours simply lounging in the open-air salon with friends and fellow passengers (French, Vietnamese and Thai on my cruise). You gaze out onto hills that rise from the water as if the land is sinking. Shadows of clouds blanket portions of the green forest. Stray shafts of sunlight radiates from the banyan and coconut leaves. Your first stop, at the village of Khone Teun, is not until early afternoon. The villagers—members of the Lao Leuan tribe—accompany you through their small community of simple wooden shacks. You observe an old woman weaving fabric on a decrepit loom. You're led uphill, past a Bodhi tree, to a temple whose interior walls illustrate the life of Buddha. The murals are crude, faded and beautiful.

As dusk nears on that first day, the *Pak Ou* approaches the Luang Say Lodge. An elevated walkway leads to a collection of private bungalows, whose wall-to-wall shutters open to expose the sun setting golden over the Mekong. After dinner on the verandah, you turn in early to sleep in a cocoon of mosquito netting. Morning arrives, and the river emerges from a bay of mist. A flock of white birds shatters the opaque green of dawn. You return to the boat, to read, nap on the floor like a child in a pre-school, or chat idly about everything and nothing at all. You're tired and content. You've become an old Mekong hand. You take this world for granted. The fleeting fragrance of jasmine. A lone elephant logging hardwood on the shore. A swirl of mud in the water, as if it's held beneath a sheet of glass.

By the time you've visited Xang Hai (Whiskey Village, where everyone buys at least one bottle of local rot-gut) and the sacred Pak Ou Caves, home to 4,000 Buddha figures, the second day is drawing to its close. In the distance, the temples of Luang Prabang shimmer. You gather your belongings. You thank your lovely guides. A premature nostalgia begins to stir. Before you are ready—could you ever be fully prepared to leave such a refuge?— the *Pak Ou* glides into shore.

Pak Ou River Cruise

I read about this cruise in a Frommer's adventure guide, which led me to **www.asian-oasis.com**. I booked it through East-West Siam in Bangkok (asian-oasis@east-west-siam.com). The company was extremely helpful and also assisted me in organizing private cars, flights and more for the rest of that particular trip.

Travelers taking this cruise either leave from Chiang Rai, Thailand, early in the morning for the border crossing from Chiang Khong into Huay Xai, Laos, or they stay overnight in Huay Xai and meet the

cruise at around nine or when everyone manages to get across the border and arrive at the boat. Read more about Huay Xai at:

WEBSITE
www.fourelephants.com/sambrown/travel.php3?sid=35

Arimid Guesthouse
Huay Xai, Laos

If you can get over the GIGANTIC spiders, this property offers charming bungalows for a few dollars a night. It is located on Saykang Street above the slow boat landing where you board the cruise.

Le Calao Inn
Luang Prabang, Laos

An amazing old French villa on the Mekong River Road (Khaem Khong Road) about 150 meters from Wat Xieng Thong walking away from the tip of the peninsula. Some of the friendliest service in Southeast Asia!

WEBSITE
www.calaoinn.laopdr.com

EMAIL
calaoinn@laotel.com

Indochina Spirit
Luang Prabang, Laos

If you are going to eat at only one place in town, this is it. It's a sprawling, romantic timber house with lots of different rooms where you sit on pillows around low tables and dine on excellent local dishes for just a few dollars per person. Ban Vat That 50-51.

EMAIL
Indochina1@yahoo.com

THAILAND
❀
Out from Chiang Mai

XXXXXXXXXXXXXXXXXXXXXXXXXXX
○○○○○○○○○○○○○○○○○○○○○○○○○○

Kat Tosi gets away from it all at the rustic Chiang Dao Nest . . .

If you're in Chiang Mai and are looking for a special escape, forget about journeying to over-visited and over-rated Pai, and head 2.5 hours north to Chiang Dao. Whether you're looking for an active eco-adventure, seeking a romantic weekend away or simply want to perfect your vegging skills, Chiang Dao is the place to do it. Stunning mountain scenery, waterfalls, cave temples, bird watching, hiking, hill tribe visits, rafting, elephant treks and good old-fashioned relaxing are all at your fingertips. Stay at the recently opened Chiang Dao Nest, with its six simple but delightful bamboo chalets. It is a gem! Owners Khun Vicha (Thai) and Stuart (English) will take you under their wings while showing you the birds. Gather around the fire at night while London-trained Khun

Vicha prepares an affordable and scrumptious meal that most four-star hotels would be hard-pressed to beat. Enjoy some wine or beer and gaze at the stars. Then collapse into your comfy bed, snuggle under your duvet and dream about extending your stay.

Chiang Dao and the Chiang Dao Nest
Start at the Chang Puak Bus Station in Chiang Mai and catch a bus to Tha Ton or Fang. Ask to be dropped off outside the Alien Bar in Chiang Dao Town. From there, get a taxi for the final 6.5 km. Or if you're going by car or motorcycle all the way from Chiang Mai, take Highway 107 north toward Fang to Chiang Dao town. In Chiang Dao Town, turn left after you see the signs (on the left) for Chiang Dao Cave. Follow this road 6.5 km. You will see Chiang Dao Nest 1.5 km past the Chiang Dao Cave right after Malee's Guesthouse.

Chang Puak Station
is north of the Chang Puak Gate on Chotana Road (a.k.a. Chang Puak Road), Chiang Mai. You may also encounter the spellings Chang Phuak and Chang Pheuak.

Chiang Dao Nest
WEBSITE
http://chiangdao.com/chiangdaone st.htm

EMAIL
chiangdaonest@lycos.com

continued on next page

Chiang Dao Region

WEBSITE
http://chiangdao.com

Candace MacKay kicks back with her family at the Hot Resort . . .

My family first arrived at this quiet resort because of my father's obsession with being near water. The Hot Resort can be found resting quietly beside the Mae Chaem River. Bungalows reside in a thin forest of pine, while the main building, which houses the kitchen and motel-style rooms, is at the center of the resort . . . all of it just a stone's throw from the river. Because restaurant seating is also near the water's edge, meals tend to be lengthy—you have the river on one side and beautifully tailored gardens on the other. The rooms and bungalows are clean, the beds are soft, and each room has its own bathroom with a shower.

Ten kilometers or so down the road from The Hot Resort (heading toward Mae Sariang) is Ob Luang National Park. This park is famous for its gorge, which you can view by just taking a short walk. If you are up for a long walk, there is a great trail that leads to the top of a high cliff. It's not a difficult trail and is clearly marked. When you reach the summit, it feels as if you are at the top of the world. The view is amazing, but if you're afraid of heights, it can be a dizzying experience.

The park also has a nice sandy shore, if you want to laze about and have a picnic. There are rafting trips during the day, and tents can be rented, if you feel like camping out. The cost to enter the park is 200 baht for foreigners, but that is the same with every national park and waterfall. I am happy to say that this park is worth the price.

This is a quiet weekend adventure for us, but it could easily be extended into a much longer trip if you have the time. For example, Mae Sariang is an untouched town worth visiting. You also pass Doi Inthanon National Park on the way from Chiang Mai to Hot—this park is likewise worth a visit. All you need is a map, a mode of transportation and a bit of money, and some unexplored Thailand is waiting for you.

The Hot Resort
Follow Hang Dong Road (Highway 108) out of Chiang Mai all the way to Hot (or Hod). On a motorbike, it takes about two hours. The first turn you make occurs when you arrive in Hot—you must take a right turn toward Ob Luang National Park/Mae Sariang. The Hot Resort is approximately 5 km down this road. Address: 239 Chiang Mai-Mae Sariang Road, Hot, Thailand.

For more on Thai national parks—and Ob Luang and Doi Inthanon, in particular—visit:

WEBSITE
www.trekthailand.net/list/
(Ob Luang is listed as Aob Luang on this site.)

For more on visiting *Mae Sariang*, go to:

WEBSITE
www.tat.or.th/province/north/
mae-son/do/mae.htm

THAILAND ✿ *Hua Hin*

Emily Huckson can't get enough of the Railway Hotel . . .

Every expat will agree that the secret to sanity while living in a foreign country is to have a special escape that you can rely on from time to time. When living in Vietnam, I discovered my "special place" while on a trip to visit a friend in Bangkok back in '96. She suggested I check out Hua Hin, a three-hour bus trip south, for the weekend.

Having knowledge of my limited budget, she recommended numerous guesthouses in the small fishing village. She also mentioned that I should, at the very least, check out the Railway Hotel. She told me it was the hotel used during the filming of **The Killing Fields** and described its various charms.

Upon arrival in Hua Hin, I went directly to the Railway Hotel and walked the grounds to see if reality matched my friend's lofty descriptions. It did. There is a topiary that is over 100 years old. There is an orchid garden where you can learn about the growing of these delicate plants. There are three swimming pools, a very cozy tearoom, a pub, a dining room overlooking a stunning garden complete with frangipani trees, an ocean, absolute peace and quiet, a gym, a library, a tennis court and a variety of daily activities (you need only sign up). And there is a *SPA!*

With each discovery of the indulgences available, I prayed to Buddha to please let me be able to stay; I approached the front desk and asked the price. The quote was about $80 US a night. I was crestfallen. I didn't know where to look. I felt like a peasant. Then I plucked up my courage and said, "This is a beautiful hotel, and I would really love to stay here, but that price is too expensive." Being straightforward is an important lesson to learn while living over here—although at the same time you have to be willing to walk away. I was taking a big gamble.

THAILAND ✿ *Hua Hin*

"Oh, just a moment," said the receptionist, "we have another single room for only forty dollars."

I was cash poor at the time, so I pulled out my credit card and announced, "I'll take it . . . for two nights!"

The porter escorted me to my room and pointed out amenities such as a TV with movie channels, A/C control, mini bar, etc. Meanwhile, I was taking in the wonderful black and white beehive flooring, outrageously thick towels and wealth of freebies in the bathroom, the wide teak-planked floor of the bedroom, the gorgeous view of ocean and gardens from my private balcony . . . immediately after he left, I jumped onto the bed and shouted, "I'm here! I'm here!"

This property will always be my marker for a first-class hotel. Since my first visit to the Railway Hotel—and I have returned many times—I've had the opportunity to stay at many five-star hotels all over Southeast Asia. *NOT ONE* compares with the hospitality, environment, service, tranquility, and beauty of the Railway Hotel. We're now into the new millennium, and rates have gone up, (it's become part of the Sofitel group), but I'm willing to pay the price for such a lovely secret retreat. Pamper yourself in the spa. Rejoice in simply being there!

Railway Hotel (Sofitel Central Hua Hin Resort)
1 Damnernkasem Road, Hua Hin.

Getting to Hua Hin
Bus: From the Southern Bus Terminal in Thonburi, Bangkok, the Hua Hin bus terminal is at the Siripetchkawem Hotel on Srasong Road near Dechanuchit Road.

WEBSITE
www.thailandhotels.net/transport/buslinks.htm

Train: From the Hualamphong Train Station in Bangkok, the Hua Hin train station office is on Damnernkasem Road

WEBSITE
www.railway.co.th/httpEng/

Air: The Hua Hin Bangkok Airways' office is at 114/7 Petchkasem Road.

WEBSITE
www.bangkokair.com

For more on Hua Hin, go to:

WEBSITE
www.frangipani.com/huahin/huahin.htm

Emily adds: Don't miss dinner on the wharf. Sit outside watching the shrimp boats coming and going, while dining on super fresh seafood. You can bring your own bottle of wine and the cafés will uncork it for you, or you can buy beer and other Thai spirits here.

The squid is the best dish—nicely spiced and unbelievably tender!

There's a great night market near the bus station. Terrific stall food at delicious prices and lots of good souvenir/craft/clothing stalls.

A great side trip is to mountain bike into the hills to the area where locals train the elephants. You can go right into the compound and get sorta close to the big beasts of burden. It's a pleasant ride, "wind in the hair, lead in the pencil" kind of thing, a bit backwoods, where the REAL Thai live, great views of the ocean, the pungent smell of pine, children yelling "hello, hello," a little hidden temple and just a great way to exercise after being a beach bum for a few days. Trips can be arranged through the Railway Hotel or on your own through one of the many "entrepreneurs" in town.

Editor's Note: Take a copy of Spaulding Gray's **Swimming to Cambodia**. It is about the making of **The Killing Fields** (among other bizarre things). The Railway Hotel played a major role in this film.

THAILAND 🏵 Koh Si Chang

*Peter J. Burns
flees to the islands . . .*

Check your travel guides. Tear through the "destinations" section of the major papers. If you have ever found anything written about it, you have accomplished something already. If you have ever found anything written positively about it, then you must be reading economic rather than travel literature. For Koh Si Chang is an important business locale but not such a prominent vacation destination. However, if you live in Bangkok or find yourself "stuck" here as so many people do, you will find it the perfect weekend getaway. An easy escape from the smog and crowds.

I learned about it almost by accident. I took a map and a 10 baht coin (roughly the same size as a quarter). I placed the center of the coin on Bangkok and then I traced a circle around the coin. That gave me roughly a 100 km radius of the area around Bangkok. Understand that I desperately wanted out of the city, but I only had two free days. I did not want to spend a great deal of my free time in a vehicle; I wanted to spend the better part of my weekend in a hammock at a nice quiet destination that could be reached easily and quickly. There were many places on the mainland within the radius of the coin, but one small island smiled at me. An island weekend seemed a nice idea at that moment.

The larger and more famous (or possibly infamous, depending on your tastes) island of Koh Samet is a very popular weekend getaway for Bangkokians. Then there is this lesser known alternative. In about two hours, from your Bangkok front door to the front porch of a scenic bungalow, you can be as far from the city as you need to be. You can hang your hammock and polish off a couple chapters of a good book, all just in time to drink in the sunset. Time could be less, depending on how long it takes you to get out of the city, which is something you can never determine accurately. Koh Si Chang is not as popular as Koh Samet for numerous reasons. However, if your goal is a quiet relaxing island weekend away from the funk of Bangkok, then it offers a perfect setting.

Koh Si Chang is a small island off the coast of Si Racha. The waters surrounding it are as busy with life as the city streets of Bangkok.

However, once the island is in sight, all remembrances of Bangkok will drift away. Well, almost. There are still the tuk tuks to contend with. Many are familiar with the tuk tuks of Bangkok. However, many may not know that the Bangkok brand of tuk tuk is almost exclusive to Bangkok and Chiang Mai. All other sizable towns and cities have their own distinct brand of tuk tuk. Many are similar but none are the same. The tuk tuks on Koh Si Chang are unlike any I have ever seen. If a Bangkok tuk tuk is like a coffee stirrer, a Koh Si Chang tuk tuk is like a high-speed blender set on puree. Of course, there are places that lie well within walking distance from the pier. Still, to really get away from it all, the other side of the island is quieter and more scenic. And the tuk tuk ride is an experience in itself. After a bus ride, then a boat ride, why not a tuk tuk ride? After all, this is a weekend getaway. Leave the walking for the weekdays on the way to work.

The tuk tuk ride will traverse the small town in a flash. It is an enjoyable little settlement complete with bank and convenience store, so there is no need to worry about a forgotten toothbrush or candy bar cravings. This is not a deserted island after all. Beyond the town, you will turn down little alleyways past brightly painted houses and shops. These stretches seem to have more of a Mediterranean feel to them. The island is quite hilly and largely undeveloped. The open areas are brushy and dense, but there are good roads and trails that make the island wholly accessible.

Following a short tuk tuk ride, the western side of the island and its cliff side bungalows await you. Most of these bungalows are built amongst the bush and trees so there are plenty of good hammock sites. After all, that is what you came here for, right? But is there anything else to do? Actually, there is. You can hike or bicycle your way around the island. You can hire a tuk tuk to tour you here and there. Or you can rent a motorcycle. Once you've chosen your mode of transportation, there is much to see, and friendly people are always willing to point you in the right direction. Swimming is easy when the tide is out, revealing small, hidden beaches at the base of the cliffs. When the tide is in, there are safe places from which to jump, for a little exhilaration. The small beaches are a great place to relax and take in some sun. Stalls offer fresh seafood and cold drinks. Lounge chairs and umbrellas provide a welcome reprieve to sunburned skin. Snorkeling is possible as the water here is very clear, although there is not much to see other than thousands of sand dollars and a large puffer fish that has always been under the same rock every time I have gone to say hello.

Koh Si Chang also has some interesting sights. On a hill overlooking the city is an old, Chinese temple. Large Buddha statues shine in the sun atop it all. They gaze toward the mainland keeping a watchful eye on all who come and go. This is a great spot to take photos and get your bearings on the island. The temple also features a cave you can climb down into. This is a special place where monks meditate, and when the light is right, it is easy to see why. Fingers of sunlight penetrate the cave from above, filling the chamber with surreal illumination. Meditation almost takes care of itself. And if you want total immersion meditation, the island features a meditation center where laymen can go and meditate with the pros.

By nightfall, the local boatmen are off after squid. Their boats will light up the entire horizon of the night sea. Of course, plenty of stalls are open with loads of great food options. The breeze is usually stirring up nicely near the cliffs. You are ready for pure relaxation. Perhaps a hammock is all you need, perhaps not. Either way, this island is a quick and easy getaway. Make of it what you will. The locals are friendly and shining. They will help you find whatever it is you are looking for.

THAILAND ❀ *Koh Si Chang*

123

Bangkok is only two hours away, but it might as well be on the other side of the world.

Koh Si Chang

Take the bus from the Eastern Bus Terminal in Bangkok on Sukhumvit Road to Si Racha. From the pier in Si Racha, catch a boat to the island.

WEBSITE
www.thailandhotels.net/transport/eastbus.htm

There are numerous websites with good information on Koh Si Chang, including:

WEBSITE
www.sawadeethailand.com/province/eastern/chonburi/kosichang/info.html

WEBSITE
www.thailand.com/travel/beach/beach_chonburi_kosichang.htm

WEBSITE
www.modernthailand.com/pattaya/koh-si-chang.htm

THAILAND 🕉 *Krabi*

XXXXXXXXXXXXXXXXXXXXXXXXXXXXXX
ooooooooooooooooooooooooooooooo

Christina Gosnell thinks that Krabi is heaven on earth . . .

A city whose motto is "Lively Town, Lovely People" remains a destination for those from all walks of life. It is made for divers and climbers, as well as those more comfortable with their feet planted solidly on the ground and who just want to bask in the sun and soak up some of God's greatest beauty. Krabi is a place that many are familiar with—even if you've never been to Asia, you have most likely seen its brilliant colors echoed in print and on screen. Numerous movies have been shot here. **The Beach, The Man With the Golden Gun** and **Cutthroat Island** are the most well-known, but many others were filmed on location in Krabi.

Are you interested in jungle exploring in the midst of waterfalls, mangrove forests and caves? How about elephant trekking on rugged limestone hills? It's all here. The province of Krabi covers 4,707 square kilometers and spans more than 200 islands. The capital of Krabi Town sits on the banks of the Krabi River, just before it opens out into the Andaman Sea. The concavity of the Krabi coastline creates numerous small-sized bays, beaches and limestone karsts. The most famous ones are Phra Nang Bay, Rai Lay Beach, Poda Island and the Phi Phi islands. Krabi also has a 75 million year old gastropod fossil, one of only three known to exist.

Considered one of the greatest rock climbing locations in Asia, Krabi welcomes climbers from all over the world . . . as long as they are brave enough to dangle from the famous limestone cliffs. The crags, which rise to great heights, cover a large range of grades. There are more than 500 routes in 40 spots. The best are said to be tucked way in the Rai Leh headland.

For water lovers, Krabi's main beach, Ao Nang, can be reached by the road north of town. (Locals insist that the best coves and beaches are accessible only by sea). Laem Phra Naeng, a long forested peninsula, juts out into the Andaman Sea from Ao Nang, and at its southern tip are three fine beaches: Ao Phra Nang and West and East Rai Leh. Concealed among the trees separating the beaches is the Dusit Rayavadee Resort.

Krabi offers a realm of possibility for anyone who dares to make the long voyage there. It is a sunrise and a sunset all wrapped into one. Whatever you want to do, you're sure to find it. Paddle a canoe along the coastline to visit the nearby islands. Want a closer view? Snorkel or dive into the blue waters and see fish and other underwater life that are impossible to find anywhere else. On Krabi, nature is what it's all about. And as the famous song "Hotel California" says, "You can check out anytime you like, but you can never leave."

This piece was originally published in a slightly different form at: **www.thingsasian.com**.

Getting to Krabi

Bus: From the Southern Bus Terminal in Thonburi, Bangkok.

Train: Trains do not go directly to Krabi.

Air: Thai Airways

WEBSITE
www.thaiairways.com

Christina suggests that visitors to Krabi should pick up a copy of the **Guide Map of Krabi**, published by V. Hongsombud.

Two great websites:

WEBSITE
www.gokrabi.com

WEBSITE
www.krabi.com

FYI: There are over 200 islands in the province of Krabi. Many belong to the Hat Noppharat Thara-Ko Phi Phi National Park, which also contains the famous Phi Phi Islands.

Kim Fay's
fact files from the
chapter introduction . . .

Dalat Palace
12 Tran Phu Street, Dalat, Vietnam.

Ana Mandara Resort
Beachside Tran Phu Boulevard, Nha Trang, Vietnam.

WEBSITE
www.six-senses.com/ana-mandara

THAILAND ❁ *Krabi*

INTO THE WILD

Getting up close and personal with Southeast Asia's awe–inspiring natural beauty.

Sometimes—when you're stuck in a taxi in Bangkok or Ho Chi Minh City, for example—it's difficult to hold onto the fact that the greater part of Southeast Asia is made up of gorgeous, natural landscapes. From its ubiquitous shimmering rice paddies to its dramatic limestone outcroppings to its tranquil unspoiled waters, this is a region in which going off the beaten path is often rewarded with encounters that will take your breath away. Granted, the cities of Cambodia, Laos, Thailand and Vietnam are thrilling, but to genuinely immerse yourself in these countries you must be willing to get up close and personal with the raw power of Mother Nature at her tropical best.

John Williams offers an overview that will make even the most shark-phobic person want to dive in the Andaman Sea, while Ray Zepp sends you into regions of Cambodia still populated with tigers. Bill Hutchins sings the praises of paddling the rivers of Laos with John Gray's pioneering company, SeaCanoe; John Gray raves about paddling the bays of Thailand and Vietnam; and Dave Williams (who Bill also paddled with) waxes poetic on the bird-watching bounty to be discovered while kayaking Thailand. Nick and Hannah Anderson reminisce about biking through Laos in a wonderful piece; unfortunately, their essay brings up an important aspect to consider when you're planning to venture into the wild. Laos has a history of random banditry that has plagued its tourism industry, but when the Andersons pedaled through the country, it was considered (relatively) safe. Since their trip, there have been two shooting incidents; in February and April of 2003, buses traveling stretches of the road that the Andersons biked were attacked. Many passengers, including tourists, were killed. Because of these occurrences, I hesitated to include the Andersons' piece in this book. In the end, though, removing it felt like admitting defeat. Laos is one of the most beautiful, awe-inspiring countries I have visited, and their travelogue captures the unspoiled spirit of the country. It is the same spirit

described in Bill Tuffin's musings on the Luang Namtha region. (Lonely Planet author Joe Cummings lists Bill's Boat Landing Guest House as one of his Top Five Laos' Attractions on page 67.)

While this section has some fabulous suggestions for unique outdoor opportunities, it also offers a reminder to look beyond the obvious. When Stephen Engle visited the Bridge on the River Kwai in Thailand, he did the usual tourist stuff and then went one step (or rather quite a few) further. The result was an experience both physical and spiritual. As far as I'm concerned, it is this union that makes travel worthwhile.

CAMBODIA 🏵 *Veal Veng*

Ray Zepp
ventures into the
Cardamom Mountains . . .

Tigers, elephants, hill tribes, jungle treks, high mountain scenery . . . tourists to Cambodia immediately envision Ratanakiri or Mondulkiri. But those areas have become highly trafficked these days. They have lost a bit of their pristine remoteness. On the other hand, very few tourists visit the Cardamom Mountains along Cambodia's western border with Thailand. This large area contains Cambodia's richest wildlife, its highest mountains and its most untouched wilderness. Best of all, it is easily accessible, and there is a guesthouse at Bramaoy, the capital of Veal Veng District.

Bramaoy is nestled between two of Cambodia's highest mountain ranges, including the second highest peak in Cambodia, Phnom Samros. In fact, the entire surrounding area is part of the Phnom Samros Natural Reserve. Bramaoy has a real frontier feeling, like Ratanakiri had ten years ago. You really feel that you are at the end of the world, but you can reach even more remote places to the west, north or south of Bramaoy.

You can arrange a jungle trek through the Forestry Service, located on the way into Bramaoy, but it may be wiser to arrange your trek from the Provincial Forestry Office back in Pursat.

The rangers can take you north into the mountains of elephant country, or south into tiger country, which is sparsely inhabited by hill tribes. I went by moto along the good road to the west, to Thmar Da near the Thai border. The first hour or so is rather uninteresting, since the area is being settled and the forests are burnt down; however, once the road starts climbing the mountain, you know you are in virgin territory. The lush forests, spectacular mountain scenery and clear, rushing streams are probably the most beautiful in all Cambodia, as the road crosses the highest mountain pass in the country. You eventually arrive at Thmar Da, whose end-of-the-world atmosphere makes Bramaoy feel like Bangkok.

South of Bramaoy, the road is virtually non-existent, but the government is improving it so that you will soon be able to travel all the way to Koh Kong. While that is good news for tourists, the downside is that the new road will open up the wilderness to development, and that will destroy much of the forest and the wildlife there. This is Cambodia's last real bastion for tigers and other rare wildlife.

The road north of Bramaoy is heavily mined and is in such terrible condition that you should not attempt to head up to Krapeu Pi and into Samlot District. But if you go with the Forestry rangers just a little ways up into the mountains, they say there are several large herds of elephants and other wildlife there.

I really enjoyed my stay in Veal Veng, and I was surprised at how accessible it was, as well as how easy it was to find accommodation and food there. Veal Veng is not mentioned in any of the main tour guides, but if you enjoy unspoiled, remote areas, you will love Veal Veng and the Cardamom Mountains.

Pursat

is on Highway 5 between Phnom Penh and Battambang, about four hours by bus if you are coming from Phnom Penh and less than two hours by bus if you are coming from Battambang. If you're traveling to Pursat from Phnom Penh, Ray recommends taking the $4 US, four hour bus ride rather than the long Phnom Penh-Battambang train trip. He adds: Bramaoy is southwest of Pursat and south of Battambang. You can reach Bramaoy by taxi from Pursat. Taxis leave early in the morning from the taxi park located a few hundred meters west of the Pursat River crossing on the highway. The trip to Bramaoy takes 2-3 hours along a good and scenic road.

LAOS ❁ *Luang Namtha*

Bill Tuffin introduces the attractions of Luang Namtha . . .

FIVE REASONS TO VISIT LUANG NAMTHA IN LAOS

To experience the warmth and friendliness of the people

Lao people are gentle and caring. They can also be very shy, and especially in the north they have a reputation for being reserved. But with a joke or smile, all reservations easily disappear, and without much more effort you find yourself on the way to friendship. The Lao love to have fun and be silly. Soon, you might find yourself sitting around having a drink and being silly, too.

To experience a totally different way of living

The Lao live in groups. They live with their families, their friends and their community. The individual identifies with his group, and not with himself as we do in the West. This is why they do not value being alone. In Luang Namtha you will see a small, insular community that lives

much as its ancestors did centuries ago. Their lives revolve around the rhythm of the seasons and the beat of rice farming. However, this is all going to change when the road between Singapore and Lisbon cuts through the province, a project started in 2004.

To help the native people appreciate the importance of their heritage

In most of Southeast Asia, the great stands of climax tropical forest have all but disappeared. The Nam Ha National Protected Area of Luang Prabang is one of the last diverse stands of northern tropical forest and habitat left in Southeast Asia. In the past, it has been protected by the province's isolation from the world. The great hope for this protected area (as it is only really protected in name) is tourism, since tourism will give it a greater value than the loggers ever can.

To help the ethnic groups learn to value their culture

In Luang Namtha, there are thirty-three different ethnic groups. They have a tremendous cultural heritage, although they consider themselves backward and poor in comparison to the lifestyles and material things of the West. They are really confounded as to why "rich" people want to come visit "poor, backward" people. Please help them to see how rich they are in their own special way. Let them know how much you value their way of life.

To taste rare and delicious food

The delectable food of Luang Namtha and northern Laos is lost in the blinding light of Thai cuisine. The world has yet to discover this unique culinary treasure. Northern Lao food is filled with all kinds of wonders to discover—pickled bamboo pastes, rattan shoots, field crab pastes, rock algae chips covered with sesame seeds and tomatoes and much, much more. Oh, I almost forgot all the spices from the forest, many of which may not even have names in English. Come and taste the food of the local people and you will see what I mean.

Luang Namtha

Bill is the General Director of the Boat Landing Guest House, whose website offers excellent information on the Nam Ha National Protected Area, as well as invaluable travel information for Luang Namtha—it even recommends other guest houses in the area. Luang Namtha can be reached by river, road or air—click on "Traveling to Luang Namtha" on the website's home page. (Note: On page 67, Lonely Planet author Joe Cummings has selected the Boat Landing Guest House as one of his "Top Five" destinations to visit in Laos.)

WEBSITE
www.theboatlanding.laopdr.com

LAOS 🏵 General

Bill Hutchins loses his heart to the rivers of Laos . . .

A dense morning mist drifted through the steep walls of bamboo that lined the Nam Tong River. I pushed my kayak along as laughing children raced across a rickety suspension bridge draped high above the water. I had been paddling the rivers of Laos for a total of about a month, and there was never a day when I wasn't wrapped in such scenes of beauty and magic.

I first kayaked the country in 1997 with a groundbreaking crew from John Gray's famous company, SeaCanoe. On that trip, we used inflatable kayaks to run three rivers in that landlocked nation of mountains and jungle. This time, my second trip, I was traveling with Dave Williams of PaddleAsia, and we were using whitewater style rafts and an inflatable kayak to navigate five additional rivers.

Every river we paddled in Laos had its unique character—its own pattern of villages, cliffs, temples and intersecting tributaries—and every one of them was a natural treasure so valuable to me that I can hardly wait to get back and paddle more. I'm not likely to run out of options any time soon.

Laos has hundreds of mountains, and scores of rivers drain the valleys between them. There are few decent roads in the country, and so the rivers are used for commerce, communication and settlement. On that first trip, we traveled overland from Thailand into Vientiane, the capital. From there, we chartered a prop plane and proceeded to pack it with thousands of pounds of people, kayaks and gear. We were so close to the plane's load limits that we could only take on half the fuel we needed to reach our destination. We had to land at another airfield halfway along and refuel, just so we could make it all the way up to our put-in spot on the upper Nam Ou River.

We flew through ranges of sharp limestone mountains that rose out of the clouds like ominous green shark fins. I prayed as we passed through opaque white sections that we would not strike anything hidden and hard . . . like a cliff face. Then the sunlight poured in against a field of blue as we banked sharply between peaks. We dropped through a needle-eye slot in the mountains as clouds streamed over the jagged

ridge like white smoke from dry ice. The plane skidded to a long, bumpy landing in the middle of a muddy field dotted with buffalo dung.

We made it! That is, we made it as far as the plane could take us. We next traveled overland on deeply rutted mud roads that snaked through endless mountain passes. Finally, we arrived at the pretty little river town of Ban Nong Khioneua, where the next day we attracted a crowd of hundreds as we pumped up our funny little inflatable yellow boats and pushed off into the swirling brown waters of the Nam Ou.

For the next couple of days we paddled through rolling green hills populated by slash-and-burn farmers tending fields of dry land rice. We slept in tiny river villages that seemed lost in a wonderful, quirky time warp. There were no phones, no electricity, no plumbing, no TVs and most of all, no hotels. We stayed wherever the villagers were kind enough to find us a protective roof, and we always made sure to reward them financially for their generous hospitality.

On the third day, we found ourselves traveling through high black walls of eroded limestone. We were hemmed in by sheer cliffs that rose straight up out of the river and resembled the spiny back of a dragon. Fog slipped over giant rock bowls a couple thousand feet high.

Black caves pocked the wall faces, and jungle trees seemed to be singing tropical bird songs, which echoed through the gorge. Giant staghorn ferns perched on thick overhanging branches draped in vines and orchids. The gorge seemed to pulse and breathe, a primeval forest of rock and wood. A couple of days later, we reached the take-out spot, but the damage was done—I was hooked. My soul was taken over by the high of the experience, and I knew I was addicted.

In the days that followed, we paddled other rivers. We paddled a lowland jungle river called the Nam Ngun, where I saw a gorgeous green snake swimming between emergent tree trunks in standing water and where we sought shelter from driving monsoonal rains in a one-room schoolhouse. Before we left Laos, we also paddled the dramatic Hin Boun River. What makes the Hin Boun so remarkable is that the river actually punches its way from one valley to another by boring through solid rock. For something like nine kilometers, it passes underground in an ink black darkness punctuated by internal rapids before emerging in a new, separate valley.

On my more recent trip with PaddleAsia, we concentrated mainly on rivers that are close to Vientiane. Our first stop was the backpacker haven known as Vang Vieng. It is a jumble of guesthouses, internet cafes and a handful of bars. It's a great jumping off point for paddling the Nam Song River, which winds through pretty scenes of karst and limestone peaks reminiscent of Chinese paintings, and is home to cave temples harboring Buddhist statuary, surrounded by tall, arching coconut palms. As well, it's a bit notorious for being a major staging area for the CIA's secret war in Laos during the Vietnam War. Air America ran a big airfield operation there, and the asphalt landing strip is still a sort of bizarre centerpiece for the town.

On this trip we also paddled the Nam Lik, Nam Tong, Nam Ngum and a bit of the Mekong. A constant highlight continued to be the river kids. Children swam out to our raft and climbed aboard. Boys jumped off high tree branches and splashed into the river beside us. Kids fished, paddled canoes and played in waterfalls. We ate lunch with them, swam with them and laughed with them. I'll never forget their radiant smiles and genuine expressions of friendship and hospitality. As soon as I earn enough money and vacation time, I'm headed back to the rivers of Laos. I'm headed back to electric green rice fields, the tinkling melodies of buffalo bells and the relaxing caress of the tropical river waters. I'm headed back to colorful flocks of wild parakeets, water dragon lizards perched on jungle branches and hand-sized butterflies drifting between thin walls of bamboo. I'm headed back, and it can't be soon enough.

This article was originally published at **www.thingsasian.com**.

Paddling Laos

SeaCanoe runs charter trips in Laos through their Ultimate Asia partners—same office, same team. For more information:

WEBSITE
www.johngray-seacanoe.com
This is the official website; beware of others claiming to be affiliated with it.

EMAIL
info@johngray-seacanoe.com

PaddleAsia can be found at:

WEBSITE
www.paddleasia.com

Along with tour information, this site has great reviews of past trips, which read more like travel narratives.

Vang Vieng

is a very small town, and the kayaking tour operators can be easily tracked down. To read more about this destination, go to Sam Brown's wonderful website:

WEBSITE
www.fourelephants.com/sambrown/
travel.php3?sid=7

Also, click into "Water Activities" at the following:

WEBSITE
www.davestravelcorner.com/articles/
vangvieng/

Chris Unno writes about a one-day kayaking trip from Vang Vieng at:

WEBSITE
www.thingsasian.com/goto_article/
tell_story.1661.html

Nick and Hannah Anderson reminisce about biking through Laos . . .

Cycling through Laos from Luang Prabang to Vientiane was pretty tough, but the rewards were high, with expansive views of towering karst limestone monoliths, villages perched high in the mountains and a road that seemed to cling for dear life to the side of rocky outcrops, only to suddenly drop away to the river valley below. Nick and I felt truly hardcore as our muscles bulged and the sweat turned to salt on our arms. Great was the relief when the afternoon rains came and rinsed us clean.

Our main concern when we decided on cycling this route was not knowing exactly where villages, food and accommodation were along the way. We soon found out that the latter two of the three were quite scarce. Our road diet consisted of large quantities of stale prawn crackers and cans of cold Nescafe—not hugely energy-giving, taking into account that we were cycling on average nine hours per day. Although we gained altitude very quickly, I was relieved to find that the climbing sections were always fairly constant, while at the same time I soon became uncomfortable in the knowledge that our descents seemed to return us to our original starting height.

Darkness in the mountains falls quite swiftly, and at five p.m. on that first day out of Luang Prabang, we approached the moderately sized village of Ban Nam Ming. It seemed stupid to try and press on, so we pulled up outside the largest of the houses. Equipped with a phrasebook (limited), we inquired about nearby guesthouses (non-existent), and it was a relief when we were invited in for the night.

Fortunately for us, we had called on the house of the village headman. Although he was also the local doctor, dentist and banker, he lived in a simple hut with his wife and four daughters. After a bath in the river and a change of clothes, Nick and I felt infinitely better, and we waited eagerly for the arrival of anything to eat. After an hour or so of sharing our limited photo selection and of an even more limited conversation, two trays of food were brought in: one for the children and one for us. We dined on bamboo soup, hot coleslaw, a bowl of *nam plaa* (tiny raw fish that we later found out was unsafe to eat) and sticky rice—all of which we consumed with that all purpose utensil, the hand. Afterwards, a bottle containing rice whiskey was passed around. We each splashed a little from the glass onto our tray as a gift to the house spirit.

We left early the following morning, after giving the family some money in payment for their kind hospitality. Strangely enough, this seemed to be expected of us, as the man of the house had scrawled down a number on a piece of paper, which he handed to us before we left.

Cycling is never boring. There is always something to look at, or somebody looking at you. Every so often we would bike through a tiny hamlet, scattering piglets and poultry. Often, scores of snotty-nosed children would run around us waving furiously. I also became aware of the number of handicapped people wandering around—a man missing both hands, a boy who was suffering from polio. I'm sure that exploding land mines were the cause of many of the terrible injuries we saw, and it was heartbreaking to see the number of adults and children with cataracts, a problem that is so easy to fix but whose cure is unavailable to these people. It was very sad.

As darkness fell that next day, we freewheeled into Muang Phu Khun. We had been turning up the pedals for a full 11 hours and had climbed 2,000 meters. This was a new record for us, and it was with great relief that night when we finally collapsed into our rickety beds at a guest house.

When we took off the next morning, a damp fog clung heavily to the corrugated iron roofs. But as we dropped out of the sky, our spirits rose. We sailed downhill, picking up speed, throwing caution to the wind as we hurtled past fast running chickens and fleeing children. Past sentry posts and bullet-scarred road signs. Past army trucks and yet more men playing with their rifles. The rain came down again as we undulated our way through a most spectacular valley, with sheer cliffs and pillars of karst rising on either side of us like the walls of some enormous cathedral. I spied children bathing naked in the running gutters, staying immersed in the dirty water to avoid getting cold in the chilled air. Past drab shops, with their bags of oil and nuts, and toilet rolls hanging from elastic bands, each shop displaying the same items while its owner slept on a mat in the back.

As we approached Vang Vieng, we were appalled to see the damage

the heavy rains had caused that year. We passed a number of villages that had been completely washed away. It was a terrible sight. When we were talking to a local man, he told us of the desperate situation, and it was with great sadness that we continued through this partially destroyed valley.

We stayed at Vang Vieng a couple of days, time enough to fill up on some carbohydrates and to be robbed of all our cash—no real fond memories there. From there it took us another couple of days to reach Vientiane, where if I remember correctly, we spent most of our time eating, sleeping, washing and most importantly, enjoying the simple luxuries of an en suite bathroom with a sit down toilet.

Cycling Laos

Nick and Hannah add: We used the **Lonely Planet Laos** guidebook, which was fine, as usual. We also borrowed **The Rough Guide to Laos**, which was useful for cross-referencing and gleaning little gems such as the fact that there is a guesthouse in Muang Phu Khun—this was omitted in the LP. It seemed impossible to get a detailed map of Laos, although since our trip, LP has published **Cycling Vietnam, Laos and Cambodia**. It covers the Luang Prabang-Vientiane route and seems to be accurate, with impressive charts of the gradients! The road is well-engineered and few hills are steeper than 1 in 20, which is a perfect gradient for a cyclist. It's just that the hills are really quite big! Some people say that the road is dangerous and at risk from insurgent activity but we saw nothing, and there was certainly plenty of traffic on it, by Laos standards anyway! (Editor's note: regarding safety, please read the introduction to this chapter).

Essential Kit Tips

1. Valium. Absolutely essential for when it's noisy, too hot, too uncomfortable and you have to sleep. It doesn't seem to affect cycling the next day.

2. Robust slick or semi-slick tires for the Luang Prabang-Vientiane route. Elsewhere in Laos, off-road tires are necessary, as the roads are supposedly very rough.

3. Thermarests for making uncomfortable places bearable.

4. Silk sleeping bag liners to make unhygienic beds hygienic.

5. Antibiotics.

6. Powdered rehydration/electrolyte drinks. These are available to some extent in Laos.

Signing in and out in Laos

At that time, **The Lonely Planet Laos** 3rd edition recommended that you sign in and out of each province as you go along, but we didn't and had no problems at all. We met a number of other people who also weren't signing in and out. I guess they may be lifting the requirement.

For more on Nick and Hannah's biking adventures, go to:

WEBSITE
http://uk.geocities.com/hannahandnick/

See next page for biking route chart.

Day	Destination	Distance	Comments
			Nick & Hannah's Biking Route Through Laos
	Starting point in Laos: Huay Xai		This small town is located just across the river from Chiang Khong, Thailand. It can be easily reached by mini-bus from Chiang Rai.
	Slow boat from Huay Xai to Luang Prabang	2 days	Very chilled out. Strap the bikes to the roof. I don't think we paid to do this. (Editor's note: the boat stops overnight in Pak Beng.)
1	Begin biking: from Luang Prabang to Ban Nam Ming	50 km	1000 m ascent, start 700 m end 780 m. Easy 200 m ascent to Xieng Ngeun (about 30 km from Luang Prabang). Many small shops here so stock up. Climb begins immediately, 1 in 20 to 1400 m. Spectacular, fantastic ride. Descent to Ban Nam Ming at bridge over river. No accommodation, but we managed to gesticulate our way onto a local's veranda. No food, so either bring your own or get in with the locals like we did.
2	Ban Nam Ming to Muang Phu Khun	73 km	2060 m ascent, start 780 m end 1660 m. WHAT A RIDE! Ascent begins immediately for about 1000 m then undulates along a ridge until Ban Kiukacham (about three hours from Ban Nam Ming) after 20 km at 1750 m elevation. Noodle shops and other supplies here so grab as many calories as you can. Descends to small river crossing, then ascent through valley, then along a ridge to Muang Phu Khun. Stay in the worst guesthouse in SE Asia. Noodle shops.
3	Muang Phu Khun to Kasi	44 km	420 m ascent, start 1660 m end 795 m. Undulations, then long descent, then flat to Kasi. Easy ride, nice scenery. Supposedly slightly dangerous (see chapter introduction). Some road work and mud. Good guesthouse and restaurants in Kasi. Buses stop here. Eat below the guesthouse, as the place two doors up gave us the runs.

Day	Destination	Distance	Comments
4	Kasi to Vang Vieng	58 km	365 m ascent, start 795 m end 630 m. Gentle ascent, short ascent for valley crossing then gentle descent to Vang Vieng. Very scenic, plenty of hill tribes, terrible flood damage in places, some damage to road in places. All foreigner amenities in Vang Vieng and loads of backpackers.
5	Vang Vieng to Thalat	100 km	Undulating. No guesthouse in Phon Hong so we had to go to Thalat 14 km east. Nice Napa Kuang Resort with air-con and restaurant. (The resort is signposted from the central market place. It is actually a fairly big resort for Laos with a bar and semblance of a restaurant.) Do not bother with the guesthouses on the way to Thalat. They are filthy and overpriced. Found out next day that there was a guesthouse on the main road 10 km south of Phon Hong. There's a gem of information for you.
6	Thalat to Vientiane	85 km	Undulating then flat. Guesthouses 10 km after Phon Hong and also at 52 and 48 km markers. A bit boring after what had gone before.
7	Vientiane to the Friendship Bridge on the Laos/Thai border	20 km	Flat, entrance to bridge on left, not the right, as you would expect. Can't cycle across the bridge so wait until someone friendly offers you a lift in a pickup. In the confusion, they didn't collect our exit fee!

THAILAND
❀
Bridge on the River Kwai

XXXXXXXXXXXXXXXXXXXXXXXXXXXXXXXXX
ooooooooooooooooooooooooooooooo

Stephen Engle takes you to hell and back . . .

I felt fortunate. I hiked the Death Railway with shoes on. I even had bottled water, a hat and bug spray. Essentials, you may say, not even to be given a second thought when setting off into the jungle. The thing is, at Hellfire Pass—where WWII prisoners were lucky to have even a clean loincloth—you do think of these "luxuries" with each and every step.

A movie made a bridge on the river Kwai famous—but it was misery and malevolence that made the entire railway infamous. Nearly 100,000 Asian conscripts and more than 12,000 Allied POWs died while building the rail line for the Japanese Imperial Army from 1942-43. Incredibly, the 415-kilometer stretch—snaking through thick mountainous jungle with every tropical disease imaginable—was completed in just 18 months.

Hellfire Pass is just a small section of the now-defunct supply line to Burma, but it exacted a terrible toll. Seventy percent of the POWs who worked here died. "The Japanese literally worked them to death," said William J. Slape, manager of the Hellfire Pass Memorial Museum.

The haunting U-shaped Konyu Cutting is perhaps the most poignant reminder of the hell inflicted by those in charge. The craggy rock walls of the 110-meter excavation tower are as high as four story buildings on each side, with room in between for light gauge trains to pass. Exhausted prisoners, under constant threat from sun and sentry, pounded at the rock by hand. At night, the flickering reflection of fire off the walls and off the emaciated faces of men gave the place its name.

"Hellfire Pass is an image of suffering," Slape said. "The whole of Asia suffered, but this was one of the worst areas."

For all this pain, the railway was only used for a year and a half until the Japanese were defeated in 1945. Too long, the builders would probably say. Most of the line was later ripped up and left for the jungle to consume. It stayed that way for half a century.

Thanks to Australian-Thai cooperation, the clearing began in the late 1990s. Four kilometers of the abandoned railway is now open to explore . . .

The hike begins at Konyu and heads northwest through six more cuttings and past several long-since collapsed trestle bridges. The tracks are also gone, but a few charred wooden crossties and iron spikes can be found along the way.

The incisor-like rocks of the rail bed jab at my rubber soles, urging me to understand—or at least not forget—what happened. A green canopy of towering bamboo now provides shelter from the sun, but not from the heat and humidity. Dehydration, I assume, would come swiftly to the ill-prepared.

I wander with my thoughts and the murmur of the jungle as my only companions, wondering if the men of '43 ever got to appreciate the stunning scenery of the river valley below. The sun slides deeper in the western sky, silhouetting the distant arching hills to resemble a herd of elephants, if you will, walking trunk to tail. It's a beautiful place, with an appalling history.

If you have just one day in Kanchanaburi, head to "the bridge" close to town for an obligatory snapshot, then get yourself to the mountains and Hellfire Pass for a grittier picture of history. But don't forget to stop first for the bug spray. The mosquitoes are bad. Did I mention the poisonous centipedes, elephant scorpions and flying snakes? It is a jungle out there, after all.

Hellfire Pass

is located about 80 km northwest of Kanchanaburi off Highway 323. From the war cemetery at Kanchanaburi, drive north for 5 km and turn left onto Route 323 and travel that for another 73 km. Access to the memorial is on the left through a Royal Thai Army farm. Give yourself at least 1 hour 20 minutes each way by motor scooter (about 1 full tank of gas each way, depending on how "hell bent" you are).

From Bangkok to Kanchanaburi, air-con buses leave the Southern Bus Terminal (oddly named because it's in the northwestern part of the city across the Chao Phraya River in Thonburi) every 15 minutes for 62 baht. The trip usually takes 2.5 to 3 hours. Same for the return.

Admission to Hellfire Pass Museum

No charge, but donations are very much appreciated. Commemorative books, videos, VCDs, polo shirts and other items are for sale, with proceeds going back to maintaining the memorial museum.

Hike Times

Those coming on an organized tour from Kanchanaburi will probably only have about 1 hour at the memorial (protest for more!), which is barely enough time to take in the museum exhibits

continued on next page

(which includes a short movie) and the nearby Konyu Cutting. If you want to hike the railway, you'll need your own transportation and some time. The official walking map (pick one up at the counter) says to allow 4.5 hours to hike the 4 kilometers to the Compressor Cutting at the end of the walking trail and back again. That's overly generous. I did it in less than 3 hours, with plenty of time to stop and reflect. It all depends on your pace, as the trail can be a bit steep where the trestles have been knocked out. Also, for safety's sake, the museum will likely equip you with a walkie-talkie and a key to the outhouse 2.5 kilometers down the line.

Veteran Visits

Former POWs who wish to visit are asked to contact William J. Slape, Manager, directly at the museum via e-mail at:

EMAIL
hellfirepass@37.com

You can also contact PO Box 61, Kanchanaburi or via the Australian-Thai Chamber of Commerce, 20th Floor, Thai CC Tower, 889 South Sathorn Road, Bangkok.

TELEPHONE
66-2100-2168

EMAIL
austcham@loxinfo.or.th

Many thanks to Steve for providing this fact file.

THAILAND 🏵 *Andaman Sea*

John B. Williams meanders through the underwater landscapes of the Andaman Sea . . .

Some of the best dive sites in the world lie off the coast of Phuket in the Andaman Sea. Manta rays and whale sharks commonly visit the sea throughout the year. In addition, our sites are home to hundreds of rare marine species not found in other areas of the world, including pipe fish, sea horses and nudibranches. Phuket is the obvious gateway to the marine national parks in Western Thailand and the Mergui Archipelago in Burma due to the island's modern infrastructure and year-round safe anchorages.

The most famous dive sites are in and around the Similan Islands, about 100 km northwest of Phuket. These nine islands offer the clearest water, the whitest coral-sand beaches and the most colorful marine life in the Kingdom. The diving environment ranges from huge boulder outcroppings to gently sloping healthy coral reefs to deep, submerged pinnacles. To the north, Ko Bon, Ko Tachai, the famous

Richelieu Rock and the Surin Islands—each a unique environment—are located near the Burmese border and are worth an extra effort to visit.

Traveling north past Richelieu Rock, we find the Mergui Archipelago, historically part of Thailand (Siam) and now governed by Myanmar (Burma). A remarkable group of over 800 islands, they have only recently opened to tourism after political closure resulting from World War II and its repercussions. With over 10,000 square miles of calm seas and uninhabited islands, the diving and water sport possibilities here are almost immeasurable. However, the dive sites and islands are far from any major port, and supplies are not available, so a visit to this area requires more days at sea.

Seven hundred and twenty kilometers to the northwest, we have the Andaman and Nicobar Islands, a part of India. This area is still much like it was 100 years ago with very little deforestation and almost no active fishing. However, permissions for dive boats are difficult to obtain, and distances between dive sites vast. Thus, lots of preplanning and at least two weeks of your time are necessary to visit these islands. It's worth it if you have the time and money.

Diving around the southern parts of Phuket is also beautiful. Famous, popular places such as Shark Point and Phi Phi Island offer incredible diving on most days. Day-trips are fun to these sites, while the other areas mentioned above generally require a multi-day live-aboard trip. However, Similan Island day-trips are gaining in popularity with recently introduced faster dive boats.

It is impossible to see all that Thailand and Burma have to offer in just one trip. People return repeatedly in order just to get a taste of it. Whether you have only a day or a few weeks, make time to dive our Andaman Sea, one of the world's treasures.

Diving the Andaman Sea

For details on diving this area and on John's diving company, check out his website. Links for the Similan Islands and Mergui Archipelago (among other destinations) can be found at the left hand side of the page.

WEBSITE
www.siamdivers.com

WEBSITE
www.thailand.com/travel/beach/beach_andaman.htm offers basic background information on the Andaman Sea.

THAILAND ❦ *Andaman Sea*

THAILAND
❀

Heading Down the Peninsula

Dave Williams spots Purple Swamphens in the Thai everglades . . .

I've dreamt about seeing rare birds in Thailand, but I had no idea that it would be so easy. Thale Noi, just north of Songkhla, is a huge freshwater marsh area teeming with life. Thale means "sea" and Noi means "little" in Thai. Since the Thai language puts the adjective behind the noun, Thale Noi equals Little Sea. It's a popular vacation spot for Thai tourists from nearby cities, including Songkhla and Hat Yai.

A friend from England and I were on a kayaking trip, hoping to see birds from fresh, brackish and saltwater areas. We anticipated spotting different species in each of the environments. When we got to Thale Noi—our freshwater destination—we were immediately taken by the beauty before us. Sturdy wooden walkways pass over the lush water bird terrain, where we could see the big leaves of Yellow Burhead as far as the eye could see. Water Lettuce, named because they look like little heads of fresh green lettuce, was everywhere. Alligator Weed and the pink flowers of the water lilies added contrast to the verdant scenery. The tiny dots of the duck weed colored the water surface. The Sacred Lotus congested the area, as well; their flowers were in bloom in every direction. It was like a green and pink water pasture.

Some birds actually have feet adapted for walking on the surface plants. Jacanas, both the bronze-winged and the pheasant-tailed, were easy to spot. Their feet are about the same length as their bodies. My friend, Nick, shot some superb video footage of a Bronze-winged Jacana walking on lilies looking for insects and tiny creatures. Thanks to the wooden walkway, he got really close to a Jacana. The handrail made a superb make-shift camera prop. Luckily, while he was shooting, the Jacana lowered its head and sped up. It cocked its neck and shot its beak forward. Something very small—sitting on a leaf, in sunny southern Thailand—became a snack for a Jacana . . . and we captured the moment on film.

At one point, we had five Purple Swamphens in front of us! A dazzlingly bright-purple, two-foot-tall adult was standing on some

6. Into the Wild

robust Yellow Burhead roots eating a chocolate brown apple snail the size of an apple itself. Nick got his camera out and zoomed right in on the snail. The swamphen's long toes wrapped entirely around the snail as it pecked, gouging out meat. This must be snail heaven for these birds. Millions of pink apple snail eggs clung to the stalks of plant life in the lake.

Since the sun would be setting in a few hours, we opted to take a quick longtail boat tour around the marsh. The traditional wooden boats—used throughout the kingdom—get their name from their long propeller shaft and their ability to navigate shallow water. We asked our driver to take us halfway around the marsh and drop us off, so we could paddle the rest of the way home.

In the longtail, we crossed over the floating salad bar. Along the way, we spotted Little Cormorants, cute little Cotton-pygmy Geese, Pheasant-tailed Jacanas, Bronze-winged Jacanas, Purple Herons, Grey Herons, Chinese Pond Herons, Intermediate Egrets, Lesser Whistling Ducks, Brahminy Kites, Ruddy-breasted Crakes and a White-breasted Waterhen . . . not to mention a range of birds usually seen in other regions of the country. Our friendly driver dropped us off late in the afternoon on the only bit

of solid land in the area, for our silent return through paradise.

For adventurous birders who want to see a large variety of birds in a reasonably short period of time, Thale Noi is a real winner. And if you have the chance, go north a few hours to Khao Sok National Park. There, you'll see the largest assortment of hornbills I've seen . . . but that's another story. Whether you have little time and use local transport or have the time to delve deeper by kayak, you'll be guaranteed a look into the spectacular wildlife habitats of Thailand.

Thale Noi Waterfowl Park
is located in Southern Thailand, 32 km northeast of Phatthalung Town. More on the Phatthalung region can be found at:

WEBSITE
www.tat.or.th/province/south/p_lung/

WEBSITE
www.thailandguidebook.com/provinces/phatthalung.html

Dave notes that his personal favorite national park is *Khao Sok*. To find out more about it, go to:

WEBSITE
www.khaosok.com

WEBSITE
www.trekthailand.net/list/

Phatthulung
can be reached by either bus or train from Bangkok.

continued on next page

THAILAND ❀ *Heading Down the Peninsula*

From the Southern Bus Terminal in Bangkok:

WEBSITE
www.thailandhotels.net/transport/buslinks.htm

From the Hualamphong Train Station in Bangkok:

WEBSITE
www.railway.co.th/httpEng/

This essay was excerpted from the PaddleAsia website. To read Dave's full article on Thale Noi, go to:

WEBSITE
www.paddleasia.com/trip-reports/thale-noi-khao-sok.htm.

Dave has also written a piece ("A Jungle Story") about Khao Sok National Park for eThailand.com:

WEBSITE
www.eThailand.com

Due to numerous problems, including illegal fishing, Dave adds: I'd really like to see Thale Noi get in more guidebooks, as the locals are really doing a good job of keeping the area natural. Tourism needs to get a strong footing in this area and the time is NOW. Like everywhere else in the world, income will be the saving grace for this very special environment. There are many fine guesthouses in the area . . . all are exceptionally clean.

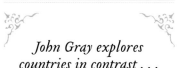

SOUTHEAST ASIA
✿
Canoeing Thailand & Vietnam

John Gray explores countries in contrast . . .

Tropical, lush, and beautiful beyond the imagination—both the complicated Halong Bay in North Vietnam and South Thailand's Phang Nga Bay have inspired Oriental tapestries. Local boatmen and bird's nest harvesters have long known that the angular limestone karst was packed with wildlife protected by terrain impossible to traverse, but Europe's great explorers left these estuaries basically unexamined. Shallow muddy bottoms laced with uncharted rocks formed graveyards for deep-keeled sailing ships; protected bays became instant mud flats. Salt-water crocodiles complicated detailed explorations in Phang Nga's wetlands until the 1970s, but *porosus* doesn't live in Halong.

When we kayak-explored Phang Nga in 1989 and Halong in 1992, we found tidal sea caves and inland lagoons within the coastlines, and so I developed a "Tidal Technology" allowing kayaks entry to these lost worlds. Ever since, naturalists paddle literally *inside* the islands to observe cliff-lined tidal sumpholes previously untouched, even by indigenous people.

Accessible only through inhospitable oyster-caves, called *hongs* in Thailand and *phongs* in Vietnam, the bays form unique tidal wetland enclaves of untouched nature, allowing observation of the most primal of species, from mudskippers and mangroves to cycads and chitons. Floating through sparkling limestone caverns into pristine tropical habitats is a sacred experience—a time machine taking you back to an age before humans walked the planet. The UK's **The Guardian** recently called our Phuket trip "a spiritual experience."

Estuarial limestone is magic because its creation was complicated. As our planet cooled, continental plates began to shrink and migrate, wrinkling Earth's skin. Over 350 million years ago, this cradle of life boasted the largest coral reef in history. Tectonic pressure uplifted the coral, creating brittle, limestone ridges that eventually broke into porous rocks—today's islands—floating across Earth's crust like ice cubes bouncing in a cocktail. Tropical rains percolated through the limestone, dissolving rock into Swiss-cheese by creating sumpholes, underground rivers and caves.

Naturally changing sea levels rotated the karst from river deltas to highland forests to tidal estuaries. Only 18,000 years ago, the Strait of Malacca was a river valley, and beaches were 100 miles west of today's Phuket resorts. Halong was a mountain range 100 miles from the sea. Sometimes mountain, sometimes island, sculpted by fresh water rivers and marine tides, these lush locations became unimaginable fairytale lands.

Thailand's oxide-stained Phang Nga Bay is colorful and delicate, while massive Halong Bay is more complicated and majestic. Fresh water corrodes alkaline limestone faster than sea water, so rivers were important in forming these bays. The trained eye can easily see submerged ancient riverbeds and how their waters sculpted the archipelagos.

Kayak exploration allows true intimacy with these unique wetlands, but you won't see the best locations when using off-the-shelf toy inflatables or Eskimo-style decked kayaks. As out of place in tropical waters as a dogsled in Tonga, decked kayaks are downright dangerous in small and intricate tidal sea caves. To do caves right, you need a highly stable, low profile, ultra-tough inflatable.

Successful exploration adapts to local conditions, and tidal caves have very specific conditions. Created

SOUTHEAST ASIA ❦ *Canoeing Thailand & Vietnam*

when tides exploit a limestone fault line, the highly irregular caves can extend kilometers through sharp obstructions, screaming tidal currents and carpets of oysters. The ceiling is usually the high tide line, so we frequently lie flat on the kayak's floor, noses scraping oysters, twisting and turning in strong currents around rocks or stalactites, jamming our custom-designed SOTAR Lexitron inflatables into oyster hotels, adding sound effects to the drama of entry.

We play a five-dimensional game—the usual three plus time and currents. Cave configuration changes with tidal levels, and each cave has its own "Windows of Opportunity," the time when it can be traversed. Tidal currents provide the fifth dimension. Two hours after a cave is dead still, cave currents can be potentially fatal, usually at the best entry level for that cave.

Both Halong and Phang Nga Bays retain their own on-the-water culture and plenty of bizarre coastal paddling. Shrimp farms are eating Thailand's wetlands, but Phang Nga still has wildlife, expansive mangroves and a few camping beaches. You can paddle Phang Nga independently, but not Vietnam. Asia is an exotic place, but for me, nature doesn't get any more "exotic" than in these two bays.

Paddling Halong and Phang Nga

More on John's company can be found at:

WEBSITE
www.johngray-seacanoe.com

EMAIL
info@johngray-seacanoe.com

Make sure to go through this website and not others claiming to be affiliated with his company.

Editor's Note: When I asked John who the "we" is in his article, he replied that he was talking about his company and added, "I do give big Orchids to Simon Warren and Adul "Mut Bong" Sagulsan who have been with me 14 and 13 years, respectively."

For more on **Phang Nga**, go to:

WEBSITE
www.phuket.com/island/phangnga
.htm

If you're interested in learning more about **Halong Bay**, a nice place to begin is the film **Indochine**, if only for its introduction to the gorgeous scenery.

Read about the legends of the bay at:

WEBSITE
www.thingsasian.com/goto_article/
tell_story.1436.html

For basic background information:

WEBSITE
www.vietnamtourism.com/e_pages/t
ourist/tourspot/natural/fr_halong.htm

Travels in Cambodia and Part of Laos

Up river, on the other bank, a protruding point throws all the waters that hit it into this bend and they turn around, in such a way that the entire mass of the waters of the Cambodia river come to surge with a speed and a thundering noise into the four or five channels which are formed by the islands at the base of the sandstone which protrudes along the right bank. Stirred by the sudden barrier they meet, the muddy waves furiously attack the bank, climb it, enter the forest, foam around each tree, each rock and leave nothing upright in their furious rush but the biggest trees and the heaviest masses of stone. The debris piles up along their passage; the bank is leveled and rises up amidst the vast sea of brilliant whiteness, full of whirlpools and wrecks—some giants of the forest, some blackish rocks still resist—while the high columns of foam gush and fall back in continual surges. It was here that we arrived with the speed of an arrow. It was most important not to be swept by these waters into the forest where we would have been shattered into a thousand pieces and also to avoid the outcrop, by following the deepest part of the channel. We partly managed this. For me, however, this was but a vision, a flash. The noise was deafening, the spectacle fascinating to the eye. ❧

A description of traveling the Mekong River through Cambodia
from *Travels in Cambodia and Part of Laos:*
The Mekong Exploration Commission Report 1866-1868 (White Lotus Press)
by Francis Garnier, translated by Walter E. J. Tips

WHEN IN ROME

A miscellany of dos, taboos, traditions and other ways to live
like a local, find ways to fit in and make yourself at home.

Of all the chapters in this book, this one contains the most eclectic collection of pieces. It offers recommendations from locals, explains how some expats live like locals, explores things expats do to fit in and delves into little ways they have found to make themselves feel at home . . . or rather, not so far from home. You will find a bit of everything here, from festivals to etiquette to everyday activities that would be considered luxuries back in London or Los Angeles. In the latter category, pedicures are a personal favorite. My salon of choice in Ho Chi Minh City was just down the lane from my house. My friend, Huong, and I went there every Thursday night for almost two years. Immersed in the smell of perm solution, we would sit amid women from all walks of life and catch up on the neighborhood gossip—Did you know that so-and-so is a lesbian? I heard that so-and-so is having an affair with so-and-so's husband—and have our toes painted for a dollar, or less if we brought our own polish. Born in the Mekong Delta and raised in Ho Chi Minh City since the age of two, Huong was not only one of my best friends; she was my ultimate insider resource. When I asked her to weigh in for this chapter with some of her favorite ways to pass her free time, she first responded with a list of the city's best known hangouts. I found her recommendations uninspired, and I asked her if these places were really where she'd go to meet up with friends, grab a bite to eat or buy a new purse. She came back to me with an entirely new list. She even removed one of our regular haunts, Vasco's, to make room for places she frequented both on her own and when friends came to town. Another friend I enlisted for this chapter was Duyen Nguyen. She is a singer and an artist; in order to make a living when her family lost everything after South Vietnam fell to the Communists in 1975, she toured the country—hill tribe regions included—in an all girl rock band. She was my translator during my first year in Ho Chi Minh City when I was writing about Vietnamese art for expat-oriented magazines. Her essays here

offer an introduction for those wanting to learn more about—and perhaps purchase—local art.

While I love all the contributions in this chapter, I felt a personal connection with many . . . it really is a small world. Eloise Brown's piece on having your hair washed in Thailand reminded me of being taken to a hairdresser for a wash before my first Tet New Year's Festival in Vietnam. Dana Sach's mention of pagoda festivals (along with Kat Tosi's etiquette tips) brought to mind my first major cultural in-country faux pas—during one such festival I was trying to maneuver around a crowd of people and stepped over a display of marigolds being sold to put on altars. There is only one thing more disrespectful than stepping over an object intended for religious purposes and that is stepping over a person. A friend of mine once stepped over his secretary who was crouched in the office hallway working on a project; she burst into tears and went home for the day.

Of all the essays in this chapter, the one that made me smile the most was Christina Gosnell's piece on salsa dancing in Bangkok. When I was teaching in Ho Chi Minh City, I had a female student who invited me to go ballroom dancing with her and her friends. I knew that this old-fashioned pastime was popular in Vietnam, and I wanted to see it first hand. When I said that I'd love to go, she told me that she would pick me up at nine. And there she was on my doorstep promptly at nine . . . a.m., which is also the very same hour that many of my Vietnamese friends like to go out and sing karaoke. These are the kinds of moments that let you know you've finally made yourself at home—when you've been in a place long enough to head out for a morning of mambo dancing without finding it the least bit strange.

More information about Vasco's, mentioned in this introduction, can be found on page 171.

CAMBODIA
❁

Phnom Penh & Beyond

Andy Brouwer hangs out at the FCC and plays kids' games (not at the same time!) . . .

I'm a simple soul, so my one extravagance after returning to Penh following my travels around the Cambo countryside, is to head for the Foreign Correspondents' Club on the riverside and indulge myself in a bowl of their scrumptious soup (whatever the flavor) and their chunky bread, as I people-watch from the balcony overlooking the Tonle Sap River.

❁ ❁ ❁

If you want to get on with the children in Cambo, learn a few simple rules of two games: "foot shuttlecock" and "sandal-throwing." The latter, as far as I know, is called *kop sbek cheung* (but don't hold me to that), and the youngsters play it all the time with their flip-flops. The former, *tot sey*, is played by a group whose goal is to keep a Cambodian version of a badminton shuttlecock in the air for as long as possible. This is also played with great skill by moto-drivers or others in the cool of the late afternoons.

Foreign Correspondents' Club
363 Sisowath Quay, Phnom Penh.

Editor's note: We tried to get the rules for *kop sbek cheung*. (The kids play a version of it in Vietnam, as well.) It's one of those things where you have to watch and learn, but once you get the hang of it, the kids will love you for joining in.

THAILAND ❁ *Bangkok*

Christina Gosnell likes to go salsa dancing . . .

Most people visiting Thailand wouldn't immediately think of salsa dancing as being a favorite pastime of the locals. But it is. Salsa is huge, and there are many places to choose from if you feel like tripping the light fantastic. Some places even have live bands, and there's no cover charge. Most also serve Mexican or Cuban cuisine, as well. The best part is that everything is inexpensive. Venues such as Salsa Club and El Niño charge a mere $3 US for a beer, while free live music plays in the background. Don't be surprised if you're asked to be a dance partner. Bangkok locals aren't known for being shy.

Salsa Club
Basement of the Pathumwan Princess Hotel, 444 Phayathai Road, Bangkok.

El Niño
Ground floor, President Tower Arcade, 973 Ploenchit Road, Bangkok. (Next to Le Meridien President Hotel.)

John Padorr spends his spare time ice skating and playing softball . . .

Asian ESPN is horrible. Turn it on and you usually get badminton, snooker or bowling. It's the rare program that shows Major League Baseball, the National Hockey League or other sports you watch back home. But that doesn't mean you can't find a place to swing a bat, throw a ball, or tool around an ice rink in SE Asia—even in Bangkok.

There are currently two ice rinks in the city, one on the eighth floor of the World Trade Center shopping mall in the city center, the other on the fourth floor of the BIG C mall on

Lad Prao 81. The rink at Lad Prao 81 has pick-up hockey on Saturday mornings and there is also regular league action and tournaments. (The Flying Farangs are the perennial winners in Thailand.)

Both rinks are relatively empty on weekday afternoons and evenings when public schools are in session. During school holidays and weekends, the rinks are crowded. Be warned: Bangkok does not have a skating culture. Teenagers rule the ice, and there are no rink guards at World Trade. Instead, they have a registered nurse patching up those who get in the teenagers' way. (Note: a new rink also opened up in Chiang Mai.)

For softball players on an extended holiday from January–March, you might try looking up **www.Bangkoksoftball.com** to see if any of the teams need an extra player. One of them often does.

The World Ice Skating Center
is on the top floor of the World Trade Center Complex on Radjamari Road in Bangkok. The complex is convenient to the Skytrain Central Station (Siam Station) where the Silom and Sukhumvit Lines meet up. Get off at the Chit Lom Station.

In Chiang Mai, *Bully Sky Ice* is located at 99/4 M.2, Huay Kaew Road, in the Kad Suan Kaew Shopping Complex adjacent to the Lotus Hotel.

For information on hitting the ice with fellow enthusiasts:

WEBSITE
www.flyingfarangs.com

Eloise Brown wants you to wash your hair . . .

Fingers running over your scalp, cool water trickling . . . ahh, the joys of the Thai hairdresser, where for a measly 60-100 baht you can have a relaxing hair wash and dry. Lie back on the bed while your hairdresser massages your scalp with her nimble fingers and scratches your cares away with her long nails. Cringe a little as she sticks her pinky fingers into your ears to get rid of the last shampoo bubbles. Give a little moan of pleasure as she rubs your temples . . . forget the girlie bars or whatever for a bit of pleasure. Get down to the local hairdresser!

Be prepared for your hair to be marveled at. Your blonde, red or brown tresses are going to be a hit at the Thai hairdressing salon. Even more so if you have curls. And another word of warning . . . watch your hairdresser once she's armed with the hairdryer. More than one young lady has walked out with a very high head of hair, having felt too shy to speak up as the hairdresser worked her magic with the dryer and a curling wand.

If you're feeling rich, why not go the whole hog and have a manicure or pedicure? For another 200 baht or so, you can sit back for another hour with your hands and feet soaking in plastic bowls of warm water, after which they're scrubbed, massaged and molded into twenty clean, shining digits that you'll want to show off!

You can easily spot a *ran serm suay* (beauty salon)—there are thousands of them in Thailand. They can be recognized by the snazzy pics in their windows of Thai pop stars and actors with their super cool hairstyles. Get in there and get that Bangkok grime washed right out of your hair . . . and out of your ears.

Beauty Salons
On the Nancy Chandler website, click into the "Planning a Visit to Thailand?" section. In the "Top Ten Things to Do in Thailand" list, the Chandlers also recommend visiting a local hairdresser. They suggest "the little salons like those atop Soi Saladaeng at Silom Road in Bangkok."

WEBSITE
www.nancychandler.net

THAILAND ✿ *Northern Thailand*

*John Hoskin
participates in
negotiating rockets
for rain . . .*

It's hot. Very hot. By 9.30 in the morning the glaring sun is already high in the sky, promising another day with temperatures pushing 40+ Celsius. The light brown earth of the paddies is parched and baked hard from the long months of the dry season. Here in Thailand's economically depressed northeast region—a semi-arid plateau—it is easy to imagine farmers praying that rains come in time for the new planting.

And that's what they are doing. Each year near the middle of May, villages throughout the area hold a time-honored festival, staging elaborate rocket-firing ceremonies to placate Phraya Thaen, the sky god, and to remind him of human needs. The biggest and best celebration is at Yasothon, a small provincial capital some 575 kilometers northeast of Bangkok.

Yasothon's annual rocket festival is known as *Boon Bong Fai*—literally: "the merit of bamboo rockets." Most Thais are Buddhist, and the concept of religious merit, which is achieved by performing ceremonial deeds, is crucial to Buddhism. But *Boon Bong Fai* is also influenced by traces of ancient animism. Ritualized rocketry is used to appease the spirit world and reinforce the social and psychological structure of traditional rural life. Combining parade, contest, holiday celebration and ritual, the rocket festival ties the themes of fertility, the generative forces of nature, sexual union and rejuvenation into what is basically a rain-invoking ceremony.

These days, the people of Yasothon see *Boon Bong Fai* less as a religious rain-making ritual and more as a time for unbridled fun. As is the case with Mardi Gras, the festival's purgative intent is fulfilled through ritualized license. Social norms are suspended, and drinking, flirting and jesting are sanctioned for the occasion.

All the dancing and merry-making revolves around the rocket, the festival's central motif. Yasothon rockets—the direct, if distant, forerunners of today's solid-fuel boosters—range from 1 to 4 meters long, excluding their tails. They are packed with up to 40 kilos of black powder to produce a burn time of 40 seconds or more. In the Middle Ages, when the ancient Chinese art

THAILAND ✤ Northern Thailand

of rocketry was exported to the West, these rockets would have been state-of-the-art.

On a sweltering Sunday, the people of Yasothon are gathering at a little park on the edge of town. Some are mere spectators, out to enjoy one of the most eagerly awaited festivals in the regional calendar; others, mostly young men, are uninhibited revelers, wildly costumed and fantastically daubed with paint and mud. They dance and prance about in high spirits—literally, in many cases. Bottles of potent rice whiskey are freely passed from hand to hand.

Among the revelers, exuberant local lads carry homemade rockets to a cluster of rickety wooden launch platforms at the side of the park. Each platform is about 10 meters high and angled skyward at around 80 degrees. In the past, rocket casings were made of bamboo, but now they are made of plastic piping that are packed with fuel. The desired blend is 10 parts saltpeter, which acts as an oxidizer, and three parts carbon in the form of homemade soft-wood charcoal; the mixture is tamped down with a wooden ramrod. The most difficult part of the procedure is boring a hollow central core through the powder for the exhaust gases. This job, performed with a pointed or corkscrew-tipped rod, requires an

expert's touch. The core must narrow gradually toward the top and be perfectly straight, with no blockages or unduly wide cavities. The top and bottom of the tube are then plugged with a mixture of clay and sugar—the latter acting as a binding agent—and capped with wooden plugs. Long, slow-burning fuses, sometimes with firecrackers, are then attached to the base of the missiles. Finally, the rockets are fitted with long bamboo tails to stabilize their flight.

On this festival day, teams ready their rockets, making last-minute adjustments and re-affixing fuses, while huddles of gamblers bet on the rockets' flights, and pranksters, in accordance with tradition, throw rocket-makers into specially created mud pools. The smaller rockets are set off first, and it is not until the afternoon that the few 4-meter monsters take to the air. One, two, sometimes three launch pads are used at once, though the long erratic fuses prevent many simultaneous launches. With much swaggering— and staggering—the teams set up their rockets and, as in a game of chicken, the most drunken member usually lingers, clinging to the frame and leaping clear only seconds before the fuse catches.

Some rockets fail to ignite, and others blow up on the launch pad, but the really good ones may reach

300 to 600 meters. Since there is no instrument for measuring altitude, the contest is judged on ground-to-ground flight time. The winning time is usually around 50 seconds, although the record stands at 70 seconds.

The last rocket isn't fired until after five o'clock. Later that night, with the roar of the rockets still ringing in the revelers' ears, rain clouds gather over the region.

Yasothon

can be reached directly by bus from Bangkok's Northern (or Northeastern) Bus Terminal on Kamphaeng Phet (or Petch) Road, north of Chatuchak Park. (It takes approximately 10 hours). You can walk to this station from the Mo Chit Skytrain stop. If you want to go by air or train, you'll have to stop at Ubon Ratchathani and continue by road for approximately 100 km.

The following websites offer helpful travel information and interesting tidbits on Yasothon:

WEBSITE
www.thailandhotels.net/transport/northbus.htm

WEBSITE
www.isan.sawadee.com/yasothon

WEBSITE
www.tat.or.th/province/e-san/yaso

THAILAND ❀ General

John Padorr ponders noise, taxis and passive-aggressive behavior . . .

Thais are polite but not necessarily considerate about things they don't care about—like noise. In general, the Thai people are social and prefer to do things with a lot of friends. Solitude is equated with loneliness, as is silence. Bring ear plugs, even to the cinemas.

❀ ❀ ❀

Taxis are cheaper than *tuk tuks* —even for short distances. Meters start at 35 baht (around 80¢ US). You shouldn't have to ask a taxi driver to use a meter. If he doesn't use the meter, just get out of the taxi. Unless it's pouring rain, there's almost always another one right behind you. There is no reason to take a *tuk tuk* unless you are carrying something that doesn't fit into a taxi, like a sofa. (Editor's note: taxis are also safer!)

❀ ❀ ❀

Thailand is a non-confrontational culture. That doesn't mean Thais don't get mad, though. It just comes out differently—often in a passive-aggressive manner, such as slowing down when you ask them to speed up, turning up the volume when you ask for quiet, etc. They get mad for the same reasons we all do. No hidden secrets here. Don't get upset if they laugh at your mishaps. It doesn't mean they think it's funny. It's just their way of dealing with embarrassments.

Oliver Hargreave walks us through the Wai and Songkhran . . .

I cringe when I see a foreign male wearing only brief shorts—not even a singlet—walking along the city streets as if he were by the pool; I have never seen a woman do this in a swimsuit. On the streets the Thais pay little attention. They are used to insensitive visitors and besides, Buddhist philosophy teaches them *my pen rai*—or "never mind." Government officials, however, and particularly immigration officials, will send such people away, telling them to dress properly.

Dressing properly is obvious to most visitors, but consider the *wai*, that graceful Thai gesture of greeting and parting made with hands held vertically, palms together. When one greets another with this gesture, it is impolite not to return it. When greeted in such a manner upon entering or leaving a restaurant, then, should you respond with a similar *wai*?

The *wai* clearly shows relative status between participants. The lower status person will usually initiate the sequence, and will raise his (or her) hands higher than the other person and lower his head more. Older people do not usually *wai* younger people first, but people of lower status such as employees will usually pay deference to seniors regardless of age. A senior will normally return a *wai*, even from a child.

Serving staff in many places of entertainment will *wai* customers when they enter or leave, but, unless a personal relationship already exists, most Thais will not return the gesture with more than a word of greeting or thanks and a smile. Of course, you can always return with a *wai* if you so choose—after all, *my pen rai.*

Editor's note: further investigation into the phrase *my pen rai* uncovered numerous variations on the definition, including the ubiquitous "no problem."

✿ ✿ ✿

Chiang Mai is renowned for its festivals, the most significant of which is Songkhran. Marking the Thai New Year (by tradition this festival falls on April 13-15), it also heralds the rainy season. This is the famous water-throwing festival in which thousands cram the streets, pile onto pick-ups—these can hardly move for all the other vehicles—and battle it out for hours, soaking anyone in range using buckets and squirt guns. For everyone except those who are trying to stay dry (this is best done by staying indoors or in a car with locked doors and the windows rolled up), Songkhran feels like a return to childhood.

For a brief period on the afternoon of the 13th, there is a momentary lull in the water fighting along Thanon Thaphae and Thanon Ratchadamnoen. The canal and tap water is put aside as people get out water specially scented with flowers and herbs for the parade of Buddha images which runs from east to west along these roads. They loft this lustral water up to bathe the revered images as they pass by on floats, each float representing a temple. Many people scoop a little lustral water that has drained from the images and collected into buckets on the floats. Taking a little of the water in their hands, they will wipe their heads with it in order to receive purification from the image

in return. With the parade having passed, they joyfully return to whatever water source is at hand, dousing each other for the remaining hours of daylight.

Songkhran and other Thai festivals

WEBSITE
www.thailand.com/travel/festival/festivals_bangkok_songkran.htm

Tara Russell experiences Songkhran in Hua Hin . . .

Songkhran is the most unique New Year celebration I've encountered to date. My first experience of the countrywide water fight took place in the southern coastal town of Hua Hin. Typically reserved Thais broke loose for a few days and used cold water to moderate one of the hottest times of the year. Thai people ranging from two to 80-years-old claimed their territory on the streets and established their "offensive" plans for attacking oncoming walkers, motor bikers and their passengers, and riders in open-aired vehicles with liters and liters of water. Some used water guns (much like Super Soakers) and others used buckets, pails and cups, while the most serious dousers sprayed those

THAILAND ✿ General

passing by with hoses. The water is supposed to mark the beginning of the harvest and is believed to bring blessings and good fortune to those who are drenched which makes it very hard to protest being soaked. Music blared from every shop and restaurant, and the Thais danced, laughed and drank without inhibition as they played in the streets waiting for their next victims to pass. Some of them rubbed white paste between their hands, creating a substance that was wiped all over people, cars and any other vessel passing by. My first pass through the streets was inside a van, which left me incredibly disappointed that I was missing out on all the fun! I only made that mistake once; I made sure to ride home in an open-backed tuk-tuk so that I could receive the "blessing" of frequent water attacks. The Thais especially love it when we *farang* take part in their festivities. By late afternoon, I was soaked, and the Thais were worn-out from the all-consuming water battles, too much time in the sun and probably one too many drinks. I can't wait until next year's celebrations.

For more about Hua Hin, go to page 120.

Kat Tosi touches on etiquette, Thai style . . .

Modesty

Modesty is a cornerstone of Thai society, so please be sure to wear long pants or skirts and cover your upper arms, especially when visiting temple grounds.

Monks

Monks have taken a vow of chastity, and women should avoid touching them or passing things directly to them.

From Head to Toe

Avoid touching or passing anything over someone else's head, as this is seen as the most sacred part of the body. The most important (and perhaps trickiest) rule of all regards your feet. NEVER point the soles of your feet at another person or a statue of the Lord Buddha. Feet are regarded as the lowest part of the body; keeping them both firmly on the ground or tucked safely behind you is the way to go. Tossing them up on the bars behind your tuk-tuk driver's head will insult him beyond words.

Table Manners

When eating Thai food, use your spoon as your eating utensil, not your fork. Eating from a fork is seen as being as rude as licking a knife is in the western world. If you really want to impress your hosts, take a bite of rice before beginning the rest of your meal. This is a gesture of respect that shows that rice is the most important aspect of the meal.

VIETNAM ❀ *Ho Chi Minh City*

XXXXXXXXXXXXXXXXXXXXXXXXXXXXXXXXX
ooooooooooooooooooooooooooooooooo

Nguyen T.P. Duyen illuminates the oft overlooked Ho Chi Minh City Fine Arts Association . . .

The Ho Chi Minh City Fine Arts Association is located in a small, unassuming building near the center of the city. It is an artistic world where more than 800 members get together to talk about art, share their creative experiences and display their recent works. This multitude of talent creates a significant force that is the foundation of the city's vivid art scene.

The Association line-up includes members from pre-1975 Saigon together with veterans from the north. A new generation of post-1975 graduates of the HCMC Fine Arts University intensifies this group,

which also includes artists of Chinese origin and overseas Vietnamese, who bring their own unique visions to this subtle spectrum.

Established in 1980, the Association has played a role in hosting exhibitions, seminars, trans-cultural projects and various activities related to the fine arts. It is considered the "promised land" when it comes to promoting an artist's career. Most of the best artists in the city maintain their Association membership, and many have gained international fame through their activities with this organization.

By visiting exhibits and artists at the Association, art lovers can discover incredibly diverse styles. This is one of the amazing aspects of Vietnam's young fine arts scene, which dates back only to the establishment of L'Ecole des Beaux Arts de l'Indochina in 1925. French colonialist rule and the French and American wars have had many effects on the development of Vietnamese painting and its singular characteristics. Numerous western schools such as Abstract Expressionism, Surrealism, Impressionism and Cubism can be seen in conjunction with traditional Vietnamese techniques and materials. Stories of the war are revealed in the emotional narratives of various pieces by veteran artists. New generations, inspired by Doi

Moi (The Renovation of 1988), have created breakthrough works.

All of the above factors define the position of the Fine Arts Association for artists and cultural organizations both in Vietnam and abroad. The varied aspects of this scene, as is evidenced by its unique and talented artists, have brought an integrated, extroverted and dynamic look to contemporary art in Vietnam.

Ho Chi Minh City Fine Arts Association
218A Pasteur Street, District 3, Ho Chi Minh City.

Ho Chi Minh City Fine Arts University
often has exhibitions. It is located at 5 Phan Dang Luu Street, Binh Thanh District, Ho Chi Minh City.

You can view Duyen's art on her website:

WEBSITE
www.duyen-ntp.com

Nguyen Thi Lan Huong chats about where she likes to hang out . . .

Ngon
138 Nam Ky Khoi Nghia St., District One
This restaurant has a very interesting look. It's a French-style house made up as a restaurant. The concept is to sell all types of street food and the kinds of food that you find in market stalls like those in Ben Thanh Market. This place is divided into three areas. Inside the house is a sit-down restaurant. Outside, around the house, there are stalls and dark wood tables and chairs in an old style not often seen these days. Upstairs in the back is a big balcony, also with tables and chairs. Numerous banana trees around the house make it look really nice. The food is served from the stalls and not from a kitchen. You can either choose dishes directly from the stalls or from a menu. The only bad thing about this place is that, because it is so nice and the food is so good, it is always busy. If I want to have a table in the area that I like, I have to choose a less busy time to go—usually late lunch after one p.m. or very early dinner at five p.m. Ngon is located kind of opposite the Reunification Palace.

Temple Club
29-31 Ton That Thiep St., District One
This restaurant is good for a nice dinner with friends and especially with a guy. The romantic walkway and stairs have candles on both sides. The Vietnamese-French colonial-style décor provides a very nice atmosphere and makes the place special. I like the Vietnamese-

style vegetarian curry here. If you don't want to eat, you can have some drinks in the bar area which is separate from the restaurant. There are tall chairs and tables in one area and a big relaxing sofa in another area. Every single friend that I have taken here loves it.

Java Café
38 Dong Du St., District One

Java Café is a friendly place with very nice, soft sofas where my friends and I always gather for chitchat all day long. In my opinion, this place looks like Central Perk in the "Friends" TV show. They play a range of music from the Café Del Mar album—this type of music is very chilled and relaxed. A large and varied selection of blended fruit drinks can provide refreshment after a long walk on a hot sunny day. For people who love coffee, this is the place. There is a large range of cakes . . . my favorites are the Italian cheesecake, chocolate cake and carrot cake. Pastas, salads and some other fast foods are also available.

Café Latin Bar & Restaurant
25 Dong Du St., District One

Café Latin is the place that I like to go to for a drink when I'm on my own or when I want to watch some sports because I will always meet friends or people that I know there. The staff is very friendly, and if I

don't have anyone to talk to, I can always have a nice chitchat with them. This is also the place where most sports' fans like to gather for drinking, talking about sports or watching some of the popular matches. It's the only place that has the Australian TV channel that shows sports all day long. There is a large menu of reasonably priced Western food for lunch and dinner.

Saigon Square Shopping Center
39 Le Duan Blvd., District One

For shopping, I like to go to Saigon Square. Similar to the Russian Market (on Le Loi Street across from the Rex Hotel), it has a large range of CDs, VCDs and DVDs. When I need stuff for traveling, such as warm clothes or a rucksack, this is a good place. They sell lots of things made for export, so the quality is very good. They also sell silk bags, shoes and clothes.

VIETNAM ✿ *Hanoi*

Nguyen T. P. Duyen introduces the Indochina Art Project . . .

Founded in 1988, the Indochina Art Partnership (IAP) initiated the first Vietnamese-American exchange project with its widely traveled exhibition, "As Seen by Both Sides," featuring artists from both countries. Its success continued with "An Ocean Apart," a collaboration designed to foster cultural understanding through shared art. This non-profit organization is a pioneer whose focus on art was at the forefront of the normalization of relations between these two countries after the American-Vietnam War.

IAP has become a very close friend of the Vietnamese artist, with its sponsorship of residencies in America for more than eighty visual artists, writers and leaders of national cultural institutions. It is also a great manager for working journeys to Vietnam for numerous American counterparts. The country's first established center of arts is known as Hanoi Contemporary Art Center, which reveals the close tie between IAP and Vietnamese national institutions such as the Vietnam Fine Arts Association. This facility exemplifies the contribution of IAP in promoting the understanding of Indochinese art through its many important exhibitions and workshops for local and foreign artists.

Furthermore, IAP is concerned with education. The concept of Sister Programs, which was initiated in 1999, has provided great advances through the exchange of scholars and students between The Maine College of Art and Hanoi Fine Arts University and between the Massachusetts College of Art and the Ho Chi Minh City University. The scope of these projects now extends to high schools and museums. Arranged by IAP, meetings and seminars among American and Vietnamese national groups engender productive processes for educational exchanges.

Indochina Arts Project
Duyen adds: Located in Boston, IAP has its offices at the director's residence—as a veteran of the American-Vietnam war, a professor of art and a printmaking artist, Mr. David Thomas has used his long-term understanding and research to lead IAP to become a popular non-profit organization aimed at conserving and

continued on next page

developing art and culture in Vietnam and the other countries of Indochina. Mr. Thomas earned a Fulbright Grant for 2002-2003 to live and work in Vietnam. His most recent project is the retrospective exhibition "From Pride's Corner to Hanoi" at the Hanoi Fine Art University. He is a dedicated organizer of Art Partnerships in Southeast Asia. Information on IAP and its art tours can be found at:

WEBSITE
www.iapone.org

The IAP website also contains a superb 5 km walking tour through Hanoi from David's house to the Hanoi Fine Arts University.

Hanoi Fine Arts University
42 Yet Kieu Street, Hanoi.

Hanoi Contemporary Art Center
621 La Thanh Road, Hanoi.

EMAIL
hanoicac@hn.vnn.vn

You can view Duyen's art at:

WEBSITE
www.duyen-ntp.com

VIETNAM ❀ *General*

Dana Sachs sheds light on motorcycles, busy bodies and pagoda festivals . . .

At the risk of jeopardizing people's health and physical safety (Vietnam has one of the highest traffic death rates in the world), I have to say that there is nothing more romantic than sharing a motorbike with someone you love . . . or like . . . or just have a crush on. The practice has plenty of room for unspoken communication and innuendo. Where will the passenger put her (assuming it's a she) hands? How close will she sit to the driver? Will they touch their heads when they talk, or just yell loud enough to hear each other? The other side of such lovely intimacies, of course, is the possibility of getting stuck with someone you don't find attractive, or don't even know. Now that *xe om* motorbike taxis—I think this term means, literally, "huggable transportation"—have become a most convenient mode of transportation in Vietnamese cities, you can easily find yourself in an uncomfortable, if not compromising position with a total stranger. One Hanoi friend of mine refuses to do it. If she needs a ride home from some distant corner of the city, she calls her husband and makes him come pick her up.

✿ ✿ ✿

Foreigners visiting Vietnam often grow annoyed by the incessant questions they get from everyone they meet—new friends, shop owners, even passersby on the streets. Equally annoying is the fact that you almost always suffer through the same set of questions. Where do you come from? How old are you? Are you married yet? How many children do you have? Though the nationality question probably stems from the natural curiosity all of us feel when a stranger comes to town, the other, more personal questions relate to issues that are particularly Vietnamese. In the Vietnamese language, the pronouns we use depend upon how old we are. In other words, you will call yourself by a different form of "I" depending on whether or not you are older or younger than the person with whom you are speaking. If the age difference doesn't seem clear, then Vietnamese speakers will ask your age in order to know how to appropriately refer to themselves in

conversation. As for questions about marriage and childbearing, most Vietnamese consider such milestones central obligations in life and they simply want to know if you've accomplished them yet.

✿ ✿ ✿

You may not make it to Vietnam for Tet, but you'd have to be pretty unlucky to miss either the Full Moon or New Moon Festivals, celebrated every two weeks at local pagodas. It doesn't much matter what pagoda you choose to visit, though you might want to get recommendations from someone who knows which ones attract the liveliest crowds. Try to visit at dusk or early evening, when the young people tend to congregate like revelers at a disco, managing to pray and flirt at the same time. If you feel like praying yourself (and many foreigners do) you'll find vendors (mostly women) selling whatever you need for offerings: fruit, flowers, incense, votive papers and various small religious objects. Don't worry if you don't know what you're doing. Someone will quickly offer to help.

SOUTHEAST ASIA
❀
General

*John Padorr
looks back fondly
on playing catch
in all the right places . . .*

I remember, at age ten, my friends and I going to the Saturday and Sunday matinee and sitting through two straight showings of **The Great Escape**, weekend after weekend for the better part of one long Chicago winter. Like all kids who aspired to be major league baseball players, the big draw for us was Captain Virgil Hilts, played by Steve McQueen, an American pilot who had the presence of mind to hold onto his baseball glove and ball when his plane was shot down deep inside Nazi territory. Throughout his captivity in a prison camp, he suffered long stretches in an isolation cell called the "cooler" his only companion that worn-out glove and ball. Virgil survived the depravations and even gained strength from them by playing catch with himself against a cement cell wall for most of his waking moments.

As an adult, over 30 years later, I still admire Virgil's wisdom in carrying along a ball and glove, and often pack the same in my own travels, especially on holidays near my home in Bangkok. Like Virgil, I take them because playing catch brings solace in strange places. Since I have the additional benefit of not being locked in a cooler during my holidays, a catch on the road actually has even greater powers. I've discovered when traveling through remote villages in Southeast Asia that a catch can make unfamiliar surroundings suddenly feel far more familiar and in the process add more than a touch of magic to the time and place.

Rural Thailand and Laos are particularly fertile in providing perfect, ready-made spots for tossing the pill with a friend or acquaintance. In most villages, an area is clearly marked by *takraw* courts (Southeast Asia's quirky version of volleyball) for sports activities, and when no such area exists, it is easy to find a clearing large enough to ensure that no errant throw will harm or disrupt anybody or anything.

The only possible drawback to a catch in these parts (and only if you are shy) is that you must be prepared to meet almost everybody in the village; as soon as you start to throw, every idle passer-by will stop and stare, and in no time a crowd will form. Having never seen a baseball or a glove, they will find the phenomenon of catch completely outside their contextual framework.

In a recent New Year's visit to northern Laos, a friend and I played catch in several hill tribe villages, and—without exception—the villagers responded with unbridled enthusiasm as if they were part of a lively, interactive performance art event. When we first arrived in one village, people were gathered around a TV set outdoors, some squatting on the ground, others sitting on fold-up chairs, watching a Chinese soap opera dubbed into the Hmong language. We picked a spot far away and out of sight from the TV audience and left them to enjoy their fantasy escape. But word got out, and as popular as Chinese soap operas are throughout Southeast Asia, this episode could not hold the audience's attention when competing with the sight of two strange foreigners throwing a small, hard orb at each other and catching it in elaborate folds of leather. Several of the kids abandoned the TV show in favor of participating in a catch, and within just a few minutes everyone awake who wasn't working the fields formed a circle around us. As always, we invited the most curious and bravest onlookers to take turns playing catch with us with

one of our gloves, which delighted the crowds who howled with laughter, needling their friends on every catch and throw.

During another catch we had a few days later, spectacularly set on a hillside plateau visible to a few surrounding Lao villages, the game once again drew crowds, some arriving on foot, others on water buffalo. Later, as sometimes happens, the village elders invited us into a hut designated for entertaining guests and plied us with *lao lao*, the country's fiery brand of rice whiskey. If we had simply walked around the village without taking out our ball and gloves, who knows if we would have received such courtesies? Probably not. In fact, the presence of foreign tourists can be extremely awkward in many hill tribe villages. The villagers do not think of themselves as being particularly exotic and may resent, with good reason, strangers gawking at them and taking their photos. However, if you forego the camera until the end of your visit and in its place engage the locals with a catch, any distrust or resentment disappears. Far from being an intrusion, you are entertaining them with something new that brings them outside of their daily routine. At the same time, you are also revealing a unique part of your culture (albeit, not a major piece of the puzzle). Most importantly, after

SOUTHEAST ASIA ✵ General

the catch is over, you are leaving many of the villagers, especially those who played catch for the very first time, with a memory of that particular day that is as strong and as fond as the one you are taking with you.

Catch is an awe-inspiring traveling companion in so many different, unexpected settings, and it is always best to come prepared. You never know when you will chance upon the perfect spot. That happened in January 1996 at Angkor Wat, when a friend and I walked into a clearing beside a few monuments that were in profound disrepair against a lush backdrop of overgrown, thickly forested jungle with dozens of species of birds playing around us in symphonies of sound and flight. We had the spot all to ourselves, and in the course of throwing our usual off-speed junk, we took the opportunity to catch our breath amid this breathtaking scene, slow down to feel the enormous scale of the temples, replay the images we had seen earlier, and get a little lost in the grandeur of it all. Today I look back on that day and see with equal clarity the majesty and mystery of both Angkor Wat and a truly colossal moment in my personal history of catch.

A classic session of a catch on the road does not require especially great throws or catches. It can even

be a sloppy and uninspiring baseball performance from a technical point of view. Age and ability are of no relevance. For a catch to qualify for Hall-of-Fame status, you simply need the presence of mind, like Captain Virgil Hilts, to pull out your glove and play when you feel like the time is right. When it is, the catch will connect you to all the other epic catches in your lifetime, from your earliest baseball memories onward.

There is probably a compartment in the brain dedicated to retaining all of life's Hall-of-Fame catches: That glorious break in the day at Angkor Wat. An epic toss in a park with my Grandfather thirty-five years back. A nighttime catch by moonlight in Hua Hin. A sunset, beachfront catch in Phuket. Several great moments by the pagodas in Pagan. It's like a treasure chest of memories.

Of course, catch is not for every traveler. Some people prefer Frisbees. Others perform music or magic tricks. The overwhelming majority of travelers rely on wit and whim alone. But if you enjoy playing catch, I dare you to take along a ball and a glove or two on your next holiday. The worst thing that can happen is they don't get used. The best thing that can happen embraces infinite possibilities.

Let's Play Ball

John recommends these essential travel items:
- 2 baseball gloves (one for you and one extra for a right hander)
- 1 standard major league hardball
- 1 softball (preferably a Clincher model), a baseball cap and sun block.
- Optional: a third glove for left handers, extra balls and/or a baseball bat.

Kim Fay's fact files from the chapter introduction . . .

For those of you who want to hit *Vasco's*, it's located under Camargue Restaurant (great terrace dining) at 16 Cao Ba Quat, Ho Chi Minh City, Vietnam. There is a pool table, and bands play on the weekends.

In Laos and Siam

The dancers roll light cloths around themselves. They strain and relax their supple bodies. They juggle with their lit lanterns which they send flying and the alternating light and dark shadows add mystery to the charm. The musicians beat ever faster with their little hammers on the big instruments with the shrill sounds and the dancers turn about without little noticeable fatigue until the first rockets go off and, falling around the That Luong, divert everyone's attention. Then a long clamor rises from the crowd and all proceed to the site of the fireworks. 🦂

The Dance of the Lamps at the Laotian New Year celebration in Luang Prabang, 1909
from *In Laos and Siam* (White Lotus Press)
by Marthe Bassenne, translated by Walter E. J. Tips

...unities for giving back to the countries you visit.

When you stop to think about it, leisure travel is an odd activity. You leave the familiarity and comfort of your home to visit a land where you don't understand the language, where a cube of ice can debilitate for days and where subjecting yourself to discomfort is considered *de rigueur*. Why do we put ourselves through it? Those who've run the gauntlet know exactly why. Travel is one of life's most exhilarating experiences. It's also one of the most rewarding. It gives so much, from great pen pals to life-changing epiphanies. Yet how often do we as 21st-century vagabonds stop to think about what we give back to the countries we grace with our presence?

I don't mean to sound like your third grade schoolteacher, but courteous and respectful behavior is a good place to start. And small gestures go a long way; for example, you can give a bundle of seasonal fruit to the proprietor of a guesthouse who made a stay unforgettable. But for those who want to add their small, flickering light to the bright sum of light (to paraphrase Billy Kwan in THE YEAR OF LIVING DANGEROUSLY), there are many exciting ways to reciprocate hospitality and have a positive impact. One of the easiest is to frequent socially responsible businesses. For instance, you can enjoy a meal at the Bodhi Tree in Ho Chi Minh City. This café was founded by a Buddhist nun and is staffed by street kids who are taught self-worth and skills for earning a respectable living. It is an admirable venture and offers a comfortable way to address what is perhaps one of the most uncomfortable circumstances a person must face when traveling in countries such as Cambodia, Laos, Thailand and Vietnam—the abundance of destitute people, especially the dirty, bare-footed, impoverished children, rushing toward you with hands outstretched. While it can be tempting to dole out candy or dollars—a temporary alleviation of an enduring problem—it's better to come prepared and offer something that can improve quality of life, such as pens and paper, both of which are

considered luxuries in many small rural villages. You can also offer to buy a child a meal. Many of the kids you see working the streets are victims of syndicates. They don't get to keep the money they bring in from selling chewing gum or lighters or from begging. A good meal is one of the greatest gifts you can offer.

Inevitably, though, there are times when you feel the tug to give money, outright. This is a tricky, controversial issue. The majority of expats I know advise against it. They feel it perpetuates a "you owe me" mentality. And in some cases this is true. But sometimes you just need to follow your heart. A friend from Australia came to holiday in Ho Chi Minh City and spent a day sightseeing with a moto driver he had hired on the street. Throughout the course of their touring, the driver told my friend that he was once a soldier for the South Vietnamese army; after 1975 he spent time in a re-education camp. Now the government had limited his work to ferrying people around town on his small Honda. The driver had two young children, but they weren't in school because they couldn't afford the fees, supplies and uniforms required. (Hooray for Communism!). This is a story I had heard a dozen times while living in Vietnam. But my friend felt that the driver was an honest and honorable man, and gave him fifty dollars. That night in a bar, when a group of expats heard my friend's story, they told him in no uncertain terms what a sucker he was. But the next day there came a knock at the door. It was the moto driver. He had brought the receipts from his children's school, along with the new supplies and uniforms, to show my friend how his money had been spent. He wished he had the words in English, he said solemnly, to express how grateful he was.

Every person has a way in which he or she feels comfortable giving. Some want to be hands on, while others prefer to contribute from a distance. This chapter offers suggestions that range from writing a check to an AIDS hospice, to getting down and dirty on an organic farm. The charities and organizations recommended in this chapter are very close to the writers' hearts. They know first-hand what a difference buying that bowl of soup for a street kid or donating a hundred dollars to a scholarship foundation can make.

More information about the Bodhi Tree, mentioned in this introduction, can be found on page 191.

CAMBODIA 🏵 *General*

Andy Brouwer offers numerous ways to return local hospitality . . .

How I repay good service and the helpful nature of the people I come into contact with is via my website travelogues. I name people so that anyone following in my wake can seek them out if they wish. I recommend moto-drivers/guides via my Cambodia Forum, as well. It's the least I can do. And I know many who have deliberately used the same people and have written to thank me. That way I know that these Cambodians are gaining work through my tales, and I hope to make their lives a little more bearable through work/reward

they might not have otherwise. On my website I also talk about charities, etc., that I come into contact with like Cambodia Trust, Veterans International, Cambodian Arts & Scholarship Foundation and Sunrise Children's Orphanage.

Andy's Website:
www.btinternet.com/~andy.brouwer

Cambodia Trust:
www.cambodiatrust.org.uk

Veterans International:
www.vvaf.org/index.html

Cambodian Arts & Scholarship Foundation:
http://cambodia.e-files.dk/casf.html

Sunrise Children's Orphanage:
www.sunrisechildrensvillage.org

Andy writes about the orphanage at:

WEBSITE
www.btinternet.com/~andy.brouwer/scv.htm

continued on next page

Sunrise Children's Village founder, Geraldine Cox, has written a book about her experiences: **Home is Where the Heart Is**. There is also a documentary about Geraldine and her work: **My Khmer Heart**.

CAMBODIA 🏵 *Phnom Penh*

Matt McKinney recommends helping the street kids . . .

Have lunch at Friends/Mith Samlanh, a local restaurant that helps the street children of Phnom Penh. Just by eating there, a tourist makes more funding available for the programs run by the staff at Friends.

Friends/Mith Samlanh

215 Ang Eng Street (Street 13), Phnom Penh. (Fifty meters north of the National Museum). To find out more about the Friends organization, log onto:

WEBSITE
www.streetfriends.org

CAMBODIA 🏵

Into the Countryside

Ray Zepp believes in helping local, non-governmental organizations . . .

Many visitors to Cambodia see the immense needs of the country and express the wish to assist in some way. This is not always as easy as it looks. While there are many local NGOs who perform a wide variety of humanitarian services—focused on health, rural development, education, human rights, etc.—a well-wishing visitor may not have the required expertise in these areas. Nevertheless, many Cambodians involved in these areas are quite competent. When I worked with local NGOs in the Battambang area for over two years, I found that the most urgent need is for first-language English speakers to help write project grant proposals and other reports in English. Even Khmers with good English language skills can benefit from the knowledge of first-language speakers who can phrase the proposals in the proper buzzwords and development-speak required by the donors.

One down side, in my experience, is that I was often disappointed by local NGOs who were in it for the money, and who found it easy to fool donors with a few photographs while spending the donations on their own personal cars and houses. Many well-meaning donors have been taken in by charming but unscrupulous local NGO directors. So before you jump into the fray, ask around to find out which NGOs are on the level. For example, the following is a small, local NGO with whom I worked closely.

Battambang-based Acts of Compassion, known locally as Tean Thor Association (TTA), works with Buddhist monks to alleviate the suffering caused by HIV/AIDS. Cambodia has the highest HIV infection rate in Asia, and the northwest is the hardest hit area. TTA trains monks to visit AIDS patients and to spread the gospel of compassion and non-discrimination, while TTA-trained nurses offer basic medical assistance to the sick and dying. Recently, TTA and the monks have moved into caring for orphans whose parents have died of AIDS; they find relatives or foster parents to care for the orphans, while providing basic food assistance for the children, educating schoolchildren in non-discrimination, and providing the

facts about HIV/AIDS. The latest initiative by TTA is a meditation center where HIV+ persons learn meditative techniques and other traditional medicine methods to keep their immune systems strong, in anticipation of the day when the AIDS symptoms may strike.

TTA has welcomed volunteers to come to the beautiful and quiet town of Battambang to assist in its small humanitarian projects. An American woman was very successful in teaching Qi Gong, moxibustion, and other traditional practices to monks and patients connected with the meditation center. A British volunteer worked with AIDS orphans and even built a house for a family of five children orphaned by AIDS. Volunteers can learn a lot from such a close-up view of community development, the AIDS situation, Theravada Buddhism and other aspects of Cambodian traditional provincial life, all the while contributing their skills to assist these small-scale but worthwhile projects.

And since all such projects require money, TTA needs volunteers to help write the proposals to attract funding, as well as to contact donors and other interested parties. My experience with many types of NGOs has been that it is these small, grass-roots organizations, rather than the big, monolithic foreign NGOs, who are best qualified to deal with local problems. But they need help in dealing with the international donor community. It is this kind of help that a well-placed volunteer can offer them.

Tean Thor Association

You can contact Mr. Ky Lok, Director of Acts of Compassion, at:
#75 Group 5 Wat Kor Village
Wat Kor Commune,
Battambang District
Battambang, Cambodia

EMAIL
teanthor@hotmail.com

TELEPHONE
012-530-436

THAILAND 🏵 *Bangkok*

XXXXXXXXXXXXXXXXXXXXXXXXXXXXXXXXX
ooooooooooooooooooooooooooooooooo

John Padorr is a fan of The Human Development Foundation . . .

The Human Development Foundation of Bangkok began 30 years ago with a single slum kindergarten school under a bridge in Klong Toey, the city's largest slum. Today, they have over thirty slum schools, a shelter for children who are abandoned, abused or orphaned, an AIDS hospice for children, another AIDS hospice for adults, a credit union for women, several slum outreach programs, and much more. Father Joe Maier, an American Catholic priest, is behind it all. Back in 1972, as the parish priest in the slaughterhouse neighborhood in Klong Toey, he originally wanted to help his parish children whose parents, predominantly 2nd and 3rd generation Vietnamese immigrants, slaughtered pigs for the market. The first school he opened was successful, so neighbors from other slum communities asked him if he could help them, too. The school system today has over 4,000 kids, predominantly Buddhist and Muslim, and the foundation itself is entirely non-denominational. Father Joe is still very much the inspiration and director of all the foundation programs, and it all works because the programs are based on a partnership with the poor. Visitors are always welcome at their main shelter/hospice at Mercy Center in Klong Toey. Volunteers are always needed. And, of course, you can always give—from spare change, to sponsoring an orphan's education, to corporate sponsorships for the schools.

Human Development Foundation of Bangkok

100/11 Kae-ha Klong Toey 4,
Dhamrongratthaphiphat Road,
Klong Toey, Bangkok.

Information about volunteering can be found at:

WEBSITE
www.fatherjoe.org

THAILAND ✿ *The Islands*

John Gray insists on keeping wildlife in the wild . . .

Whenever I visit my favorite Phuket beach, I see a pair of White Belly Sea Eagles flying free, enjoying their aerobatics as soaring birds do. But these mated eagles aren't here to hunt or play. They come to visit their baby, stolen from the nest three years ago so that a beachfront bungalow could attract tourists. Despite the cage, the family remains unbroken, with the mother and father visiting their captive baby every day.

Ironically, this captivity wasn't necessary. Any raptor rehabilitator knows the biggest challenge is getting a release to leave a steady diet and loving home. Of course, it's too late once the nest has been raided, but the bungalow owner could have just set out fresh fish daily, built a bond with the birds, and then watched them fly in the wild.

This dream can never happen when tourists frequent establishments with captive wildlife, or get their pictures taken with a bird or a snake.

When wildlife is good for business, mother gibbons are shot, eagle nests raided and forest families broken. The Discovery Channel encourages us to keep emotional wildlife documentaries in mind when we travel, yet we forget those impressions once we board the plane, dooming our relatives to solitary confinement, unnatural surroundings, bad diets and shortened life spans.

Your commitment can be minimal. Don't frequent a business that keeps captive animals. Tell the owner why you aren't spending your money there. If you want to be effective, remember *Jai Yen* (Cool Heart), and quietly leave once you make your point. When bookings decrease, maybe the eagles will be reunited in the wild.

This article was originally published in the "Caveman's Babble" column at **www.johngray-seacanoe.com/reading/index.htm**

THAILAND
🏵
Out of Ayutthaya

*Robert Power
explores the benefits of
alternative agriculture . . .*

In the courtyard of an antique wooden guesthouse in Bangkok, I discovered a browning collection of **Bangkok Posts**, and an article discussing the response of a small farming community two hours north of the city to the debilitating impact of industrialized agricultural practices. Having just spent a month working on and photographing an organic farm in central Thailand, and with one month left to explore the country, I decided to check it out.

It was mid-January and high tourist season; after four hours in a hot, vinyl-seated bus, my evening arrival in the town of Ayutthaya guaranteed me a night in a guesthouse dormitory on the main road. I woke early to the sounds of un-muffled motorbikes. Over a fruit shake in the attached restaurant, I read a well-worn issue of a Thai Development Newsletter that was devoted to Alternative Agriculture and the National Education and Development Plan.

Implemented around 1957, the plan was intended to industrialize and capitalize on the agricultural bounty of Thailand. An export-oriented, cash crop economy, coupled with developing industry, would end poverty and conflict, educate and develop, and bring wealth to all. Unfortunately, this idea was largely dependent on the adoption of a Western industrial agricultural model. Petroleum-based nitrogen—left over from WWII weaponry production—was blended with phosphorous and potash to create a synthetic fertilizer. But these fertilizers neglected necessary plant nutrients and eventually led to soil deficiency. As well, chemical pesticides were prescribed—poisons that completely ignored the pest-predator relationship inherent in diverse, balanced ecosystems.

In the beginning, Thailand was touted as the developmental exemplar of Asia, but ultimately, universal agrarian prosperity did not materialize. On the contrary, Thailand's shift away from centuries-old indigenous farming practices destroyed biological and cultural diversity, created ecological instability and increased poverty. Fortunately, the tide is beginning to turn. Though still in its infancy, an

Alternative Agriculture movement has recently blossomed. This movement is intended to meet the needs of local farmers and adapt methods to the local ecology.

As I finished reading the newsletter, morning was ending, and the tiny eatery had filled. I grabbed the cook's attention and asked how I might reach the Marawichai Community. Suddenly, a motorcycle rumbled up, silencing our conversation. A man in brightly colored surf attire, sporting oversized sunglasses and a gun, sat down beside me. He was an undercover police officer whose job, he explained, was to arrest tourists who play with drugs. When told of my destination, he offered to show me detailed maps that were kept at the police station. After a heart-stopping motorcycle slalom through the congested streets, and a brief interrogation at the station that prompted fears of being arrested as a scapegoat for the influx of tourists seeking to sample—in so many of its various forms—the legendary local poppy, he took me to a bus stop. A short ride later, the bus skirted the road's edge and stopped, abruptly. After a whistle and a wink from the driver, I hopped off. The driver pointed to a dusty road that seemed to extend into nowhere. It was now late afternoon. The sunlight was thinning. I reclined beneath a tree and waited for connecting transportation.

A motorcycle taxi eventually bounced up, and a man asked where I was going. Using the article as a guide, the driver and I agreed on a fare, and I climbed on. I was let off at an intersection amidst the frantic gait of early evening traffic. I had no idea where I was or where I was going. Beneath a canvas overhang attached to a storefront, a family celebrated the evening meal. I nervously interrupted, waving the now rather wrinkled newspaper clipping. The group, in concert, grinned and aimed their beverages at a house across the street. To the young man who opened the front door, I explained that I was from Canada, interested in Alternative Agriculture and seeking the Marawichai Community.

In the past, the Marawichai Community in Baan Sakhli, Ayutthaya, was a community connected by agriculture; farming had held together the economic and social fabric. But the bonds began to loosen with the introduction of modern farming practices. The increasing costs of cultivation, combined with an unstable, centralized rice market, forced many farmers into debt. At the same time, the drive to modernize brought factories into the community. Many farmers sold their land to developers.

Others simply defaulted on their agricultural loans. Thousands of young people, witness to their parents' poverty, fled to the factories or to the city in search of work. The community and its social structure collapsed.

Appalled by what he saw, a community leader and former schoolteacher named Surin Kijnitchee devised his own plan. He imagined that the community could strengthen and rebuild itself if it could adopt a sustainable, self-reliant system of agriculture and organize a community bank. In 1990, community members pooled their financial resources to create a fund to help start small-scale community businesses. Borrowers agreed to repay loans in full, once they reached self-sufficiency. Business shares were sold, and yearly profits divided among members.

Luck was on my side. It turned out that I had been directed to Surin's house. Surin was in Bangkok, and the young man who welcomed me was his son, Pairat. Shyly, but fluently, he asked if I had eaten and where I planned to stay. He then brought a large bowl of spicy pork noodle soup and declared that I would sleep at his house that night. While I inhaled the soup, Pairat explained that the following morning at nine, a guided tour of the Marawichai Community was planned for two members of the Royal Thai Government. In response to the recent economic crash, they were being sent to examine the inner workings of a self-reliant community. My haphazard timing turned out to be perfect.

The next day our tour began as we crossed a steep, rickety, wooden bridge leading to the inside of a long, brick house, where an area was sectioned off with glass walls. Behind the glass, crouched on the floor, a man bottled a clear, viscous liquid. He smiled and waved us in. Stacked in crates behind him was an assortment of beverages and wines made from locally grown fruits and herbs—the drinks would eventually be sold in local shops, at community events and in various locales in Bangkok. Down at the end of a narrow, dusty road, underneath a wooden overhang, another man stirred a deep pot of green goo. His family was making herbal soap and shampoo using bouquets of multicolored plants in full bloom. A young girl shyly approached me, offering a freshly filled container. After six weeks of travel, soap was a welcome gift. At least, I hoped it was a gift, rather than a tactful suggestion.

A mixed system of diversity-based agriculture flourishes in the Marawichai Community. No chemicals or synthetic fertilizers are used, and combining a variety of crops and techniques ensures a plentiful year-round harvest. Inside a stilted house, where chickens were kept on the left and goats on the right, a man was tenderly bottle-feeding a newborn kid. Animal droppings slid between cracks in the bamboo floor, causing a feeding frenzy among the fish below. Fattened with feces, the fish are an excellent source of protein and bring much-needed income. Water from the nutrient-rich ponds is used to irrigate crops.

The next morning I rose before the sun and quietly crawled outside Pairat's house to watch the morning unfurl. It dawned as hot and humid as the previous. Sitting on a wooden table, I watched the sun slowly rise from behind a jostle of shacks, shifting the shadows on the wall beside me. With my camera, I exposed the subtle light and what it revealed: a young mother in a tropic-colored "pah-sin" guiding her child's first steps; an elderly man enjoying a hand rolled smoke as he pedaled his bike; solemn-faced, uniformed school children; smartly dressed factory workers and well-covered farm laborers, packed into the backs of pickup trucks, on their way to work.

My bus for Bangkok would depart the community market at noon. I said my good-byes to Pairat and his family, thanking them for their hospitality. He handed me a bottle of herbal wine. "For the trip," he said. I raised my hands to my face, palms together, and lowered

my head—a show of respect in Thailand. Carrying the heat of the coming day on my shoulders, I snaked along a muddy footpath. In the distance, under the shade of conical straw hats, farmers were deep into their daily toil, oscillating between the rows of green with backbreaking monotony.

Decentralized, community-based land economies such as Marawichai are being resurrected around the world, but the progress at ground level is painfully slow. For significant, meaningful change to take place, the goals of the corporate food economy will have to shift, from power and self-gain to nourishment and conservation. Farming is perhaps the noblest profession, I thought, and Alternative Agriculture is an ancient concept putting down roots in a new day. I felt fortunate to have met some of the pioneers.

Baan Sakhli
is located in the Sena District (Amphoe Sena) on the outskirts of the city of Ayutthaya in Ayutthaya Province. Although Sena is on the way from Bangkok to Ayutthaya, it is probably best to use Ayutthaya as your base. From Ayutthaya take the bus to Sena, and once there, at the station, ask for the bus to Baan Sakhli—it's a local bus and the ride takes about 30 minutes due to frequent stops.

continued on next page

Getting to Ayutthaya

Ayutthaya is about 76 km from Bangkok, in central Thailand. Trains going to Ayutthaya leave from Bangkok's Hualamphong Station on Phra Rama IV Road. Buses (both sweltering and air-conditioned) leave from Bangkok's Northern Bus Terminal—a.k.a. Mo Chit—at Kamphaeng Phet 2 Road near the Chatuchak Weekend Market. Information on taking the train can be found at:

WEBSITE
www.railway.co.th/httpEng/

For More on Organic Farming in Thailand

Earthnet
greennet@asiaaccess.net.th.

The Khao Kwan Foundation
daycha@loxinfo.co.th

Rural Reconstruction Alumni & Friends Association
rrafa@loxinfo.co.th

Excellent information on all of these organizations can be found at:

WEBSITE
www.oxfamgb.org/easteasia/thaila nd/thaipart.html

THAILAND 🏵 *Chiang Mai*

Candace MacKay takes her fourth graders to visit the Forru Tree Nursery . . .

Climb the mountain up Huay Kaew Road to Wat Prathat Doi Suthep and then continue on about another 500 meters and take a right into Doi Suthep Park Headquarters; for your efforts, you will find yourself in a quiet, evergreen rain forest where, slightly below the park's office complex, the FORRU Tree Nursery is located. Here, a group of scientists is working to help accelerate the reforestation process—deforestation is one of the most serious environmental problems in northern Thailand, and at FORRU you can witness some of the things that are being done to help the situation.

One of the ways the FORRU team wants to battle deforestation is through education. They have set up a program for schools and other institutes to visit. I took advantage of this program and brought my fourth grade students on a field trip to

FORRU. My students learned about the different aspects of the reforestation process from various scientists, all of whom spoke excellent English. Individuals are also more than welcome to come to the nursery, take a look around, ask questions and even help out if they wish.

The highlight of my students' field trip was a trek through the rainforest. With over 300 different bird species and almost 2,000 different kinds of ferns and flowering shrubs, there's a lot to see. One of my students spotted the rare Raffelisia flower along the side of the path, but the real excitement came when we arrived at a giant fig tree. We were shocked at the enormity and beauty of it. It is called a "strangling fig," and this one had certainly strangled many a weaker tree in its day. The final result of its struggles is a trunk that has many hollows with lots of room to crawl through and around.

This is an excellent outing for those who want some quiet or who seek knowledge about reforestation techniques, or for families who want to appreciate nature at its best; the trek is not too difficult, so young children can enjoy it, as well. There are also longer trails, which range in levels of difficulty. You need to talk to someone at the office if you're planning a longer trek.

Doi Suthep National Park

Take public transportation up Huay Kaew Road until you reach the Prathat Doi Suthep Temple. Just past the temple on the right hand side of the road, you'll see the sign pointing the way to the park office.

WEBSITE
www.trekthailand.net/north11/index.html

For more information on the park, you can contact FORRU Tree Nursery at:

EMAIL
forru@science.cmu.ac.th

THAILAND
✸
Out of Chiang Mai

XXXXXXXXXXXXXXXXXXXXXXXXXXXXXX
oooooooooooooooooooooooooooooo

Stuart Cavaliero believes in practicing hilltribe payback . . .

We at Chiang Dao Nest have been arranging treks around the locality of Chiang Dao in North Thailand for a few months now, and we are constantly striving for the best ways to help the hilltribe villages we visit. We have decided to include a small donation in the price of the treks; although this is not popular with everyone, since some feel it is not right for "enforced donations," we find it an acceptable solution that eases the pressure for most. What do we do with the money, and how can individuals in similar situations give? First, let's look at what not to do. Buying sweets/drinks and giving money to the random selection of kids you meet is probably not the best thing to do, although those kids will be delighted. Entrusting funds with the people that lead tours, own accommodations and supply food and drinks to tourists can create unnecessary suspicion and jealousies. Finding the local school, we have decided, is the best way to help. Actually, buying the books, pens and such ourselves, rather than handing over cash, is a good way of avoiding funds being misappropriated. School lunches are a constant source of concern for very poor schools/villages. We have bought chickens for the school, which has proved very successful, (apart from the few that were killed in pig biting incidents!). Women's groups in the hilltribe villages have also been reliable recipients of cash. While it is probably against the natural instincts of most Westerners, the donations are best given very publicly. This again avoids misappropriation, and also demonstrates that there is a benefit to the village from these

strange foreign visitors. But money isn't everything! When you visit these places, if you can educate or entertain any of the villagers for even a very short period, they will be most appreciative.

Chiang Dao Nest Guesthouse
Read more about it on page 117. For tour information, contact Chiang Dao Nest at:

EMAIL
chiangdaonest@lycos.com

THAILAND 🏵 *North*

Jim Algie investigates an innovative approach to teaching English . . .

The life of an English teacher in Bangkok is beset with such woes as two-hour bus journeys to teach yawning business drones in industrial wastelands. Or trying to teach teenagers with vastly different levels of English, in one of those franchise-style schools, where you have to repeat questions like, "Does Mary make good coffee?" day after day until tedium turns into an intellectual black hole, and you find yourself living in a guesthouse and "liquidating" every evening in different dens of promiscuity.

But the life of a Volunthai English teacher in the northeast of Thailand is enlivened with attending weekend language camps in national parks, being invited to eat grilled geckoes and drink rice wine at 10 a.m., riding water buffaloes, signing autographs for the students and being asked whether you know Leonardo DiCaprio. If you can handle the hordes of screaming, kinetic adolescents, as well as communal living, a pauper's ransom of a salary and having the locals put on an Eagles' CD every time you walk into a bar, then you should send in an application.

Many of the impoverished youngsters who come to these two-and-half-day camps have rarely seen a *farang* before, let alone spoken to one. For them, the experience (filled with songs, games, skits and even a brief disco) is akin to American kids going off to summer camp, claims PJ Fleig, a 27-year-old teacher from New York. "Except that the kids are much more respectful towards their teachers here. And the thing that surprises me the most is how poor most of them are, but they're just so happy all the time."

The nine Thai teachers from different schools who brought 160 of their charges to a recent camp in a pastoral part of Chaiyaphum Province (about five hours northeast of Bangkok) also learn a lot of valuable activities to implement in their own classes. Khomkrit Raksombat, who is 50, believes that these weekend retreats are the most effective way for students to learn English, largely because their regular classes consist of local teachers explaining the ABCs of spelling and English grammar in Thai, while the young learners receive very little speaking or listening practice. Without a proper grounding in the world's lingua franca, the chances of any of these students gaining admission to a decent university are scant, and the possibility that they'll end up slaving away in some Bangkok sweatshop or brothel looms large.

The Thai education system frequently comes under fire for its reliance on rote learning and its inability to get the students to think for themselves. But once these strictures are removed at the Volunthai camps, the students (who are between the ages of 12 and 19) respond with bursts of creative enthusiasm—particularly during the English skits that they perform based on Thai folktales, says Andy Rose, a 25-year-old native son of Kansas. "We try to get the students to make 'em funny and stuff, so they change the endings. One time, the girl comes out and she's real ugly, so the thief and the guy are about to fight, and then they see her and they're like, 'You have her.' 'No, you take her,'" laughs Andy, and adds that in another version of the folktale, the two male characters pretended to be gay and walked off together.

PJ often marvels at his students' natural artistic gifts, which manifest themselves during the ice-breaking activities at the start of each camp, when the students are put into different groups, and have to give their squad an English name, elect a leader, make a costume for him or her, and then come up with their own special dance. "The kind of costumes these kids can invent with just some flowers and branches and a few scraps of paper really blows me away. It just goes to show how they can make do with so little."

The founder of Volunthai is Michael Anderson. After graduating a couple of years ago with a bachelor's degree in Asian Studies, Michael spent several months backpacking in Thailand and then a longer spell as a volunteer English teacher in the northeast. An article he wrote for **The Washington Post** about these experiences attracted the attention of the Keenan Institute in North Carolina, and they agreed to sponsor the program. The big advantage of Volunthai over programs like the Peace Corps is that within a couple of days of passing a phone interview with

Michael, you can be out in Isaan observing some of the classes.

How much English anyone can learn in two-and-a-half days is not really important. Many of the foreign instructors reiterate the same sentiment: Volunthai helps to break down some of the stereotypes of Westerners propagated by Hollywood—or older sisters and brothers who've worked at bars and massage parlors in Bangkok—and to cure some *farang*-phobic young people of their fear. PJ of New York, who still hasn't met Leonardo DiCaprio, recalls a Thai teacher speaking at the finale of one of the camps. "The last line of his speech was, '*Farang* will not eat our children.'" No, but Hannibal Lector might, and he speaks English eloquently.

This essay was excerpted from **www.ThingsAsian.com**.

Volunthai

Jim adds: In the next few years, Volunthai wants to run camps every weekend. They're also hoping to expand their sphere of influence into other parts of Isaan and Chiang Mai. Anyone who's interested in applying should check out:

WEBSITE
www.volunthai.com

You can also look around for their ads at various Khao San Road guesthouses in Bangkok. Ordinarily, he prefers younger teachers in the 20-27 age group who have a little teaching experience (though it's not essential), and he expects a minimum commitment of a month.

THAILAND 🏵 *General*

Kat Tosi
offers suggestions
for responsible travel . . .

Thailand has no shortage of people begging on the streets, including amputees, blind karaoke singers and mothers with children. Yes, these people are desperate, but what you might not know is that they are often victims of mafia-like organizations that exploit them. Buy them some food, water or milk instead of giving money, and that way you'll be sure who is receiving your donation. Also, Thailand has many people eager to learn English, but have no means to do so. Why not teach your kind taxi driver what "left" "right" and "stop" mean, or share some counting skills with the group of children that has gathered around you to giggle and stare?

Have some free time? Volunteering to teach English is a great idea! You could also choose to sponsor a needy student who probably would not be able to afford to go to school otherwise. Contribute through the Bangkok Post Foundation; $25 USD goes a long way in Thailand. See **www.bangkokpost.com/bnf/bnfhome.htm** for more information on this.

Another option is to support small family businesses. Stay at a small guesthouse and shop at the local markets. Mega-stores and international hotels are making it difficult for mom and pop establishments to survive. Besides offering a more authentic and personal experience, these businesses typify the color and uniqueness that is Thailand.

Last but not least, don't forget that most of the people you will meet along the way typically live on less than 200 baht ($5 US) a day. Small tips are always appreciated. Bargaining at the markets is an enjoyable experience, but don't bargain to the extreme. Ten baht isn't much to you. To the vendor it could represent lunch.

VIETNAM 🏵 *Hanoi*

Graham Simmons urges you to visit KOTO Restaurant . . .

If you want to take concrete steps to aid some of Vietnam's most needy and yet most worthy citizens, visit KOTO restaurant, in Hanoi. KOTO ("Know One, Teach One") is a fully operating restaurant and training school, created to provide working opportunities for former street kids. The school was established by Vietnamese-Australian Jimmy Pham. In late 2002, the school's largest number of graduates took up employment at some of Hanoi's leading restaurants and hotels.

The 80-seat restaurant opposite the popular Temple of Literature is now run by thirty trainees, a number of Vietnamese national supervisors and staff, and several western volunteers. It boasts an extensive menu and has branched into the catering of corporate and private functions around Hanoi.

A training curriculum has been developed in the areas of Cookery,

Front of House Bar and Service Operations, as well as English Language for the Hospitality Industry. The trainees complete 36 hours per week of combined practical training at the KOTO restaurant and theoretical training at the KOTO dedicated training center, which is situated a short distance from the KOTO restaurant.

Towards the end of their training, the KOTO trainees take part in a work experience program. For a short time, the KOTO trainees gain experience at restaurants and hotels in Hanoi, where they can hone their skills and develop confidence, which aids the trainees' transition from KOTO to the workforce and wider community.

KOTO
61 Van Mieu Street, Hanoi.

For more information on this and other worthy projects, visit:

WEBSITE
http://streetvoices.com.au/default.htm

VIETNAM 🏵 *General*

Dana Sachs believes in giving locally . . .

Give money to charities that work in Vietnam! One that does particularly marvelous work is Operation Smile, which provides medical services to children with cleft palates. The American Friends Service Committee has programs throughout Vietnam that help poor rural people move toward self-sufficiency.

Operation Smile
www.operationsmile.org

American Friends Service Committee
www.afsc.org

Kim Fay's fact files from the chapter introduction . . .

Bodhi Tree
175/6 Pham Ngu Lao (located down a small side lane), Ho Chi Minh City, Vietnam. This ultra-budget vegetarian café also has a few rooms for rent.

VIETNAM 🏵 *General*

BOOKING YOUR TRIP

A collection of resources for planning and enhancing your travels.

I was an independent bookseller for almost six years before I moved to Vietnam. During that time, I worked on compiling a comprehensive reading list for the store's travel section. As a result of that project, combined with my obsessive love of travel literature, I could write (and probably will someday) a volume devoted to Southeast Asian writers and literature; it would also include a section naming all of the great bookshops I've encountered during my travels. In this chapter, you will find a selective collection of reading suggestions from both the contributors and me.

This chapter also contains a section of useful and interesting websites, as well as a few movie recommendations, although as far as the latter is concerned, not nearly as many as the medium deserves. There have been so many wonderful movies either set in or made about this part of the world. Of course, the subject of the Vietnam War dominates a majority of them. I have seen some well-done and thought-provoking war films, but if I were to offer any guidance at all for films about Vietnam, I would steer you away from the battlefields and recommend THE SCENT OF GREEN PAPAYA, CYCLO and THE VERTICAL RAY OF THE SUN. In regard to subject matter, they feel—at least superficially—as if three different people made them, but when it comes to tone and passion, and the feelings they evoke, they all bear the distinctive stamp of writer and filmmaker Tran Anh Hung. While I found THE VERTICAL RAY OF THE SUN the most visually mesmerizing (the colors are unforgettable, as are the scenes set to songs by Lou Reed), CYCLO made the deepest impression on me. It was painfully honest, and although it was emotionally brutal, it made me long to return to Vietnam. It felt true.

As for Cambodia, anyone visiting this country must watch THE KILLING FIELDS. I bought a copy of this movie on the black market in Phnom Penh and watched it as soon as I got back to

Ho Chi Minh City. I had already seen it once, years before, but this time—as the grainy video played in the dark night in my small cement house, and the thick tropical humidity swelled over my skin—it was accompanied by visions of the stark Tuol Sleng Holocaust Museum and the Killing Fields at Choeung Ek that I had visited just one day earlier. In addition, numerous books have been written about the Cambodian genocide, and two that I would recommend are THE DEATH AND LIFE OF DITH PRAN by Sydney Schanberg and FIRST THEY KILLED MY FATHER: A DAUGHTER OF CAMBODIA REMEMBERS by Loung Ung. They're not light holiday reading, but they're important, and if you care at all about understanding what happened in this country, they are a good place to start.

This, of course, is the dilemma; once you've become mesmerized by Southeast Asia, once you've started nibbling on the wealth of resources that shed light on this enigmatic region, your appetite will become insatiable. Hopefully, this chapter will help you curb at least a few of the hunger pangs.

CAMBODIA ✿ *General*

Donald Gilliland directs you to a few great online and print resources . . .

Check out Gordon Sharpless' monthly column in the Cambodia section of "Tales of Asia", **www.** **talesofasia.com**. Andy Brouwer also has a comprehensive site devoted to Cambodia, with lots of travel articles, information, photos and links. His "Cambodia Tales" is located at **www.btinternet.com /~andy.brouwer/**. Other good books: Elizabeth Becker's **When the War Was Over: Cambodia and the Khmer Rouge Revolution** and Loung Ung's **First They Killed my Father**. Good for travel: Ray Zepp's **Cambodia Less Traveled**.

Cambodia Less Traveled

Word has it that Ray Zepp's book is tough to get your hands on, although you should be able to pick up a copy once you're in Cambodia. For a few highlights from Ray and a review of his book go to the following:

WEBSITE
www.btinternet.com/~andy.brouwer/miscz.htm

WEBSITE
www.btinternet.com/~andy.brouwer/highway2.htm

A few of Ray's insights can also be found on pages 113, 128 and 176.

Andy Brouwer sends you to his own website for hot tips . . .

On my website, see my book tips on the "Hot Off The Press" page and a Cambodia Bibliography at **www.btinternet.com/~andy.brouwer/biblio.htm**.

THAILAND 🌸 *Bangkok*

John Padorr recommends a columnist for the Bangkok Post . . .

Check out the **Bangkok Post's** Saturday issues with Ung-aang Talay, the newspaper's restaurant critic. His pseudonym means "toad" in Thai. An American who has lived in Thailand for decades, he writes very articulately about street food and modest shop house restaurants in Bangkok.

THAILAND 🌸 *Chiang Mai*

Jeff Petry reviews a great guidebook by a good friend . . .

**Exploring Chiang Mai:
City, Valley, & Mountains**
by Oliver Hargreave

Far more than simply "the best guidebook on Chiang Mai city and province," this is a labor of love and *tour de force* by photographer, journalist, photo editor, cartographer, motorcyclist and mate Oliver (Oli) Hargreave. Chock full of insights into the land called Lanna—its history, geography, language, culture and attractions—Oli's book shares with the reader his love and experience of this gentle realm. Profusely and beautifully illustrated by the author, and literally exploding with information and enthusiasm, this book offers far more than any tourist could ever hope for in a "guidebook," or hope to accomplish on a mere visit to northern Thailand. In fact, we who live here view it as much for "us" as for "them." After buying it for less than 500 baht, the reader's return on investment occurs in the tuk-tuk ride back to the guesthouse.

Ordering Information

The newest edition of Oliver's book was published in 2003 by Odyssey. You can order it from—among other sources—the Elliott Bay Book Company in Seattle.

WEBSITE
www.elliottbaybook.com

*Kat Tosi
reveals her passion for
the written word . . .*

Wondering Into Thai Culture
by Mont Redmond

This book is an absolute must for anyone looking for in-depth, articulate and insightful explanations about the whys and whats of Thai culture. A challenging read, but worth poring through every page.

The Thai and I
by Roger Welty

This is a user-friendly and valuable read for anyone considering relocating to Thailand or wishing to learn more about Thai culture. The book offers plenty of practical advice and gives useful explanations on a wide variety of "everyday life" subjects, including "How to Use a Squat Toilet."

Postscript
by Roger Crutchley

"Postscript," written by Roger Crutchley, is a weekly column in the Outlook section of **The Bangkok Post**. One of Thailand's most humorous expatriates, "Crutch" will take you on a side-splitting ride through his world. Just a few of the noteworthy features include taxi rides from hell, people falling into gigantic potholes, miscommunications with his maid, misspelled and misspoken English, witty commentary on Thailand's often absurd politics and true criminal tales, where would-be robbers decide to take naps in front of the safe they are trying to break into and end up getting caught. "Postscript" appears every Sunday in the **Bangkok Post** and can also be accessed through the newspaper's website, **www.bangkokpost.com**.

Metro Magazine

To find out what's happening in Bangkok, pick up a copy of the monthly magazine **Metro**, available at most English language bookstores and in some hotel lobbies. The magazine has a website at **www.bkkmetro.com**.

Kinokuniya Bookstore

Bangkok's best bookstore? The largest selection of English language books in the country can be found at Kinokuniya Bookstore, located on the third floor of the massive and trendy Emporium Shopping Centre.

Kat's Window on Thailand

Follow me as I attempt to explain Thai culture as seen through my western and often confused eyes. The 130 articles put you on a roller coaster ride through daily life in Thailand and provide insight into the whys and hows of Thai culture. **www.katswindow.net**.

Wondering Into Thai Culture
At the time **To Asia With Love** went to press, this book could be found at:

WEBSITE
www.amazon.com

WEBSITE
www.abe.com (used books)

The Thai and I
This book is available from Community Services of Bangkok, 15/11 Sukhumvit Soi 33.

TELEPHONE
02-254-5652

EMAIL
csb@loxinfo.com

Roger Crutchley's "Postscript"
dates back to 1979. You can buy a copy of Crutchley's book (a compilation of his columns), **Forgotten But Not Gone**, at:

WEBSITE
www.bangkokpost.com/postbooks/

On the "Post Books" page, don't be put off by all the weird symbols. Just type the name of the book—not the author—into the search square at the top left. Follow the trail from there. You can also access it through "Bangkok Post

continued on next page

Columns" on the left side of the page. (Note: Crutchley contributed a piece to this guidebook; it can be found on page 17).

Kinokuniya Bookstore
Emporium Shopping Center at 622 Sukhumvit, near Soi 24, Bangkok.

VIETNAM 🏵 *General*

Dana Sachs suggests Hanoi bookshops, compelling documentaries and works in translation . . .

On my website, **www.Vietnam Universe.com**, I have a long list of Vietnamese literature. Also, the bookshops on Trang Thien Street in the center of Hanoi offer lots of good reading (English and Vietnamese) at excellent prices. There are a number of used bookshops along Ba Trieu Street, but those are mostly for readers of Vietnamese.

🏵 🏵 🏵

I suggest two excellent and provocative documentaries about Vietnam and Vietnamese Americans—**Mai's America** and the Oscar-nominated **Daughter from Danang**. Also, the film about Vietnam that I made with my sister, **Which Way Is East**, is available on videocassette from Women Make Movies.

Mai's America
www.marloporas.com

Daughter from Danang
www.daughterfromdanang.com

Which Way is East?
You can read more about this on
Dana's website or order it from:

WEBSITE
www.wmm.com

Kim Fay
*adds her own two cents on
Vietnamese literature . . .*

I had been living in Ho Chi Minh
City only a few months when I found
a copy of **Time and Other Stories** on
a shelf in a tailor-cum-clothing shop
on Le Thanh Ton Street near the
former Hotel de Ville. The pages
were parched, stained brown from
years of suffering the damp of the
tropics. This volume was proof that
no self-respecting book should ever
have to endure such unforgiving
weather. Containing stories written
by Vietnamese writers between 1975
and 1985, it was published by the
Foreign Languages Publishing
House in Hanoi—a publisher, I later
discovered, that translated Vietnamese
literature into English, using translators
whose eclectic and imaginative skills
lent a telling hue to the already
colorful stories.

I bought the book for a few
dollars. That night I took it to the
house that my boyfriend was renting.

The house was a typical, narrow,
three-story structure squashed
between like-minded architecture
down a side lane off a main street. It
was relatively unassuming, with the
exception of its rooftop terrace.
Darkness fell. We lit candles. We
climbed into our hammocks. I chose
a story, randomly, and I read aloud—
"The Traffic Policeman at a Crossroads", by Nguyen Manh Tuan . . .

It is one year after Vietnam's
liberation from the Americans, and
there are not enough jobs to go
around for the former North
Vietnamese military officers. One of
these officers is assigned to work as
a traffic policeman on a street corner
in Ho Chi Minh City. He cannot figure
out how his life—once devoted to a
noble cause—has been ceded to
this most trivial of occupations. Every
day he observes the crush of people
passing on their motorcycles; every
day he finds himself watching for a
particular young woman who drives
by at ten-to-seven each morning
and twenty-to-five each evening. He
begins to count on her. Her comings
and goings set the rhythm of his
days. Gradually, with a sense of
both acceptance and loss, he
resolves himself to his new, less
grandiose profession.

When I finished reading, we
were silent. Wax flowed down the
sides of the candleholders. We were
both thinking about the stringy, surly,

green-uniformed men who wildly waved their batons and pulled people over on street corners all around the city. To us they had always been jokes, Vietnam's version of the Keystone Kops. But after this story, we would view them differently. We might still find them annoying, but we would see them as more than just local color.

The book was filled with many such glimpses into the minds of a people whose language I did not speak, whose culture was so unlike my own. It was as much a guidebook as it was a story book. Its "Legend of the Phoenix" is a must for anyone visiting Hue—an elderly archaeologist travels to his childhood home to complete a project on ancient citadels; Le Boc Road is no longer recognizable, the ginger confectionaries are gone, and the dimple in the face of his childhood crush, Boi Hoan, has become a wrinkle "like a deep cut." In my opinion, there are few better ways to learn about a place than to read the fiction of its people. While much can be lost in translation, a steadfast essence remains. Style and technique may suffer, but voice and vision can never be completely repressed.

Time and Other Stories was merely the first of numerous insightful literary encounters during my four years in Ho Chi Minh City. While I could appreciate the

significance of **The Lover** and the photocopies of photocopies of **The Quiet American** (the latter was one of my favorite books long before I moved to Vietnam) that were sold on street corners throughout the country, it was in fact a handful of unanticipated run-ins with works by Vietnamese writers that helped me best understand my new home. **Impasse** was eye-opening. This novel was published by Red River Press, which may or may not be the same as the Foreign Languages Publishing House—this was a mystery I never solved. It was written in 1938 by Nguyen Cong Hoan, a man who firmly believed that deprivation of education was the driving force behind the exploitation of peasants in his country.

Nguyen wrote of Pha, a young farmer who loses everything he owns to the French administrators and their Vietnamese mandarins, all because he cannot read the laws and therefore stand up for his own interests. I was an English teacher at the time I was reading this book. My students were between the ages of 20 and 60; they were imperfectly, enthusiastically and amusingly proficient in the English language. When I showed them my copy of **Impasse**, they smiled. They were proud of me for having discovered this thoroughly local story. The book was to them as **The Pearl** or **The Old**

Man and the Sea had been to me during junior high school. Required reading. **Impasse** is a work that imprints its simple but universal truths into young, impressionable minds. More importantly, as far as the country of Vietnam as a whole was concerned, it was a document of social injustice, a time capsule that preserved poll taxes, backbreaking rice harvests and opium abuse—all of which had been translated with an abundance of rollicking British slang.

My free-wheeling education continued. **In the Shadow of the American Embassy** (Giai Phong Publishing House, 1972) makes good use of words such as "aggression," "warlords" and "neo-colonialist henchmen." **Women in Vietnam** (Foreign Languages Publishing House, 1978) refutes the stereotype of a "weaker sex" in a country that is considered to be Confucian and patriarchal. **Vietnamese Literature** (Red River Press) weighs in at over 1,000 pages; this Vietnamese version of a Norton anthology is filled with poetry, short stories, novel excerpts and political essays, including passages from Ho Chi Minh's prison diaries, which are well worth buying in their entirety.

Almost every book I came across during my years in Ho Chi Minh City was discovered haphazardly, in an off-the-beaten-path stall or in a small shop down a side lane. Hunting for a new literary treat was like being on a wild goose chase, blindfolded. But each time I discovered a gilded egg, it was well worth the hours spent on my bike pedaling through congested, polluted back streets. Once, by chance, attracted like a moth to the colorful flame of a large map hanging in a shop on Ly Chinh Thang Street selling Vietnamese textbooks, I noticed a stack of offerings from the—who else?—ubiquitous Foreign Languages Publishing House. They were tucked on a bottom shelf in a corner. I had only a few dollars with me. I bought as many books as I could afford. After reading them, I returned for more. The entire shop was gone.

This experience taught me two important lessons. The first is that you never know what you're going to find, no matter where you are, and so you need to keep your eyes open and be vigilant—chances are, you will eventually be rewarded. Secondly, get it while the getting's good. When it comes to books in Vietnam, many volumes are one-of-a-kind. While there may be another copy floating around in Da Lat or Hoi An, you can't just go home and place your order on the Internet. If you want it, and if you can afford it, buy it now.

Thus said, I would like to mention one last book that is relatively easy to come by and that you can count

VIETNAM ❀ General

on finding, inasmuch as you can count on anything in Vietnam. A tale of love and loss, **Kim Van Kieu** is the Vietnamese adaptation of a Chinese novel. Its local publication in 1813 integrated it into Vietnam's literary heritage. The story is schmaltzy and the translation I got my hands on was poor, but reading it is essential if you care at all about scratching beneath the surface. There is a reason that this story caused such nostalgic musings when I mentioned it to my students. Its romance and sentimentality and exuberant drama mirror characteristics that have deep roots in the Vietnamese culture. The last time I checked, you could buy an English edition at the Xuan Thu bookshop at 185 Dong Khoi Street, across from the Continental Hotel, in Ho Chi Minh City. Happy hunting.

SOUTHEAST ASIA
✿
General

Jim Algie talks up
FARANG *magazine . . .*

To quote **National Geographic Traveler**, "**FARANG** magazine is an irreverent yet reliable guide to Thailand, Cambodia, and Laos." Offering up-to-date listings and travel info for the three countries, this gonzo mag has also run feature stories on everything from the Moose Festival in Chibougamau, Quebec to Rastafarian road-trips through Jamaica. It contains a monthly column from an American heroin trafficker doing hard time in Thailand's worst prison. **FARANG** was launched as a bi-monthly in September, 2001, and then went monthly in February, 2002, when it secured a Thailand-wide distribution deal with **The Bangkok Post**. The 88-page magazine is also distributed in Cambodia and Singapore. Its website is: **www.farangonline.com**.

Kim Fay
recommends visiting
White Lotus Press
in Bangkok . . .

"The first book was an accident," insists Diethard Ande, the owner and publisher of White Lotus Press in Bangkok. "I was in the antique business. I told this guy, 'If you ever want to write a book on Yao painting, I can sell it.' Some friends said I'd lose my shirt on it. I didn't. It was a great success academically. That was the glorious start of my career as a publisher."

Ande is standing, barefoot, in the middle of his "office," a warren of humid showrooms huddled deep at the end of a tree-shaded lane in Soi 58. His gray hair is swept back from his face. He's wearing boxer shorts and a white tee-shirt. A pink and green Thai silk scarf is tucked like a cravat into the neck of his tee. He reigns confidently over these rooms that are just a bit too warm, infused with a sleepy quiet and languid aquatic light. In one corner, a pot-bellied Chinese businessman silently examines a volume on ancient Thai ceramics.

Having traveled to Asia in the 1960s, Ande returned to Bangkok from Germany in 1970. He'd just finished university, had a one-way ticket, and was looking for a reason to stay. Little did he know that a commitment to a small volume on Yao painting would blossom into a rogue independent publishing empire responsible for over 15,000 titles, which include rare and out-of-print books, and White Lotus titles ranging from original texts to translations and reprints of centuries-old travelogues.

"Anything that happens in this area," he says, "I'm interested." His catalogs certainly attest to this. Skim through and you'll see titles as diverse as **Siam's Rural Economy Under King Chulalongkorn, Glutinous Rice Eating Traditions in Vietnam and Elsewhere**, and **A Guide to the Temple of Banteay Srei at Angkor**, originally published in 1926. As well as being marvelously eclectic, Ande's books are, in and of themselves, a treat. The paper is smooth and thick. Wonderful reproductions of drawings and photographs accompany the text. Back pockets contain maps that you can unfold and examine as you travel through the book.

"This developed. It wasn't planned," he explains. "It's like having the thread of a pullover in your hand. You pull and you pull, and the next thing you know, you have a nude girl." He chuckles, mischievously. The analogy is signature Ande, as idiosyncratic as the man himself. One moment he's challenging you to tell him how many teeth an elephant has, and the next, he's very seriously explaining a type of palm once thought to be extinct and now the subject of one of his books. Yet no matter which mood he's in, one thing is clear. Ande found the best of all possible reasons for staying in Bangkok.

White Lotus Press Showroom
11/2 Soi 58 Sukhumvit Road, Bangkok. Telephone: (602) 332-4915 or (602) 741-6288-9. I took a cab to the showroom from across town, and it only cost $5 US, but Ande suggests: Go to the end of Skytrain On Nut, from which it's a 15-minute walk, or take the bus and get off at Soi 89, which is opposite Soi 58.

BOOK RECOMMENDATIONS

Those who don't have time to venture out to the showroom can find many travel-oriented White Lotus titles at Asia Book locations throughout Bangkok.

WEBSITE
www.asiabook.com/contactus/maps.asp

You can also go to the White Lotus website at:

WEBSITE
http://thailine.com/lotus

Editor's note: I recommend visiting the showroom, where you'll also find an exceptional selection of antique prints and maps pertaining to the region.

White Lotus titles I have purchased and enjoyed include: **The French in Indochina**, first published in 1879; **Travels in Cambodia and Part of Laos** and **Further Travels in Laos and in Yunnan**, fascinating travelogues based on the Mekong Exploration Commission Report from 1866-1868; and **Travels in Siam, Cambodia, Laos and Annam**, by Henri Mouhot, who rediscovered the Angkor Wat ruins in the 1860s. Next on my list is **Three Years in Vietnam**, the 1907-1910 diaries of a doctor's wife in Nha Trang.

ADDITIONAL BOOK RECOMMENDATIONS FROM KIM FAY

This list is very selective and does not include many classics that have been written about these countries. I am simply noting a few that stand out for me. Check out the recommended reading sections in a Lonely Planet, Rough Guide or the like for more suggestions. The website **www.abebooks.com** is a good source for tracking down used or out-of-print books.

Books on Cambodia

When it comes to visiting the Khmer temples in Cambodia, there is a trio of books that will truly enrich the experience. In whole or in part, all were inspired by the exploits of Andre and Clara Malraux. (Many know of Andre as the Minister of Information under Charles de Gaulle.) In the early 1920s this young French couple decided to loot the neglected temple of Banteay Srei about 30 kilometers from Angkor Wat. They were intellectuals and they were supremely arrogant—the latter was both the reason they believed they could get away with their crime and the reason they were almost immediately caught. **The Royal Way**, a novel by Andre, and **Memoirs**, an autobiography by Clara, are a kind of he said-she said about this event. Clara's book is highly personal and emotional, while Andre's fictionalized account does not even mention that a woman, let alone his wife, was an integral part of this journey. For a more unbiased version, pick up a copy of Axel Madsen's **Silk Roads**. Or perhaps it is better to read this book first and then allow the Malrauxs to weigh in on the subject.

❁ ❁ ❁

I picked up a copy of **A Pilgrimage to Angkor** by Pierre Loti at a stall in the Old Market in Siem Reap. I think I paid almost 20 dollars for the 107-page volume, but the splurge was worth it. Loti visited Angkor Wat in 1912. From his sense of self-importance, you'd think he had spent half a year exploring the area, but in fact he was there only a few days. Nevertheless, his reminiscence stands out for its descriptions and the mood of the era that it captures.

Books on Laos

If you plan on taking a trip on the Mekong in Laos, order a copy of Marthe Bassenne's **In Laos and Siam** from White Lotus Press (see page 204). Bassenne was an intrepid French woman who traveled the river up to Luang Prabang in 1909. If you follow her route (you can—see page 115), you'll be delighted to discover how little has changed in so many places along the way. The book contains the beautiful black and white photographs that were published in the original edition.

❁ ❁ ❁

Forget Clancy and LeCarre for adventure/espionage reading during your holiday in Laos. While **Shooting at the Moon** by Roger Warner is a bit heavier (literally) than your typical mass market read, its heft is worth its weight in insight and intrigue. This is the story of the CIA's involvement in Laos at the beginning of the 1960s. The characters involved are as fascinating as the facts of the matter. This is a great introduction to the role that Laos both chose to play and was forced to play during the American war in Vietnam.

Books on Vietnam

Twenty-first century Vietnam has been shaped in great part by the countries that strove to dominate it during the 19th and 20th centuries. To understand Vietnam, you must understand these influences—both their idiosyncrasies and their rampant contradictions. I feel that Marguerite Duras' **The Sea Wall** and Graham Greene's **The Quiet American** are two

BOOK RECOMMENDATIONS

of the most revealing and significant novels on this tender and touchy subject. Duras' book takes place during the waning days of French colonialism, while Greene's sheds light on the dawning of American involvement in the region. I have read each of these novels at least half a dozen times, and I learn something new every time.

❀ ❀ ❀

Neil Sheehan is acclaimed for his coverage of the Vietnam War for **The New York Times**. His less celebrated wife, Susan, has also written about this controversial era. Written in 1967, **Ten Vietnamese** is exactly what its title suggests—ten essays about ten Vietnamese individuals, ranging from an orphan to a North Vietnamese prisoner. If you want to understand the human side of the war, this is a smart place to start.

❀ ❀ ❀

Speaking of Neil Sheehan, William Prochnau's **Once Upon a Distant War** is the telling of a few adventure-filled years in the life of Sheehan and his fellow journalistic cowboys, David Halberstam and Peter Arnett. While this book purports to be the tale of these men's struggles with editors, the government and censorship as they covered the

Vietnam War during the early 1960s, it is much more than that. This compelling history lays out the events of the crucial few years that led up to America's entrenched involvement in Vietnam. It's over 500 pages long, and I read it in three days.

Books on Southeast Asia

When I was planning my second big trip to Asia in the early 1990s, I picked up a copy of a book called **The Lands of Charm and Cruelty** by Stan Sesser. It is comprised of five essays that were originally published in "slightly different forms" in **The New Yorker**. At the time, I was particularly interested in the sections on Singapore and Borneo. It was only later that I read the chapters on Laos and Cambodia. Sesser is a personable, clean writer, and this is a good primer to get you started on understanding these two countries.

❀ ❀ ❀

Norman Lewis traveled through Indo-China in 1950, and the result was **A Dragon Apparent**. This travelogue sets the standard for its genre. Lewis is attentive to the details of a region that is both in transition—French colonialism is about to topple—and at the same time wedded to the traditions it has nurtured for centuries. I bought a used Jonathan Cape copy over the web, and it's filled with great photographs and a pretty little fold-out map.

⚛ ⚛ ⚛

Vietnam. 1976. The Americans were long gone. And it was as if the country had vanished from the face of the earth as far as most westerners were concerned. In **Brother Enemy: The War After the War**, Nayan Chanda chronicles those ghost years in Vietnam, as well as in Cambodia and Laos, from the end of the war to 1979. This is undoubtedly one of the most important books on America's involvement in the region, as the end is a very telling indictment of the means.

⚛ ⚛ ⚛

Travel writing and food writing make the perfect literary pairing. Yet there are no MFK Fishers or Elizabeth Davids for Southeast Asia. Fortunately, Jeffrey Alford and Naomi Duguid have infused their cookbook, **Hot, Sour, Salty, Sweet: a Culinary Journey Through Southeast Asia**, with essays that can stand with the best of them. Their love of the region's food is equaled only by their love of the region itself. This book is also a testament to the fact that where and how you eat can be just as important as what you're eating. While reading these pages, you'll be inspired to add a few new destinations to your itinerary.

SHOPPING FOR BOOKS:
A FEW EXTRA NOTES

Looking for some great reading material to complement your trip? Cambodia bound travelers should check out Andy Brower's website (see following) for author interviews and recommendations, as well as the Canby Publications website (page 208) for both books and where to buy them in-country. **The Bangkok Post** publishes its own tomes, and their selection features many highlights from their own writers. Pick up a copy of **But, I Don't Give a Hoot!** by Jennifer Bliss. It's the unauthorized biography of controversial Bangkok writer Bernard Trink. At **www.silkwormbooks.com** you can get your hands on—among other titles—a copy of Matt Jacobsen and Frank Visakay's **Adventure Cambodia**, which comes highly recommended by contributor Janet Brown.

WEBSITES

While there have long been many wonderful, comprehensive guidebooks to Southeast Asia, websites have just recently come into their own as credible resources for intrepid travelers. They can be updated in a timely fashion (on the flip side, they can sometimes be out-of-date without you realizing it), and they tend to be more specialized and personal than the majority of their bound counterparts. The following list is just the beginning when it comes to great online gold mines.

Websites: Cambodia

WEBSITE
www.btinternet.com/~andy.brouwer

Along with being authoritative, this website is just plain fun. **To Asia With Love** contributor Andy Brouwer adores Cambodia, and it shows in every word he writes. He has been visiting the country for years, and his travelogues are both informative and inspiring. From literature to noble causes, to the heartfelt friendships he's formed during his travels, this tribute to the land of the Khmers is essential reading.

WEBSITE
www.canbypublications.com

This is a comprehensive and well-organized website with all the basics a traveler needs for planning a trip to Cambodia. It is essentially an online version of Kenneth Cramer's free (in-country) Visitors' Guides to Phnom Penh, Siem Reap, Sihanoukville and a few other select destinations. While the first two cities have numerous publications and web pages devoted to them, Sihanoukville is often neglected. It is one of Southeast Asia's best off-the-beaten-path destinations, and this website is an excellent resource for making the most of it.

WEBSITE
www.tourismcambodia.com

Official tourism site with some decent basic information.

WEBSITE
www.gocambodia.com

General tourism plus extras like recipes, MP3 songs you can download and a cool collection of folk tales and short stories: (**www.gocambodia.com/cambodian_tale**).

WEBSITE
www.theangkorguide.com

A translation of Maurice Glaize's comprehensive and detailed 1944 guide to Angkor Wat.

Websites: Laos

WEBSITE
www.visit-laos.com
Official tourism site. Click into "News & Stories."

Websites: Thailand

WEBSITE
www.katswindow.net

Kat Tosi's contributions to **To Asia With Love** are inspired by many of the pieces that she compiled during her 2.5 years writing her "Kat's Window on Thailand" column for the **Bangkok Post**. This website contains a complete archive of those columns covering a range of subjects. If you want information on how you can train at a Thai boxing camp or need advice on how to drink the local rice whiskey, log on!

WEBSITE
www.fourelephants.com/sambrown
Containing articles written for **The Nation**, **Bangkok Metro Magazine**, and numerous other publications, this site lets you in on what it means to live in Bangkok. Your questions about going to the dentist and joining the right golf club are answered here. This website isn't as practical as many others devoted to traveling Thailand. On the other hand, it doesn't purport to be the next Lonely Planet. Instead, you'll have the opportunity to go behind the scenes and beyond the standard "insider" ramblings about language mishaps and red light districts.

WEBSITE
www.khaosanroad.com
Fascinating. There is no better word to describe this website. Focused on the backpackers' hub of Khao San Road in Bangkok, it is an online bulletin board where information from the site's expert creators mingles with comments from travelers. Read descriptions of the street's Israeli restaurants and learn where to get the best Internet access. You'll also find a few unusual offerings as well, such as the "Missing Persons" section (I'm disturbingly captivated by this) and information on how to visit foreign prisoners at the Bang Kwang Prison. This is also where I discovered the column, "Ask El." Eloise answers questions on a variety of Thai-travel-oriented topics and has contributed some of her insights to this guidebook.

WEBSITE
www.nancychandler.net
Nancy and her daughter, Nima, are known as being the experts on shopping in Thailand. In fact, on my last trip to Bangkok, I ended up setting aside my regular guidebook and using their map not only to find markets, but also to find my way around in general.

It got me to the Jim Thompson house, as well as to an interview with a publisher in an out-of-the-way pocket of the city. Visit this website for information on picking up these maps of Bangkok and Chiang Mai. And click on the "Planning a Visit to Thailand?" section for a small, interesting reading list and recommendations of "insider" things to do while in-country; they even suggest going to the hairdresser for a wash and scalp massage. (See Eloise Brown's take on this unique indulgence on page 155.) The Chandlers' excellent contribution to this guidebook can be found on page 51.

WEBSITE
www.tat.or.th
General tourism. In particular, go to their web magazine:
www.tatnews.org/emagazine/
This section includes great articles about things to do around the country. Philip Cornwel-Smith's piece, **Eco-Life**, explores Home Stay programs in Thailand and recommends two environmentally conscious tour companies that can set up home stays: Lost Horizons (**www.losthorizonsasia.com**) and REST (**www.ecotour.in.th**).

WEBSITE
www.thailandforvisitors.com
Excellent in-depth information on sightseeing throughout the country. It is associated with **http://chiengfa.com/**, which offers magazine style pieces on more out-of-the way destinations.

WEBSITE
www.sawadee.com
General tourism offering information on everything from Thai fruits to zoo listings to golf course locations.

WEBSITE
www.thailand.com/travel
General tourism including well-written, in-depth monthly articles on a variety of subjects, such as the relationship between mural paintings and Buddhism.

WEBSITE
http://welcome-to.chiangmai-chiangrai.com
Information on northern Thailand, recommended by **Time Magazine Asia**.

WEBSITE
www.chiangmainews.com
Information on Chiang Mai as well as other timely articles from **Chiang Mai Citylife Magazine**. This is where I discovered **To Asia With Love** contributor Candace MacKay.

WEBSITE
www.topthaisites.com
Click into the "Travel" section. Among many great offerings is

comprehensive transportation (buses, trains, planes and more) information.

Websites: Vietnam

WEBSITE
www.vietnamuniverse.com

Dana Sachs is the author of **The House on Dream Street: Memoir of an American Woman in Vietnam**. Her website offers some good, very personal travel information, some of which you'll find in **To Asia With Love**. But the best part of her site is the section devoted to Vietnamese literature. Dana has translated numerous Vietnamese novels and short stories into English. The website's bibliography includes a wonderful list of fiction that includes works translated by Dana. You can also read a selection of translated short stories and a folk tale. Although no one story can completely capture a culture, since no culture is ever that simple, stories such as "Crossing the River" offer insight into the unique outlook and sense of humor of the Vietnamese. (One of Dana's favorite folk tales from her most recent book can be found following this chapter.)

WEBSITE
www.jandodd.com/vietnam

To Asia With Love contributor Jan Dodd co-authored **The Rough Guide to Vietnam**. This website provides a hodgepodge of updates to that guide both by Dodd and travelers. It also includes information on some of Dodd's personal favorites in the country. For a distillation of that list, go to page 88.

WEBSITE
www.vietnamtourism.com

Official general tourism site. It also contains a series of sections dedicated to a variety of topics that include such interesting offerings as "Traditional Villages"—a group of essays on destinations that specialize in pottery, flowers, incense, stone carving and more.

WEBSITE
www.vnn.vn/english/

News and feature stories. It offers articles on art, culture and society, as well as listings of "goings-on" about Hanoi and Ho Chi Minh City. The "Vietnam Diaries" section is particularly interesting.

Websites General: Southeast Asia

WEBSITE
www.ThingsAsian.com

Without this website, this guidebook would not exist—ThingsAsian is both the inspiration for and publisher of **To Asia With Love**. Beginning in the 1990s as a print magazine called **Destination: Vietnam**, ThingsAsian has evolved into an e-arena where travelers can publish essays about culture, art, food and adventure throughout Asia. It is constantly adding new stories, but one of its best features is that it maintains a library of all past stories.

WEBSITE
www.pmgeiser.ch

This is a good website if you're looking for lots of facts supplemented by quirky commentary. The site's creator, Peter Geiser, provides the basics and then some. The layout isn't the most user friendly, and it may take you a minute to get in tune with the style, but it's worth checking out for little tidbits such as the email address of a man who can give you information on the Bolaven Plateau in Laos, and telling insights like this one from the section on Phnom Penh accommodations: "Generally, the medium-priced hotels, and also some of the expensive places, double as brothels. This may appeal to some travelers, but it certainly doesn't make for a good night's sleep."

WEBSITE
www.visit-mekong.com

General tourism. Make sure to check out the "stories" section for essays by fellow travelers.

WEBSITE
www.talesofasia.com

Insights by Gordon Sharpless on travel throughout Asia and particularly Cambodia. The site also contains current news stories and reports by travelers. Noted by **Time Magazine Asia**.

WEBSITE
www.exotissimo.com

I relied on this travel company during the four years I lived in Vietnam. They arranged my flights, as well as one particularly memorable group outing. Get on their mailing list to receive information about unique excursions. They're not for the budget backpacker; at the same time, as with many things in Asia, most of what they offer won't break the bank.

WEBSITE
www.asiahotels.com

I organized all the hotels for my last trip to Asia through this website. It doesn't offer the most user-friendly format, but it's manageable. Its listings are comprehensive, and its bookings are reliable and legitimate.

ALL THE NEWS THAT'S FIT TO PRINT . . . AND THEN SOME

WEBSITE
www.camnet.com.kh/cambodia.daily/

A limited version of the **Cambodia Daily**. It's not much to look at on the screen, but it has a few interesting news pieces from time to time.

WEBSITE
www.phnompenhpost.com/
A link to the weekly **Phnom Penh Post**. Click into the free online edition for a selection of articles on current events and the disturbing "Police Blotter."

WEBSITE
www.laosnews.net
Lots of news articles about Laos and the surrounding countries. It also has links to Lao related websites.

WEBSITE
www.vientianetimes.com
A more Lao-centric version of the **Laos News**. The site offers good overall coverage, although it seems to have a political agenda—it's hard to tell what its criticism of the Lao government is intended to accomplish. It also includes many current news items about the Hmong community in the U.S.

WEBSITE
www.bangkokpost.com
The ultimate online source for news in Thailand. The restaurant, entertainment and travel sections are particularly valuable.

WEBSITE
www.vietnamnews.net
The Vietnamese version of the **Laos News** website. You'll find lots of crossover regional articles along with pieces about Vietnam.

WEBSITE
http://vietnamnews.vnagency.com.vn/Home.htm
This is the virtual version of the local daily English-language rag read by the majority of expats who live in Vietnam.

WEBSITE
www.cnn.com/ASIANOW/southeast/
Full-on regional coverage from the editors of **Time**, **Newsweek** and CNN.

WEBSITE
www.time.com/time/asia/
The Asia-oriented edition of **Time** magazine. Good for in-depth pieces on current events in the region. The travel section is of particular note.

READING FOR THE ROAD

*A classic Vietnamese folktale to get you in
the mood for your upcoming trip.*

Dana Sachs and Nguyen Nguyet Cam
weave a traditional Vietnamese folktale . . .

A Daughter's Love

Long ago, Au Lac's king, An Duong Vuong, ordered his subjects to build a large and solid rampart surrounded by a deep trench, to protect the tiny nation from invasion.

An Duong Vuong expected the rampart to be magnificent, but before the work was half complete, something very strange and terrible happened. The king and his subjects woke one morning to find that all the work they had accomplished the day before had somehow been destroyed during the night.

That evening, the king ordered one hundred of his brightest soldiers to stay awake to catch the culprit. From sunset to sunrise, none of them so much as blinked an eye. But they saw nothing, and the next morning, the king awoke again to find that some mysterious spirit had destroyed all the previous day's work during the night.

At this rate, the ramparts would never be completed, and Au Lac would always face the fear of invasion. An Duong Vuong decided to watch the place himself. That night he didn't sleep at all, but he, too, discovered nothing. The next morning, as before, everything they had accomplished lay in ruins.

The king was full of sorrow. How could he protect his people if he couldn't even complete the ramparts to defend them? In desperation, he built an altar to pray to heaven and earth and to call for the help of the gods. For many days he stayed in this shrine, hoping that by renouncing the luxuries of his royal life, he could prove his true and faithful heart. The king's wife had died, and the only person he would see during this time of prayer was Mi Chau, his only daughter. She cooked her father's simple meals of rice and vegetables and she washed his tattered beggar's clothes.

One night during this period, the king had a dream. An angel appeared in the form of a golden turtle and said to him, "I am Kim Quy Divine. I am moved by your prayers and I will help you in your wish to protect your people. You are right to build a rampart, but the shape is wrong. Build a rampart that wraps into itself like a snail's shell, and you will be able to finish it soon." Then Kim Quy disappeared and the king woke up. Before the sun rose over the distant mountains, the people of Au Lac had already begun work on the new ramparts, following the golden turtle's advice exactly.

Just as the turtle had promised, one month later the rampart, called Loa Thanh, was complete. No one, not even the most ancient woman in the kingdom, who was over 130 years old, had ever seen such a solid, imposing structure. The rampart walls curled into themselves like the shell of a snail, and no invaders could figure out how to get inside.

An Duong Vuong returned to royal life and held a great feast to thank Kim Quy Divine. That night, the golden turtle appeared to the king in another dream. Handing the king one of its golden claws, the turtle said, "Now I offer you this to defend your territory. Make a bow's trigger out of it and you'll have a miraculous weapon. This bow will never miss its mark, and it will kill thousands of enemy soldiers with every shot. But I also have one word of warning. Keep the golden claw very carefully. If you lose it, you will lose your country!" With that advice, the turtle disappeared.

The king woke up and found the claw at his side. He picked it up carefully and called his most skillful bowmaker to construct the bow. Nine days later, the bowmaker presented the king with the weapon, which shone like the moon and was so big that only the strongest soldiers could lift it. An Duong Vuong kept the precious gift next to his bed.

At that time, Au Lac's worst enemy was the country of Nam Hai, which is now a part of southern China. Year after year, the king of Nam Hai invaded, but An Duong Vuong used his divine bow to defeat the enemy every time.

The king of Nam Hai, Trieu Da, was a clever man. Although he knew nothing of the golden bow, he realized that in order to win Au Lac he would have to find a way other than military force. He wanted to discover An Duong Vuong's secret strength and destroy it. For that purpose, he came up with a tricky plan.

Trieu Da sent a peace delegation to Au Lac, at the head of which was his only son, Trong Thuy. Trong Thuy carried a message from his father suggesting that the two countries cement their new alliance of friendship through marriage. Trieu Da proposed that his son should take the hand of Mi Chau, King An Duong Vuong's daughter.

King An Duong Vuong was glad to establish peace with his former enemy. He was not yet willing to agree to the plan of marriage, but he welcomed Trong Thuy into the palace.

In those days, love never played a major role in the marriage plans of princes and princesses. Rather, kings used the hands of their children to strengthen their own positions of power. The relationship between Trong Thuy and Mi Chau was special from the start, though. Trong Thuy was instantly moved by the divine beauty of the princess, and Mi Chau could not fail to notice the handsome young man. In addition, Mi Chau played the lute more exquisitely than the finest musicians Trong Thuy had ever heard, and when the prince sang to accompany her, the lovely tones of his voice moved Mi Chau to tears.

Trong Thuy hadn't even been at the palace a month before the love between the two young people became apparent to everyone. Even the king enjoyed the sight of the happy couple

talking for hours while they sat on a large white rock in the palace garden. King An Duong Vuong didn't feel suspicious at all when he saw his daughter and the son of his former enemy wandering through the secret passages of the rampart. Recognizing the love between the two young people, he agreed to let Mi Chau marry the Nam Hai prince.

The couple lived in harmony, playing chess, reciting poems, and spending quiet afternoons admiring the beautiful flowers in the palace gardens. Day after day, night after night, their life passed in peace and serenity. Mi Chau was so happy she thought that life would always be this way.

One night, when the moon was very bright and the stars flickered like diamonds in the sky, Mi Chau and Trong Thuy were sitting on the big rock in the garden, looking out over the high ramparts. They had been there a long time when a cold wind suddenly blew through the trees. Large white clouds began to roll across the sky.

Mi Chau started to shiver and Trong Thuy pulled her closer to him. Then he whispered, "My darling, now we are as dear to each other as two people can ever be. We must always be truthful with one another, and so I want to ask you something. Is there a secret reason why your father's kingdom has never been defeated?"

Mi Chau turned to her husband and said, "There's no secret, my love! Au Lac has a high, strong rampart and a deep trench. It also has a divine bow that can kill thousands of enemy soldiers with every shot. How could anyone defeat us?"

Trong Thuy asked Mi Chau many questions about the bow, and she finally led her husband to the king's bedroom so that Trong Thuy could see it for himself. Even in the dark night, the golden claw glowed as if it were imbued with light. As Mi Chau explained to Trong Thuy how to use the bow, Trong Thuy listened quietly, looking closely at the trigger and at the particular size and shape of the instrument. Then the young couple put the bow back in its place and went back to their own quarters to sleep.

The next morning, Trong Thuy asked for An Duong Vuong's permission to go back to Nam Hai to visit his father, Trieu Da. Within a few days, the young prince was telling his father the whole story of the divine bow. Trieu Da was thrilled with the information, and ordered his servants to make a false trigger out of the claw of an ordinary turtle that would look exactly like King An Duong Vuong's magical trigger. Trong Thuy then hid the new trigger in his clothes and returned with it to Au Lac.

An Duong Vuong held a huge party to welcome his son-in-law home. At the party, Trong Thuy held up his glass of wine and offered toast after toast to his new family. An Duong Vuong and Mi Chau drank many glasses of wine, but Trong Thuy himself drank only a little. Soon the king and Mi Chau were fast asleep. Trong Thuy sneaked into the king's bedroom, stole the golden trigger, and replaced it with his false one.

The next morning, Mi Chau thought her husband seemed worried and restless. "What is bothering you, my darling?" she asked.

Trong Thuy looked at his wife and said, "I have to leave. My royal father has told me that I must return to Nam Hai immediately so that I can accompany him to battle very far away in the north. It's possible that I will be gone a long time."

Mi Chau looked at the ground and said nothing. Trong Thuy took her hand and continued, "I have no idea when we will meet again, my love, but I know that we will. We must think of a way to find each other, because if there is a war you may have to leave this place. I can't live without you, and so I have to know how to find you."

For several moments, Mi Chau said nothing. Then finally she whispered, "I have a goose-feather coat. Wherever I go, I will drop feathers along my way. You can follow that trail of feathers to find me."

Trong Thuy was pale now. He knew that if he didn't leave quickly, he would never be able to leave at all. The young lovers hugged each other. Neither one could even speak. Then Trong Thuy gathered his things and left. For a long time, Mi Chau stood by the window staring down at the garden below her, the tears streaming down her cheek.

Back in Nam Hai, Trong Thuy gave his father the golden claw. Trieu Da held the magic trigger in his hands and proclaimed "This time, Au Lac will be mine!" Trong Thuy said nothing. He simply turned and walked away. A few days later, he and his father led the entire military force of Nam Hai across the border and into the kingdom of Au Lac.

When An Dung Vuong heard that Nam Hai had invaded his kingdom, he swore at King Trieu Da's deceit. However, trusting the power of his divine bow, he made no preparation for battle. Not until the enemy had nearly reached the ramparts did he pull out his precious weapon and shoot. It was only at that moment, when the shot failed to have its magical effect, that the king realized the depth of his misfortune.

The Nam Hai soldiers rushed the rampart gates and, within minutes, the solid walls began to crumble. An Duong Vuong pulled Mi Chau up onto his horse with him, and they escaped through the back gate. From her seat on the galloping horse, Mi Chau plucked goose feathers out of her coat, and left a trail so that her husband could find her.

The mountain roads were rough and dangerous. For several days, their horse ran without rest. Finally, late one afternoon, the road climbed Da Son Mountain and led to a cliff overlooking the Eastern Sea. The king and the princess stopped and got off the horse. An Duong Vuong looked at the sun setting over the horizon and realized he was trapped. Although the road continued along the edge of the cliff, it was too narrow to travel at night. At the same time, they couldn't rest or turn back, because the enemy troops might be right behind them.

An Duong Vuong knelt down and whispered the name of Kim Quy Divine. Suddenly, the wind picked up, blowing sand and dirt in all directions, shaking the leaves, shaking the trees, shaking the whole mountain. Then the clear image of the golden turtle appeared within the fog of dust. "The enemy," the turtle said, "is at your back." With that, Kim Quy disappeared.

King An Duong Vuong looked around. In the fading light, he saw the trail of feathers on the ground behind them. Now he knew the truth. Without another thought, he took out his sword. Mi Chau closed her eyes. Then, with one fatal stroke, King An Duong Vuong cut off his daughter's head. He stood for a moment, looking down at the body of his precious child, and then he hurled himself over the cliff into the sea.

Back at the capital, Trieu Da's soldiers had taken over the whole Loa Thanh rampart. As soon as he saw that the battle was over, Trong Thuy got on his horse and rushed off to find his love. For days, he followed the trail of feathers, through forest and hills, then up into the mountains until he finally reached Da Son Mountain at the edge of the sea. There, beside the cliff, lay the body of Mi Chau. Trong Thuy fell to his knees and covered his face in his hands.

Two days later, Trieu Da, his soldiers, and all the people of Loa Thanh saw Trong Thuy riding slowly back to the rampart with the body of Mi Chau. Though his father and all his friends tried to get the young man to speak, he said nothing, and he wouldn't

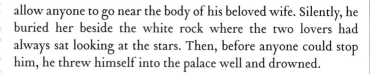

allow anyone to go near the body of his beloved wife. Silently, he buried her beside the white rock where the two lovers had always sat looking at the stars. Then, before anyone could stop him, he threw himself into the palace well and drowned.

Nowadays, at Co Loa village just outside Hanoi, the well called Trong Thuy sits in front of An Duong Vuong's temple. According to Vietnamese legend, when the king killed his daughter, her blood flowed into the sea. Oysters drank those drops of blood and produced pearls that were large, but glowed only dimly. Local people say that if the pearls are washed in the water of Trong Thuy's well, they will shine with a translucence as bright and beautiful as the moon.

❀ ❀ ❀

There is also a modern Vietnamese poem that recalls the tragedy of Mi Chau and Trong Thuy:

> *Tears become the other side of trust*
> *Ultimately love is death*
> *But the beautiful girl, even headless, still has beauty*
> *And love, even with betrayal, is still love.*

This story is excerpted from **Two Cakes Fit for a King: Folktales from Vietnam**, compiled by Nguyen Nguyet Cam and Dana Sachs, introduced and illustrated by Bui Hoai Mai. (Honolulu, University of Hawai'i Press, 2003).

EPILOGUE

Walking meditation teaches one contributor how
to bring the spirit of her journey home.

Phuong Tran takes home the perfect souvenir . . .

"Nam Mo A Di Da Phat."
"Praise to the Buddha."

It was not yet dawn. The nuns' chants enveloped me with their rhythmic, almost melancholic tones. I was seated in the half-lotus position, numb and drunk from lack of sleep, adjusting to the thick perfume of incense and the dimly lit interior of the Chua Tay Linh Temple in Hue, in Central Vietnam. The abbot, Su Co Nhu Minh (Sister True Wisdom), took my hand and that of my friend and led us out into the courtyard. After a series of stretches, she started pacing around the courtyard in even, measured steps.

> *"Have you ever walked and arrived at your destination but forgotten how you got there?"*

She continued to walk in slow circles. Two steps—she inhaled, silently. Two steps—exhale.

> *"This helps you to be aware of each step.*
> *Walking in constant mindfulness of the journey."*

We walked and meditated until the sun appeared, a rose flame that wrapped the courtyard in a protective halo.

❀ ❀ ❀

Earlier in Hanoi, my friend and I met a Vietnamese-American monk from the University of California at Berkeley who was on a Fulbright Fellowship, conducting research on temple architecture. When he learned that we wanted to visit Hue, he told us about Su Co Nhu Minh and said that we should pay a visit. When we arrived at the temple, we were greeted by a series of nuns who led us to Su Co Nhu Minh. She quietly sat us down to tea and removed her conical hat. She didn't speak much, nor did she ask us where we were from, how we knew

Chua Tay Linh, how long we intended to stay or what we hoped to learn. Nor did we know the answers to these questions had she asked them. Travel has the liberating effect of allowing one to visit for the sake of curiosity, to speak to fellow travelers without ulterior motives or a business card exchange, to live without guaranteed outcomes. We know our stay in a particular place is finite and that we will soon leave it; the rationale is to experience it deeply, widely and without expectations.

We couldn't stay overnight at the temple because we weren't Vietnamese citizens, and as foreign passport holders, it would have required advance permission from the local authorities. We elected instead to stay at an area guesthouse and to meet Su Co Nhu Minh in the morning. Would we like to join her for the morning chants, she asked? It was exactly what we hoped for, to be folded into temple life and to taste a contemplative way of living we often idealized—seclusion from the material world of avarice and ambition. Yes, we would be honored to meet her. At 4 a.m. During that night, I woke up to a persistent mosquito in my net, fluorescent hallway lights and disquieting dreams of over-sleeping an important appointment. By the time 3 a.m. came, my friend and I were both wide awake, alert with an inexplicable fear of missing our meeting.

Our morning started with the chants, which lasted approximately one hour. Then Su Co Nhu Minh asked us to join her in the temple courtyard for morning stretches. When the sun rose, she began to walk in a circle, tracing the halo of light on the concrete with measured steps. We followed her as we had during the morning stretches. There was no explanation, no introduction to distinguish the walking from the bending, reaching or toe touching. *Two steps, inhale. Two steps, exhale.* This was the only instruction we had received from her about walking.

This activity wasn't called walking meditation by Su Co Nhu Minh. In fact, it was years later when I learned that was what I had been taught. With Su Co Nhu Minh, it was simply a morning exercise along paths lined with lotus ponds. It was a way to get to the market and its rows upon rows of scallions, mangoes and garlands of garlic and flowers. *Two steps, inhale. Two steps, exhale.* This walking was a way to travel to homes as she checked on families in the area. How are you doing? The kids? The business? *Two steps, inhale. Two steps, exhale.* But as we did these morning errands with her over two days, something in my step changed. Yes, I still didn't know this was a form of meditation because we didn't walk particularly slowly—she's a fast woman, one of the quickest nuns I have met. Wasn't meditation supposed to be slow, a respite from our hurried lives, an imposed speed bump as we slowed to listen to birds, without being terribly productive? Yet here was Su Co Nhu Minh walking with her bags from the market, carrying scallions and roses and a baguette. In addition to her abbot duties at the temple, she was overseeing the building of a second temple, continuing her social work activities in the community, and hosting two guests. However, as she carried out her day's work, her feet always kept the same rhythm, touching the ground with equanimity, calm and resolve. Her steps were measured and in her flip-flop sandals, her toes would tap the ground; then, like a wave on that dry dirt, the balls of her feet, her arch and her heels would roll over the ground.

Two steps, inhale. Two steps exhale.

The idea of meditating typically conjures images of a still sanctuary and reverent silence. To learn a kind of meditation that you can carry with you in the streets of Vietnam, among the chaotic pedestrian traffic, street vendors, a mob of women diving into watercress bins, tourists drowning in the oppressive August heat, the cacophony of students and business persons in the city . . . now that is another realm of mindfulness entirely.

I was reminded of Zen master Thich Nhat Hanh's words, "The real challenge is not to walk on air or water, but rather to walk on earth." We were with Su Co Nhu Minh for only two days, but she remained at my side, in my steps, for my entire stay in Vietnam, lending me quiet strength through this metronome of mindfulness: my breathing and my footsteps.

The rhythm—two steps inhale, two steps exhale—seized me as I chose fabric at the tailor, drank at coffee shops that played Bananarama and Lionel Richie (*Hello, hello, is it me you're looking for?*), and when I lingered over *che* pudding desserts at a midnight market. This mindfulness chased me through the country like the lizards that climbed my aunt's walls. It pinned me down and made me feel the burnt coals under charcoal flames, sense the wind from the flap of a white *ao dai* school gown flowing from the back of a bicycle, hear the singsong chants of the vendors who sold lilies, sandals and coconuts, and read the weathered expressions of old women in black silk pants with their betel nut stained teeth, women who had endured sun, water, fire and history. This unflappable mindfulness allowed me to connect with languid water buffaloes, a painting of an archway I thought I recognized but could not have possibly passed under in my lifetime, a retired Communist soldier intrigued by my family's history, and two tailors in Hoi An who found me—by American standards slender—portly. Fat, to be exact. An undercurrent of subtle rhythm, I discovered, as I focused on my meditation, seemed to permeate Vietnam's streets, hypnotizing workers who shaved ice for *sinh to* shakes, cooked *pho*, painted calligraphy, signed trade agreements, sewed silk pajama sets, painted ceramics, dried squid, built hotels, sang opera, controlled water puppets, enticed foreign investors, barbequed pork, developed beach resorts, and opened KFC and Baskin Robbins franchises.

But when I left Vietnam, I found that this attention to my breathing and walking stayed behind with the lotus ponds, women in conical hats who sell sticky rice wrapped in banana leaves at train stops, iridescent pink dragon fruit shaped like long grenades, children who shine shoes and sell cigarettes, tea, and photocopied editions of the Lonely Planet. I returned to the United States as I had left it, rushing to my next destination, impatient and too myopic to notice the details that make memories so vivid. Maybe this is inevitable with travel—the stimuli are more sexy, noteworthy and ultimately memorable than those in our daily surroundings. Perhaps that is why travel photography comes out so great; friendships formed on the road are so intense and sometimes even more intimate than our relationships back home; epiphanies, Kerouac musings and travel journaling so liberating; love affairs so satisfying; food so delicious; and people so attractive.

I am now back in New York City, guarding the fragile mindfulness cultivated in Hue's Chua Tay Linh Temple. I carry it with me like a folded and refolded recipe, the dog-eared page of a beloved poem, a creased grade school love note (*Will you go with me?*). On some days, mindfulness revisits me when I least expect it—I will be crossing the long underground tunnel between Port Authority and Times Square, waiting in line at Rite Aid to pay for my Peppermint Patties, or crossing Broadway to Zabar's or Barnes & Noble. Suddenly I will focus on the mustached violinist subway performer in his fedora, the rhythm of the cash registers opening and closing, the sound of receipts being printed, or the blood red Gerber daisies at the corner deli.

Two steps, inhale. Two steps, exhale.

For a moment Vietnam and a perfect unity with the intrinsic rhythms of daily life don't seem so far away.

Chua Tay Linh Temple

The temple is located on Ton That Thuyet Street, Hue, Vietnam. It is quite well-known, and any taxi or Honda driver should be able to take you there. If you need assistance, call 054-525-711 and ask for Su Co Nhu Hai.

Meditation

If you're looking for some basic background information on the practice of walking meditation, check out:

WEBSITE
www.wildmind.org/meditation/walking/overview.html

WEBSITE
www.yogateacher.com/text/meditation/on-line/walking.html

A good primer is **The Long Road Turns to Joy: a Guide to Walking Meditation**, by Nhich Nhat Hanh. It can be ordered from the usual online sources, as well as at:

WEBSITE
www.parallax.org

While on this site you should also look for his book, **Peace is Every Step**, and his autobiography, **My Master's Robe**.

General Resources

You could search the web for hours and still not discover all the many pages devoted to various meditation centers in Southeast Asia. A good starting point is:

WEBSITE
www.buddhanet.net/asia.htm

This website is also helpful:

WEBSITE
http://meditationthailand.tripod.com

Meditation Centers

Among many destinations of note, Phuong Tran recommends a visit to Van Hanh Buddhist University at 716 Nguyen Kiem Street, Ho Chi Minh City, Vietnam. Meditation sessions in English are offered here.

Contributor Matt McKinney writes: In Phnom Penh, stop by Wat Langka on a Monday or Thursday at 6 p.m. for meditation with the in-house monks. It's a beautiful wat, and the monks will assist you with basic meditation techniques—a wonderful way to clear your head before moving on to the next tourist stop. The wat is located near Independence Monument on Sihanouk Boulevard.

See Candace MacKay's piece on Wat U Mong in Chang Mai on page 100 in Chapter Four.

For more on Buddhism and meditation for readers of Vietnamese, Nhat Phuong recommends:

WEBSITE
www.lotuspro.net

Information about extended (four week minimum) Buddhist Temple Stays in Thailand can be found at:

WEBSITE
www.cultural-ecology.com

CONTRIBUTORS' PROFILES

Jim Algie

Canadian Jim Algie, a self-described "sentient being and weirdsmith", has published hundreds of feature stories, won awards for his short fiction, and is the managing editor of **FARANG**, a travel mag based in Bangkok. Throughout the '80s he played in various underground rock bands, and was dubbed "the Keith Richards of the bass guitar" by **The Montreal Gazette**.

Nick & Hannah Anderson

Nick and Hannah Anderson cycled through Laos as part of a year's cycling trip to New Zealand, Australia (a small bit of!), Thailand, Burma, Laos and Malaysia.

WEBSITE
http://uk.geocities.com/hannahandnick/

Lori Ashton

Hailing from Canada, Lori studied costume design and spent 13 years designing and producing sleepwear and bridal gowns, winning the Award of Excellence for her work. Eight years ago she and her husband headed to Asia for an 18-month break; they have been there ever since. She was working in public relations in Phuket when she recognized the need for an art and culture guide. For further information on **Art & Culture South, Art & Culture Lanna** (and coming soon: **Art & Culture Bangkok**), "the definitive guides to studios, shops and special places," contact Serendipity Designs Co., Ltd.

HEAD OFFICE
12/13 Viset Road,
Rawai, Phuket 83130,
Thailand

WEBSITE
www.ArtAndCultureAsia.com

EMAIL
info@ArtAndCultureAsia.com

Cindy Brown

Cindy Brown first visited Hanoi in 1997 with her husband Allen, after living in Japan for one year. It was during this two-week stay that they were ruined for life. Hanoi haunted them like a bad dream until they decided to return and make it their home for six months in 2002. Maybe it was all the near miss encounters with young male moto drivers, women in elegant *ao dais* riding by on bicycles, and farm women carrying 50+ pounds of colorful fruits balanced on their shoulders by a stick and two baskets. Whatever the case, after exploring much of Southeast Asia, such as Cambodia, Laos, Indonesia, Burma, Thailand, Singapore, and Malaysia, Vietnam continues to provide a source of endless fascination and wonder for both Cindy and her husband.

Eloise Brown

Adventures in Thailand on school exchange inspired Eloise Brown to pursue Asian Studies at universities in both Australia and Thailand. Fluent in Thai, Eloise has worked in translating and research, and has also been a student counselor and freelance consultant, based in both Bangkok and rural Thailand. She is currently far from Thailand working as a governess on a remote cattle station in Western Australia. For more on her insights into Thailand, check out the "Ask El!" link at:

WEBSITE
www.khaosanroad.com

Janet Brown

Janet Brown found a true home in Bangkok and lived there for four years. She now shivers and sells travel books in cloudy, chilly Seattle, where she dreams of Thai street food and of all the Khmer *prasats* that she has yet to explore.

Joshua Samuel Brown

A nomadic freelancer, Joshua Samuel Brown's travels have spanned two millennia and two hemispheres. In Asia, his travel and leisure work has been published in **Beijing Scene**, **South China Morning Post**, **City Weekend**, **That's Beijing**, **China Week**, and nearly every English publication in Taiwan. In America, his work appears regularly in the **Albion Monitor** and the **Rocky Mountain Bullhorn**. His column "Politics and Other Dirty Words" has savaged left and right since the summer of 2000, and his political essays appear occasionally at:

WEBSITE
www.antiwar.com

JSB's work can also be read at:

WEBSITE
www.josambro.com

EMAIL
jsb@monitor.net

Andy Brouwer

Words cannot adequately describe the extent to which Andy Brouwer's passion for Cambodia has grown since his first, white-knuckle visit nearly ten years ago. The warmth and resilience of the people, the awe-inspiring temples, and the variety of locations and adventures all go into the melting pot to make Cambodia the fascinating and life-enhancing destination that he has been so fortunate to experience.

Peter J. Burns

Peter J. Burns grew up in the American Midwest along the banks of the Mississippi. He has been teaching English and Lit for five years; for three of those years he has been in Thailand. Currently living and working in the mountains outside of Chiang Mai, he still travels frequently and chronicles his trips through photography and journal writing.

Stuart Cavaliero

Stuart Cavaliero is formerly from Norwich, England, but now lives in Chiang Dao, Thailand. He and his wife own Chiang Dao Nest Mini-Resort, a lovely little place in the mountains with amazing views and amazing food.

Kenneth Champeon

Kenneth Champeon is an American writer based in Chiang Mai, Thailand. He spent six months in Bombay and has lived in Thailand for over three years. He contributes regularly to **ThingsAsian** and writes reviews of Asian literature for **BookPage**. Visit his web page at:

WEBSITE
http://kenneth.champeon.com

EMAIL
kenneth@champeon.com

Nancy & Nima Chandler

Nancy Chandler and her eldest daughter, Nima, publish Nancy Chandler's Maps of Bangkok and Chiang Mai, unique guides to shopping, dining and sightseeing, including lots of local secrets. Both have spent many years in Thailand, sharing their favorite finds with other expatriates and tourists through their maps. For more information, please visit:

WEBSITE
www.nancychandler.net

Samantha Coomber

Sammy Coomber is a freelance travel writer from London, but now resides in Sydney and Vietnam. Her extensive travels (especially in Asia and particularly Vietnam) have led to many internationally published articles. Samantha has updated three **Rough Guide to Vietnam** guidebooks and is now based in Hanoi, Vietnam, as an editor/writer for an English-language tourist magazine.

Richard Craik

Richard Craik is the director of marketing of Exotissimo Travel Group, headquartered in Ho Chi Minh City.

Roger Crutchley

Roger Crutchley hails from Reading in England. In 1969, at the age of 22, he set forth from London on an overland trip to Australia. He got as far as Thailand and has been there ever since, most of the time working on the **Bangkok Post** newspaper. He finally made it to Australia 27 years later. He is the author of two books based on his weekly column, the most recent being, **Postscript: Forgotten But Not Gone**, available at Asia Books and other leading bookstores or from:

WEBSITE
www.bangkokpost.net/postbooks/

Joe Cummings

Joe Cummings is a prolific and highly regarded travel writer, whose many publications include the Laos, Thailand and Southeast Asia on a Shoestring books for Lonely Planet—among many, many others. He is a two-time winner of the Lowell Thomas Travel Journalism Gold Award and two-time finalist for the Thomas Cook Guidebook of the Year.

Jan Dodd

Jan Dodd spent six years exploring Southeast Asia before moving to southern France, where she is now established as a freelance travel writer. In addition to the **Rough Guide to Vietnam**, Jan co-authored the award-winning **Rough Guide to Japan** and has worked on guides for Lonely Planet, Insight and a number of other travel publishers. She also contributes to web sites, newspapers and journals on a regular basis, and can be found on her own informative website at:

WEBSITE
www.jandodd.com

Stephen Engle

Seattle native Steve Engle first went to China in 1990 to "fall off the face of the earth for a while." The charming rust belt of Manchuria was his jumping off spot, and he is still tumbling. He has since lived in Japan, Taiwan, Guam, Singapore and Hong Kong, where he works as a television news anchor "to pay the bills to be a backpacker."

Peter M. Geiser

Peter Geiser works as a director for a major Swiss bank. He holds diplomas in Computer Science from ETH Zurich and in Business Administration from the University of St. Gallen (HSG). A part-time teacher, he also writes travel guides and has created a web portal for mineral waters around the world. Check out his SE Asia website at:

WEBSITE
www.pmgeiser.ch

Donald Gilliland

Originally from Orlando, Florida (USA) where he operated a record store and bookshop for 12 years, Donald Gilliland moved to Bangkok, Thailand in 1996 and worked there as a manager for Tower Records. He also taught English and worked as an editor and copywriter for a travel website and a marketing company before going to Siem Reap, Cambodia in August 2002 to open up the Lazy

Mango Bookshop. Although still a diehard baseball fan (Minnesota Twins and Atlanta Braves), when he has free time, he likes to sneak away to a local basketball court and pretend he's Michael Jordan.

Christina Gosnell

Christina Gosnell is a full-time freelance writer who has written extensively about Southeast Asia. As a contributor to ThingsAsian since 2001, she has published over 20 articles, including one entitled, "Krabi: Lovely Town, Lovely People" (see page 124). Her first novel is set to be released this year, as well. Christina makes her home in the Southern U.S.

John Gray

Lifelong waterman and wildlife rehabber, John "Caveman" Gray crawled into California's surf at six months and surfed The Wedge long before his 1957 SCUBA certification and Honolulu's 1978 High Surf Ocean Lifesaver charter class. Gray's 1983 pre-ecotourism business model became Hawai'i's first sea kayaking company, featured in the 1985 Emmy award winning **Moloka'i's Forgotten Frontier** and Travel Channel's 1988-89 **Inside Hawai'i**. Caveman developed his limestone sea cave entries while exploring South Thailand in 1989 and Vietnam's Halong Bay in 1992. After

numerous awards and dozens of documentaries, the 14-year Phuket resident still kayaks at every opportunity. Despite competitors' claims, John Gray's SeaCanoe is Caveman's only company. Make no mistake.

EMAIL
info@johngray-seacanoe.com

Han Thuy Giang

Han Thuy Giang was born in 1965. He is a poet and translator of literature and lives in Hanoi.

Oliver Hargreave

Oliver Hargreave has lived in Chiang Mai since 1991. He is the author of **Exploring Chiang Mai: City, Valley and Mountains**, first published in Thailand in 1997. The first international edition is now being distributed worldwide under the imprint of Odyssey International Guides.

John Hoskin

British-born writer John Hoskin has spent half his life living and working in Asia, based mostly in Bangkok. His latest book is **Falcon at the Court of 17th Century Siam**. An extensive listing of articles by John can be found at:

WEBSITE
www.travelthailand.com/hokstory/hokdex.htm

Emily Huckson

After spending far too many winters in her hometown in Northern Ontario, Emily Huckson moved to Ho Chi Minh City in 1995 and has put all her underwear in one drawer. Apart from giving advice to numerous travelers in her "host" city, she is also involved in raising money for disabled children via "treading the boards" in theatrical productions. She has a cat, a fridge and a hammock, so one can assume she is there for the duration!

Bill Hutchins

An accomplished journalist and avid environmentalist, Bill Hutchins died March 20, 2002.

Liza Linklater

Liza Linklater is a Canadian photographer/writer/editor who has lived in Bangkok, Thailand for the past five years, plus two years in the 1980s. During that time, she published a book on international development projects and a photography book, as well as innumerable travel and international development articles. She holds degrees in social anthropology, photography and journalism.

Candace MacKay

Candace MacKay is from Nova Scotia, Canada and has been living in Asia for eight years, four of those in Chiang Mai, where she thoroughly enjoys teaching grade four at the international school. Candace has grown to love Thailand for its beauty, people, culture and food. Her little girl, Willow, was born in Thailand and also enjoys the country, perhaps in part due to the ridiculous amount of attention she is given.

Matt McKinney

Matt and his wife, Molly, ditched their professional attachments to home and wandered into Southeast Asia in 2001, intending to stay for a year. Enlightenment struck, and they stayed for two and a half years, working with Cambodian journalists, artists and orphans. Although they cherished their life in Cambodia, they have now returned to the U.S., where they think about their Cambodian friends every single day.

Nami Nelson

Nami Nelson is a 25-year-old Australian who spent about two years living on the Thai-Cambodian border working for CARE Cambodia on their HIV/AIDS projects. She is a graduate of Asian Studies (Thai and

Vietnamese) and currently studying toward a Masters of Primary Health Care. Nami has a deep-seated belief that good food is a luxury you should always be able to afford, and that it can be found in the most unusual and unexpected of places.

Nguyen T. P. Duyen

Nguyen T. P. Duyen is an artist who received her Bachelor of Fine Arts from the Massachusetts College of Art in 2003. Her experience includes working in public relations for the Ho Chi Minh City Fine Art Association and being vice president of the Galaxy Women Artists' Club in Vietnam. She is a dynamic painter who has had many exhibitions in Vietnam, France and the USA since 1997.

Nguyen Thi Lan Huong

Nguyen Thi Lan Huong was born in 1976 in a little town called Tan Hiep close to My Tho in the Mekong Delta, and her family moved to Saigon when she was two years old. Now working as a consultant for the relocation company, Orientations, she enjoys the fun of living in Ho Chi Minh City.

Nguyen Nguyet Cam

Nguyen Nguyet Cam is an instructor in Vietnamese language at the University of California, Berkeley. She has published numerous translations of works from English into Vietnamese, including two of E.B. White's children's novels, **Charlotte's Web** and **The Trumpet of the Swan**.

John Padorr

Originally an advertising copywriter based in Chicago and New York, John Padorr has lived and worked in Southeast Asia since 1991. He currently splits his time between Brooklyn and Thailand, writing and consulting for aid organizations. You can email him at:

EMAIL
johnpadorr@aol.com

Jeff Petry

Jeff Petry is a cyber-cultural anthropologist based in Saraphee, Thailand, six kilometers south of Chiang Mai (near Krua Pee Khun Chai!). For the past 15 years, he has been studying the Karen people of Thailand and Myanmar and working on his forthcoming ethnography of the Karens. In order to sustain himself, he does occasional anthropological projects in the nearby mountains as well as website promotion. He is a middleman, farmer and namer of cats. This Pennsylvania Dutchman has wandered (and wondered) far from his hometown to his new home.

For more information on northern Thai culture, art, tourism and travel, anthropology, etc., *and* to promote your website (SEO), contact him.

WEBSITE
www.lanna.com

WEBSITE
www.lanna-website-promotion.com

Robert Power

Robert Power has spent nearly three years living and working in Asia as a researcher, photography instructor and freelance photographer. He currently works as a designer for an e-learning company in Victoria, British Columbia, Canada. Robert misses traveling, and he is off to follow his camera around Asia in the coming months. More of his work can be viewed at:

WEBSITE
www.balanceimages.org

Tara Russell

Tara Russell, from Portland, Oregon in the USA, is a professional nomad, currently calling Bangkok, Thailand home. She is eager to experience any new place and culture and enjoys sharing her experiences with everyone she knows. Tara has fallen in love with Asia, and considers it to be the most strangely enchanting place on Earth.

Dana Sachs

Dana Sachs is the author of **The House on Dream Street: Memoir of an American Woman in Vietnam**, which tells the story of her experiences living in Hanoi in the mid-1990s. Her translations of Vietnamese literature have been published widely and include the co-translation of Le Minh Khue's collection of short fiction, **The Stars, The Earth, The River**. With her sister, Lynne Sachs, she made the award-winning documentary **Which Way is East?**

Mick Shippen

Mick Shippen is a freelance writer and artist. Originally from the UK, he has lived in Thailand for over 7 years. He is presently based in Chiang Mai, northern Thailand. With a strong interest in local arts, Mick is currently fulfilling a commission for a book that will document the life and work of the traditional village potters in Southeast Asia. Along with his Thai wife, Suwimon, he also runs an arts and crafts export business.

WEBSITE
www.orientations-online.com

Graham Simmons

Graham Simmons is a freelance travel writer/photographer, based in Byron Bay, eastern Australia, and a full member of the Australian Society of Travel Writers. His work appears regularly in publications including **CNN Traveller**, **Tatler** (Singapore and Hong Kong) and **The Star** (Malaysia). He is also a founding member of the Global Travel Writers' Syndicate.

WEBSITE
www.globaltravelwriters.com

Jason Smith

Jason Smith is an American by birth, and a Chiang Mai resident by choice. He is currently teaching English at Chiang Mai University and working on a novella set in northern Thailand. In addition to a love for travel, he enjoys his football, northern Thai food and stringing his hammock up in the islands. Contact him at:

WEBSITE
neilknows2002@yahoo.com

Katherine Tosi

Katherine Tosi grew up in Vermont, U.S.A. She lived in Switzerland from 1996-1998 and in Bangkok, Thailand from 1999-2002, where she worked as a freelance journalist for the **Bangkok Post** and wrote a popular weekly column called "Kat's Window on Thailand." These articles can be found at:

WEBSITE
www.katswindow.net

Currently, Katherine is attending graduate school in Sydney, Australia.

Phuong Tran

Phuong Tran was born in Weatherford, Texas, but whenever asked where she is from, she has always said Vietnam. Recently, she was in Vietnam on a film shoot for Discovery International. Phuong now lives in New York City, where she works as a radio journalist, makes smoothies and is attempting to put together an IKEA shelf.

Bill Tuffin

Bill Tuffin is the General Director of the Boat Landing Guest House in Luang Namtha, Laos. He is from Pueblo, Colorado and his eclectic career has included work with numerous humanitarian groups. Among his many talents is the ability to speak—among other languages— German, Thai, Lao and Tai Lue.

WEBSITE
www.theboatlanding.com

Katy Warren

After discovering that working as a temp wasn't as glamorous as expected, Katy Warren lost her mind, put her stuff in storage and moved to Ho Chi Minh City for 14 months of writing, teaching English and traveling around Southeast Asia. Fortunately, most people who live in Ho Chi Minh City are a little bit nuts, so she fit right in.

Dave Williams

Dave Williams is a lifelong naturalist. His passion for kayaking started over 25 years ago. He feels the same today as he did the first time he sat in a boat. PaddleAsia is the result of his accumulated knowledge of flora and fauna coupled with his intense love of paddling. You can share his excitement at:

WEBSITE
www.paddleasia.com

John B. Williams

John Williams is the author of three dive guides on Thailand, Burma and the Andaman Islands, including the recently published **Lonely Planet Diving & Snorkeling Thailand**.

For more information about diving in the Andaman Sea, visit his website at:

WEBSITE
www.siamdivers.com

EMAIL
john@siamdivers.com

Raymond Zepp

After spending 20 years teaching in universities in developing countries, Dr. Ray Zepp came to Cambodia in January, 1995, as part of a Georgetown University team to strengthen the Faculty of Business in Phnom Penh. He was one of the first travelers to explore the outlying areas of Cambodia, and his book,

The Cambodia Less Traveled, was a pioneering effort in the field. During his seven years in Cambodia, he has written a series of books and articles, including, **A Field Guide to Cambodian Pagodas**, and **A Field Guide to Siem Reap Pagodas**, available in most markets and bookstores. Other regional publications include **Around Battambang**, **More Cambodia Less Traveled 2001-03**, and **More Around Battambang 2003**, available in selected locations in Battambang, such as the Riverside Balcony Bar.

Kim Fay

Seattle native Kim Fay fell in love with Southeast Asia when she traveled to Thailand in 1990. Journeys to Borneo, Singapore and Bali followed, and in 1995 she moved to Ho Chi Minh City, where she worked as an English teacher and travel writer until 1999. She now writes and edits for travel websites in L.A. She recently finished **In Yellow Babylon**, a novel about the looting of the Khmer temples, set in Indochina in 1925.

Kim's favorite ThingsAsian stories:
- The Kindness of Strangers: September 11 in Laos
- Hoi An Hoard: Excavation, Collection and Theories
- Christmas in Cambodia
- Wedding in the Countryside
- Dalat Tapestry

Julie Fay

Julie Fay's most recent trip to Thailand, Laos and Vietnam inspired her to return to school to study photography. Before pursuing this newfound passion, she majored in drama at university, worked for the Four Seasons Newport Beach and spent the last six years establishing a career in the film industry. She now resides in Los Angeles.

Note cards featuring photographs found in this book can be ordered at **www.ThingsAsian.com**.

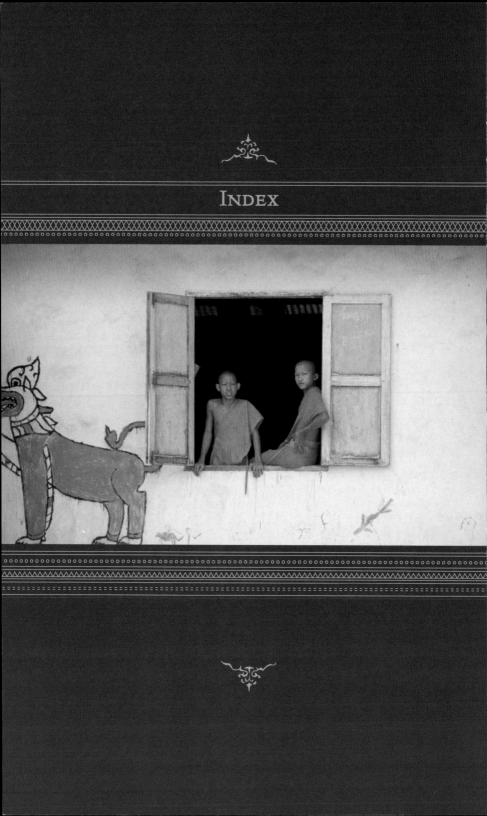

Index